Monterey County

The Dramatic Story of Its Past

Monterey County

The Dramatic Story of Its Past

by Augusta Fink

WESTERN TANAGER PRESS

1982

To Margaret
who always gave generously
of her time and of herself.

Western Tanager Press/Valley Publishers
1111 Pacific Ave.
Santa Cruz, CA 95060

ISBN 0-913548-60-X — Cloth Cover
ISBN 0-913548-62-6 — Soft Cover
Library of Congress Catalog Number 72-76931

ACKNOWLEDGMENTS

To all the many people who made this book possible I am deeply grateful.

I wish especially to express my appreciation to Mrs. Hans Ewoldsen for providing documentary material on the Pfeiffer family and for editing the south coast chapter of the book, to Mrs. Hester Harlan for family material and pictures, and to Mrs. Edward Hohfeld for contributing to the Carmel chapter.

Special thanks also are due Byington Ford, Marion Crush, and Mr. and Mrs. Frank Porter for extensive assistance in connection with the Carmel Valley chapter, and to Mrs. Winnifred Beaumont and Mrs. Kenneth Shields for sharing their reminiscences of early Pacific Grove.

Enough appreciation cannot be expressed to Mrs. Amelie Elkinton for providing original source material, including genealogical data, and for reading the manuscript and making corrections and suggestions.

Among the many other persons who gave generously of their time and assistance are Harry Downie, Edgar H. Haber, Mrs. F. H. Herrick, Mrs. Frank Lloyd, Emmet McMenamin, Harry Dick Ross, Judy Todd, and Mrs. Van Court Warren.

For guidance in research and selection of pictures, I am grateful to Mr. John Barr Tompkins, Head of Public Services in the Bancroft Library of the University of California at Berkeley. I am also indebted to the staffs of the city libraries of Monterey, Pacific Grove, and Carmel, the Monterey County Library, the Pacific Grove Museum of Natural History, and the library of the California Historical Society.

Finally, I wish to express appreciation to Mayo Hayes O'Donnell for the inspiration provided by her voluminous writings on the Monterey heritage and the fine collection of materials in the library which bears her name.

Augusta Fink
Carmel
January, 1972

Contents

Promises on the Land

Between the bustling cities of San Francisco and Los Angeles lies a storied land, a land of myth and legend, a land where California history began. Before either of California's major metropolises was more than a bright seed in the Spanish dream of colonization, Monterey was its capital. The history of Monterey County is the history of California in microcosm—a story that can best be told through the dramatic interplay between the land and the people who spent their days and their dreams in shaping its evolution.

The character of the land, which directed how this story would unfold, was determined long before man walked the earth. The present vista of valleys and mountains is relatively recent, having been sculptured within the last thirty million years. When the Miocene period began, a great inland sea covered most of present-day Monterey County and extended over a large portion of central California. Two long island masses occupied the approximate areas of the Gabilan and Santa Lucia Mountains, and a third rose from the sea in the location of the Santa Cruz Range.

For millions of years, processes of erosion contributed vast quantities of sedimentary debris from these ancient land segments to the adjacent sea. Mixed with the skeletons of innumerable tiny marine animals, the deposits formed a thick, mud-like substance. Then great forces of upheaval lifted, folded, and crumpled the sediments of the ocean floor, raising and enlarging the mountain ranges and introducing some of the present-day geographical features.

The last million years, coinciding with the Ice Age, saw a succession of violent storms and inundations and withdrawals of the sea. During this period, the spectacular present-day formation of the Santa Lucia Mountains took place as extensive erosion carved the rugged peaks, valleys, and canyons that characterize the range. Finally, a period of gradual uplift established the coastline as it now exists.

The County of Monterey now comprises 3,324 square miles, or more than two million acres of land. Stretching along the coastline for about 125 miles, its contours consist of a long narrow valley cradled between two rugged mountain ranges. On the seaward side, this lowland—the Salinas Valley—is bound by the bold escarpment of the Santa Lucias, rising abruptly from the shore and threaded by a thin marine terrace hundreds of feet above the surf. Approximately eighteen miles in width, the multi-layered coastal mountains soar to peaks almost 6,000 feet in height. The Gabilans form the eastern boundary of the county. Heavily wooded to the north, the range becomes rough and barren in its center portion, then softens to low rolling hills at the southern end. Through the rich soil of the central valley, the Salinas River winds and twists, third longest in the state, tumbling at last into the deep blue waters of oval-shaped Monterey Bay.

For centuries the long stretch of coastline that is now Monterey County, with its soaring mountains, sheltered valleys, lovely wooded slopes, and stunning shoreline, lured men with the beckoning promise of a better life. They came for a variety of reasons; some for adventure, others in search of souls, many for security, most in the hope of material gain, a few just to partake of its blazing beauty.

First in the procession were the Indians, making their way from colder regions to the mild hospitable climate of central California. Their claim rested most lightly upon the earth. No real ownership was involved. How can a man possess something to which he believes that he himself belongs? Their title was confined to the rights of hunting, fishing, and food gathering.

Then the Spanish explorers came, hungry for gold and eager to claim more land for the crown, thus reaping the rewards of royal favor. Accompanying them were the missionaries, led by Father Junípero Serra. In his heart burned an incandescent zeal for converting the heathen to Christianity, and he saw the docile, brown-skinned natives as priceless jewels to be collected for the Church. The Spanish also brought the Laws of the Indies, rigidly prescribed rules under which the land might be occupied. During their regime, missions, presidios, and pueblos came into being and the rancho period began.

Next in line were soldiers and settlers from Mexico, simple folk and for the most part desperately poor. They yearned for a piece of land on which they could herd cattle and live in peace and security. With the advent of Mexican independence from Spain, these simple, accepting *Californios* invited exploitation by enterprising foreigners who perceived a way to capitalize on the isolation of the young settlement.

Monterey became the headquarters of these entrepreneurs as they created a market for foreign commodities and established the trade in hides and tallow that sustained the economy for forty years. These ambitious men were the vanguard of the American occupiers, who brought even more startling changes to the land.

The Americans had a different philosophy of life. They saw another kind of promise in the green and golden hills and meadows. Before long, the great herds of wild cattle were replaced by dairy herds and agriculture, and the steel ribbons of railroad tracks had cut through the land, following the long valley that lay in the heart of the newly created County of Monterey. In the wake of the railroad, typical small American towns sprang up and people came to settle in them, seeking a part in the burgeoning real estate bonanza of this fertile and beautiful land.

Next in the long procession were those dazzled by the potentiality for resort development along the unique seacoast. They bought huge tracts of land, surveying them into "paper towns" and building hotels designed to attract others to the beautiful country. They launched the promotional campaigns that made Monterey County a mecca for millions of people to whom it still represents an attraction as compelling as the cities of silver and gold the Spaniards sought.

Always, the contour of the land influenced the character of its development. Out of the configuration of mountains, valleys, and shoreline emerged the economic and social patterns that made Monterey County evolve, ultimately, into six principal regional units. Three of these—the cities of Monterey, Pacific Grove, and Carmel—are on the Monterey Peninsula. With beneficent climate and spectacular natural attractions, they grew into tourist centers. The Salinas Valley blossomed as an agricultural district; and, until very recently, the Carmel Valley was also mainly devoted to fruit orchards and dairy farms. The south coast, isolated by its precipitous terrain, has remained a sparsely populated region, with its spine-tingling beauty unspoiled.

In the final six chapters of this book, the story of each of Monterey County's six geographical sections will be told, beginning at a point in time when the first significant change in the evolution of each took place. The preceding chapters deal with the land and its peoples as a whole, beginning with the gentle Indian tribes and ending with the tumult of the constitutional convention in Monterey and statehood for California.

The whole Monterey area represents a unique segment of the California heritage. During its first 80 years, Monterey was the focal point

of the California story, and each subsequent episode of its evolution
parallels that of the state. In addition, the land, the buildings, and the
ambience that symbolize the romance and reality of early California
are preserved in its cities and countryside to a remarkable degree. Here
can still be seen the rugged coastline, the wilderness of mountains, the
missions and great land grants, much as they were in the days of the
padres and pioneers. One can walk through the fine old adobes and
historic buildings and feel the presence of the past. Only the dramatic
story of the people and the parts they played is needed to make this
past come fully alive.

1

The Gentle People

For thousands of years before the first white men sighted the shores of Monterey County, the region was inhabited by a simple and serene people, who held the beautiful and fertile land in reverence and reaped from it all that they needed to sustain a carefree and unencumbered existence. By nature they were generous and friendly, knowing neither ambition nor avarice and expending effort only as the demands of the day required.

Three different tribes of these docile Indian people occupied the region. Those who dwelt along the coast as far south as Point Sur were named Costanoans by the Spaniards, from *costaños* or "coast people." They extended inland along the lower courses of the Carmel and Salinas rivers and occupied the Salinas Valley to about the vicinity of present-day Soledad. Linguistically, they belonged to the Penutian family.

The other two tribes, the Esselens and Salinans, lived in the rugged Santa Lucia mountains and belonged to the Hokan linguistic family— although their dialects bore only a slight resemblance to each other. The Esselen group lived in the coastal mountains from Point Sur to Point Lopez and inland along the upper reaches of the Carmel and Arroyo Seco watersheds. At the south, their terriory extended to Santa Lucia Peak, where it adjoined that of the Salinan group. The Salinans occupied the area comprising the southern reaches of the mountains to the Santa Margarita divide, as well as the Salinas Valley north to the Costanoan border.

Each tribe was organized into several villages, called *rancherías* by the Spanish, which were no more than clusters of huts located on level sheltered sites close to a supply of fresh water. No complete record exists of the number or location of these communities, but ample evidence of their existence has been uncovered in ancient kitchen-middens, or refuse heaps. These remains are most noticeable along the coast, where shell fragments and fire-blackened rocks are not concealed by grass and shrubs.

The villages were seldom permanent places of residence. Their inhabitants regularly left to gather seasonal harvests of seeds, nuts and other food, and sometimes inclement weather would drive them away temporarily. Periodically, when the condition of a village became intolerable from fleas or filth, the villagers simply burned their huts and rebuilt at a nearby location.

The hemispherical huts that housed individual families could be constructed within a couple of hours. Poles were fixed in the ground in a circle about six feet in diameter and then pulled together and bound at the top. Bundles of brush formed the walls, although more than half of the hut was usually left open, with extra bundles kept handy for use in bad weather. The interior apex of the hut was about four feet from the earthen floor, making for pretty cramped quarters. But with the exception of sleeping, all family activities took place outdoors.

It is estimated that the population of the Salinan tribe at the time of their discovery by the Europeans may have been around 2,000. They were distributed principally in villages on the San Antonio and Nacimiento rivers. Journals of the explorers mention six villages in the area, and mission records indicate at least eight. One of these, which was called Holamna, is believed to have been near the site of Jolon. In the southern Salinas Valley there is evidence that villages may have existed near the present-day towns of Bradley and King City.

Very little information has survived about the Esselen group. They were small in number and the first of the Monterey County tribes to become extinct. Apparently there were village sites in the Tularcitos area of the upper Carmel Valley, and one authority states that some Esselens lived at what is today called Tassajara Hot Springs.

The Costanoan tribe is believed to have been the largest of the three, numbering about 3,000 at the time of their discovery. Mission records have preserved a long list of village names for the Costanoan group. The San Carlos Mission was founded near the Costanoan village of Achastan, and the village of Rumsen was a short distance up the valley, on the south bank of the Carmel River. At one time, a village called Tamotk apparently existed in the vicinity of present-day Monterey. Excavation of the old Spanish fort in Monterey uncovered Indian kitchen-midden deposits extending to a depth of nine feet and indicating a habitation of 1,500 to 2,000 years at that site. There are also indications that at least five Costanoan villages existed along the Salinas River.

According to Spanish reports and drawings, the Costanoans—the best known of the tribes—were not a prepossessing people. Somewhat short and stocky, both the men and women of this tribe kept their abundant, coarse black hair cut or burned off in ragged strands of about five inches. Some of the men plucked their faces clean, which was considered to be the ideal, but the more indolent among them had bushy beards. Tattooing was very fashionable among the women.

Nakedness was the custom for men and children; the women wore short aprons woven of grass fibers. A short rabbit or otter cape was sometimes used by the women in cold weather, while the men plastered themselves with mud. A robe fashioned from knotted strips of rabbit fur served as both blanket and bedding.

The men spent a substantial portion of their days hunting and fishing, although shellfish and seeds were the staples of the Costanoan diet, and the garnering of these was the responsibility of the women. The fishing was carried out in small, fragile craft built by lashing together bundles of tules. Seals were hunted on the rocky shores of the bays and salmon were taken at the mouths of rivers. When a whale washed ashore, there was abundant food for many days.

The hunting method on land was ingenious. When stalking deer, for example, the Costanoan men covered themselves with the skin and head of the animal and proceeded on all fours. Approaching a herd of deer, they imitated the movements of the creatures, then quietly made their kill with two or three arrows.

The women devoted long hours to gathering and preparing mussels and all manner of seeds. They also foraged for acorns, pine nuts, berries and mushrooms. The seed was roasted in bark utensils over hot embers and then pounded into a fine flour, which could be mixed with water and cooked as a bread or porridge. Meat and fish were roasted over flames or hot coals. Seaweed was sometimes combined with foods for flavoring.

Strong familial ties characterized these affectionate people. Great love existed between mothers and their children, and husbands held their wives in high regard. Monogamy was generally the rule, with matrimonial alliances arranged by the parents but consented to by the boy and girl.

Affection and strong ties also ordered the life of the villages. Food and material possessions were freely shared, keeping one's word was a matter of honor, and help was readily given to those in distress. If antipathy existed between certain people, they simply avoided each other or settled their quarrel quickly. When two men fought, they stood body to body, striking each other with small spatulas made of deer bone until blood was drawn. Then, instantly, the fight ended. Much the same principle applied in battles between tribes. Attacks were swift and sudden, but when two or three warriors had fallen, the field was abandoned.

The government of a village, or group of villages, was under the rule of a chief, usually hereditary, who commanded obedience and respect. Apparently the chief's prerogatives were dependent upon the acquiescence of the people, for he held no punitive powers. His responsibilities were to be the leader in war and to provide a sufficient supply of bows and arrows to his warriors. He was expected to be an expert archer, and his principal privilege was the right to have as many wives as he wished.

The shaman, or medicine man, was also a very influential figure in the community, for the people had absolute faith in his ability to cure sickness. Although some of the shaman's practices were outright charlatanism, he knew the secret uses of many native roots and herbs, which were effective in relieving such ailments as fever, inflammation and dysentery.

The sweat house was a regular recourse for most illnesses, as well as for fatigue and even for pleasure, but its use was restricted to men. Constructed of a circular ditch covered with branches, the sweat house was made oven-hot with a blazing fire near the very small opening left for a door. The patient sweltered inside for as long as he could endure the heat and, during the interval, scraped his body with the same kind of spatula used in combat. At the end, he staggered forth and jumped in a nearby pool of water or a river.

Women had a different version of the sweat bath for use in recovery from childbirth. A pit was dug in the floor of the mother's hut and, in it, a fire was built. Several large, flat stones were placed in the fire, and when the flames died down, these stones were covered with aromatic grasses. The mother lay there with her child until she felt the heat diminishing. Then, she rose and plunged into cold water. The process was repeated several times daily for about a week.

Costanoan religious beliefs and ceremonial practices were simple. According to their creation myth, the world began when a single mountaintop rose from the sea. In the beginning, the land was inhabited by the coyote, the eagle, and the hummingbird. Then, after the waters receded, these three created all other living things. The sun, the moon, and large redwood trees were also considered to be sacred, and it was believed that powerful deities dwelt in the sky. Puffs of tobacco smoke or handfuls of seed were directed towards these deities as indications of devotion.

Cremation was the preferred method of disposing of the dead, but if there were too few friends or kinfolk to gather firewood, the deceased was buried. Seeds, shells, and other tokens of affection were scattered over a corpse. Then all property of the deceased was immediately destroyed and every effort was made to eradicate his memory. The dead were thought to journey across the rim of the sunset sea and to return only in the dreams of the living. Evil persons were believed to come back as grizzly bears, and the killing of a grizzly was cause for great rejoicing.

Though not as highly skilled as some of the Indian tribes of California, the early inhabitants of the Monterey area practiced some arts and crafts. They fashioned fine bows of flattened wood and deer sinew. Their arrows were straight and true, feathered, and headed with carefully worked flint or chert. They wove excellent utilitarian baskets out of willow twigs; and from bone they devised awls for sewing basketry, tools for prying abalone loose from rocks, and a variety of scraping instruments. Lighthearted and fun loving, these people also devoted much of their time to simple music, singing and dancing, and friendly games of chance.

For the Esselen tribe, no specific knowledge has survived the years, and for the Salinans only limited details are available. It is known that there was bitter animosity between the Salinans and the Costanoans and that contact between them was confined for the most part to war. It is also known that the Salinans lived in larger and more complex dwellings than those of the Costanoans. Quadrangular in shape, their houses averaged ten feet square. Supporting posts were driven into the ground at each of the four corners and in the center of the space. The roof then was constructed of a lattice of poles thatched with tules, which were lashed on by strips of bark. A fire pit was placed in the middle of the house with a smoke hole in the roof above it.

As acorns were abundant in a large part of the area inhabited by the Salinans, they formed the basic staple of their diet. The acorns were prepared by drying them in the sun and then pounding them into a fine flour. The Salinans were also known not only to smoke tobacco but to eat it mixed with lime.

Indications are that the Salinans were quite adept at basketry. They had two varieties of coiled baskets and used reeds as well as willow twigs. Large sloping granaries, three feet across and two feet high, were woven of willow to store acorns, and other baskets were shaped like jars and coated inside with pitch. Apparently, the only decorative material used by the Salinans was black, extracted from the roots of bracken.

The creation myth of the Salinans was like that of the Costanoans except for the substitution of the kingfisher for the hummingbird. Apparently, the only significant difference between the beliefs and practices of the two groups was the Salinan use of elaborate ritual and drugs for the initiation of boys to mature status in the community. After several days of rigid fasting, the youths partook of a highly intoxicating and narcotic drink, which was brewed from a poisonous plant, commonly called Jimson weed, that grows in dry places over much of California. A ceremonial dance ensued, during which the boys collapsed in a stuporous sleep and had visions which were supposed to guide them throughout their lives. Today, this same practice is termed the *toloache* cult, from the Spanish transliteration of the Aztec word for the plant, and is found among many Indian tribes.

For several millennia, these gentle people occupied the beautiful hills and coastal plains of Monterey County, believing that the land and its plenty, like the air, was free and belonged to all, and knowing that, like the air, that land was necessary to the life of their race. Then another kind of people came, with different concepts of property, and laws and soldiers reflecting these concepts. Ultimately, these strangers claimed and took for themselves the good earth that had nurtured the Indian culture. It all began when Juan Rodríguez Cabrillo, a Portuguese explorer in the service of Spain, discovered Alta California, and it ended, ultimately, with the displacement and extinction of the three Monterey tribes.

In the remote reaches of the coastal mountains, caves still harbor the mute testimony of these forgotten people in pictographs painted on the smoke-darkened walls. One of these, in a shallow cave above Tassajara Hot Springs, was the subject of the poem "Hands," by Robinson Jeffers. In the painted patterns of lines depicting a multitude of hands, Jeffers found a moving message from the ancient inhabitants of the "beautiful country":

    . . . All hail
    You people with the cleverer hands, our supplanters
    In the beautiful country; enjoy her a season,
        her beauty, and come down
    And be supplanted; for you also are human.

2

Sails against the Sea

In 1519, the golden city of Tenochtitlán, capital of the Aztec empire in central Mexico, fell to the ambitious *conquistador*, Hernán Cortés. A year later, Juan Rodríguez Cabrillo, a Portuguese navigator then in his early thirties, arrived in the hot and humid Atlantic port of Vera Cruz. He was a soldier in an expedition sent by the governor of Spanish Cuba to punish Cortés for overstepping his authority.

The charismatic Cortés, using promises of wealth and prestige, swiftly brought members of the expedition into his own camp; and in a matter of weeks, Cabrillo found himself in the service of the man he had come to humble. He played a key role in the destruction of the city of the Aztecs, by building the fleet of thirteen brigantines that were used by Cortés for the amphibious assault over the great lake surrounding the capital. And by 1536, Cabrillo had forged an important reputation as a member of expeditions responsible for the conquest of the rest of Mexico and most of Central America. Culminating his military career as one of the founders of the capital of Guatemala, he subsequently engaged in shipbuilding and mining operations from which he reaped a sizable fortune, high honors, and several huge grants of land.

He had married, established a beautiful home, and started a family when Pedro de Alvarado, the governor of Spain's newly founded empire in Central America, approached Cabrillo with a business proposition. He wished to build a fleet of ships to explore the still unknown reaches of the Pacific. There were legends of fabulous riches to be found to the northwest, and the mythical Strait of Anián, or Northwest Passage, was yet to be discovered. Would Cabrillo join him in the venture?

Bored with his secure but uneventful existence, Cabrillo agreed, investing a substantial portion of his wealth. Construction of the ships was a long and complicated task, and it was not until Christmas Day 1540 that the fleet of thirteen vessels stood ready, anchored on the western coast of Mexico in the harbor at Navidad.

Immediately, trouble and long delays began. The newly appointed viceroy of New Spain, Antonio de Mendoza, wanted to be cut in on the enterprise and therefore withheld approval of the expedition. Months of haggling ensued; then Alvarado was killed in an Indian insurrection, and Cabrillo was left to deal with Mendoza alone. After much hedging and many more delays, Mendoza took possession of the fleet but permitted Cabrillo to remain in command. Finally, he consented to let him sail with two of the ships, the *Victoria* and the *San Salvador.*

On June 27, 1542, Carbrillo left Navidad on the voyage that would lead him to the discovery of Alta California. His ships were small and of the caravel type, similar to those of Columbus. Despite four long years in construction and Cabrillo's arduous efforts, the ships were poorly built, badly provisioned, and ill-prepared for the rough waters off the coast of California.

The explorer and his crew of inexperienced conscripts sailed up the coast of Mexico, across the Gulf of California, then north along the shores of the Baja peninsula. Though the weather was good, they progressed only about fifteen to twenty miles a day. On September 28th, they entered the waters of a great harbor which Cabrillo named San Miguel, in honor of Michael the Archangel. They had reached the port of present-day San Diego.

A party went ashore and encountered the Diegueño Indians, who indicated by signs that they had seen bearded men with dogs, weapons, and horses. Clearly, the Indians of the Southwest had an excellent grapevine, since the soldiers to whom they referred were undoubtedly those of the Coronado expedition, which had probed into Arizona and New Mexico during the years 1539 to 1541.

After spending six days in the sheltered port, the explorers proceeded up the coast and, at daybreak on October 7th, they anchored off the island that is now called Santa Catalina. Cabrillo gave it the name San Salvador after his flagship and recorded in his log that the Indians were exceedingly friendly, "shouting, dancing, and making signs that [we] should land." Some of the islanders even sailed out to meet the Spaniards on one of their canoe-shaped rafts and welcomed them ashore.

The following morning the ships moved into the open roadstead that would become Los Angeles Harbor. Seeing the smoke of many fires on the surrounding hills, which were heavily populated by Indians, Cabrillo named the place *Bahía de los Humos,* or Bay of Smokes. He made no attempt to land, but continued northwestward, sailing close to the coast and anchoring at several points along the Santa Barbara Channel. On Wednesday, the 18th of October, they reached the rough waters of Point Conception, which they called Cape Galera, a word signifying distress. Indeed, from Point Conception on, the expedition was dogged by disaster.

The weather had turned ugly, and they were now surrounded by some of the roughest currents of the Pacific coast. Cabrillo made port at a small island he called San Miguel (now Cuyler Harbor) and waited out a raging, week-long storm. In the course of that storm, the weary commander, now in his fifties, stumbled and broke his arm near the shoulder. On the 25th, despite the agony of his injured arm, Cabrillo insisted that the expedition sail on through the angry seas.

For weeks, the small vessels were battered back and forth between Point Conception and present-day Goleta, unable to make any progress. They were in the fifth month of their tortuous voyage, provisions were running low, and many of the men suffered from malnutrition. Finally, they managed to move northward, only to be struck on November 11th by a severe storm off the headland later known as Point Pinos. The storm drove the ships six leagues out to sea, and when the gale finally calmed three days later, the voyage northward was immediately resumed. The explorers never even saw the great bay just beyond Point Pinos that someday would be called Monterey!

For four more days they beat their way northward, as far as the vicinity of Fort Ross, but they could find no shelter. The terrifying swell of the ocean and the high, mountainous coast prevented them from approaching the shore. Desperately, they turned around and sailed back to San Miguel Island.

There, the severe winter weather detained them for nearly three months, while gangrene began to develop in Cabrillo's arm. On January 3, 1543, the iron-willed commander died on the bleak, windswept island. His dying orders were to push the exploration northward whatever the cost and as soon as possible. His successor carried out this command, sailing as far north as Oregon before returning to Navidad in April of 1543.

For 50 years, Spain paid slight attention to the accomplishments of the Cabrillo expedition. Then in 1566, the first successful trading expedition between Acapulco and Manila was accomplished, and a California port became essential. The Manila galleons made annual voyages across the Pacific laden with Mexican silver and gold, which they exchanged for the fabulous luxury goods of the Far East. Profits ran high and, frequently, extra cargo was crowded into space that should have been allocated to food and water. Thus, during the rugged seven-month voyage from Manila to Acapulco, the crews suffered from starvation, thirst, and scurvy and the vessels were often damaged by the rough seas. There was a great need for a port of call on the California coast where provisions could be obtained and repairs made.

Another reason for such a haven had also developed during those years. As news of the treasure-laden galleons got around the world, they became fair game for freebooters. Particularly the English pirates, like Francis Drake and Thomas Cavendish, made tremendous hauls hijacking the huge Spanish ships. Furthermore, Drake had landed at what is today called Drake's Bay and had taken possession of all of the Pacific coast in the name of Queen Elizabeth. His claim threatened the sovereignty of Spain in the region, and Spanish authorities were finally bestirred into action.

Sebastián Rodriguez Cermeño, the galleon commander for the Manila voyage of 1595, was commissioned by Spain to search for the site of a possible port on his return voyage. After an especially harrowing passage across the Pacific, he anchored his ship in the bay where Drake had landed sixteen years earlier. There, the ship was driven aground by a gale and pounded to pieces. An exceedingly valuable cargo was lost, but Cermeño and his 70 men survived and managed to return to Mexico in a small open boat. In his official report, Cermeño accurately described many points along the coast, including the site of the future port of Monterey. But his accomplishment was not credited, and it was decided to risk no more galleons, laden with treasure, in coastal explorations for a safe harbor.

Instead, an expedition was organized specifically for the purpose of surveying the coast of California. Sebastián Vizcaíno, a robust, energetic man of about 50 and a merchant-seafarer with ambitions to become a *conquistador,* was chosen to be its commander. Vizcaíno invested a considerable amount of his own money in the expedition, which consisted of three ships and 200 men. The flagship *San Diego* and the *Santo Tomás* were vessels of moderate size; the *Tres Reyes* was a small frigate. On board, in addition to the carefully selected crew, was an expert cartographer and three Carmelite friars. The expedition set sail from Acapulco on May 5, 1602.

More than six months later, on November 10th, the expedition reached the huge harbor which Cabrillo had named San Miguel. The voyage had been exceedingly difficult because of head winds, and many of the men were ill due to a serious shortage of water, which had leaked from the poorly made water barrels.

On the 12th, which was the day of San Diego, mass was celebrated and the port was renamed in honor of the saint. The expedition tarried for a few days to give the sick a chance to recover and to repair the ships; then they sailed northward again, anchoring at Cabrillo's island of San Salvador and mainland *Bahía de Los Humos*, which Vizcaíno renamed Santa Catalina and San Pedro in honor of the feast days that occurred during the sojourns.

Or December 14, Vizcaíno sighted the formidable coastal sierra, which he named for the feast day of Santa Lucia; and toward sunset, on the 15th of December, the ships rounded a great pine-covered headland, which they called *Punta de Pinos*.

Then, a large bay burst into view. The *Tres Reyes* was sent ahead to determine if it constituted a good port, while the other ships anchored at sea. The following day the captain of the frigate reported that indeed an excellent harbor had been discovered. That same evening, all three vessels sailed into the bay, which Vizcaíno named Monterey in honor of the viceroy of New Spain, the Condé de Monterey.

In the morning, a party went ashore with instructions to reconnoiter the terrain and build a shelter where mass could be said. They found a huge oak with great spreading branches near the shore. Not more than twenty paces beyond was a small ravine with pools of fresh water. In the shadow of the venerable oak, they built a hut for the sanctuary and an arbor for the nave; then the rest of the expedition landed, and one of the Carmelite friars conducted the solemn service.

As it ended, fog which had shrouded the shoreline since early morning suddenly cleared. Brilliant sunlight shone on the sparkling blue water and dark green forest. Vizcaíno was delighted with what he saw. He reported the port to be sheltered from all winds, failing apparently to notice its vulnerability from the northwest. In all other matters, however, his perception was accurate. There were many pines suitable for the construction of masts and yards, as well as large oaks, which would provide materials needed for the repair of galleons that might put into the harbor. A good supply of water was available, and it soon became obvious that there was an abundance of wild game. His enthusiasm pervaded the report and had considerable influence on developments in California a century and a half later.

Camp was set up, and Vizcaíno turned his attention to the pressing problems of the moment. The voyage had already taken over seven months. Supplies were seriously depleted, and 45 men were sick with scurvy. He decided that the *Santo Tomás* should return at once to Acapulco, taking back those men who were in the worst condition and carrying a report of the discoveries made to date. Thus, on Sunday, the 29th of December, the ship sailed with 34 men aboard. All had received holy communion and those in danger of death had been anointed. Of the whole brave company, only nine would reach Mexico alive.

Meanwhile, preparations were under way for the *San Diego* and the *Tres Reyes* to continue the exploration northward. Vizcaíno reported in his log that the work was hampered by the cold and inclement weather; on New Year's Day, for example, the nearby mountains were covered with snow, and water holes were "frozen over more than a palm in thickness." In addition, the work on the two remaining ships was interrupted often by visits from the Indians. They were friendly and unafraid, offering gifts of food and indicating by signs that there were many Indian villages inland.

On January 3rd, when all was in readiness for departure, Vizcaíno and a party of eleven explored inland to the southeast for about three leagues. There, they discovered "another good port, into which entered a copious river descending from some high, snow-covered mountains." Many black and white poplars and willows grew along the banks of the river, which Vizcaíno named *Rio del Carmelo* in honor of the Carmelite friars in his expedition. They then returned to Monterey and, at midnight that same day, set sail in search of other ports to the north.

A horrendous voyage ensued. Driven by furious winds and blinded by fog and rain, the two ships were separated within a couple of days— not to be reunited until they had both returned to Mexico. So violent were the storms that men were pitched from their bunks, and Vizcaíno suffered broken ribs in such a fall.

Finally, on January 21, having passed Cape Mendocino, Vizcaíno ordered the *San Diego* to turn back. It was already too late. The men were so desperately ill with scurvy and the remaining provisions so rotted that the return voyage became a race with death. On February 18, Vizcaíno and the only five men who were able to walk finally went ashore at Mazatlán. The *Tres Reyes*, which had been driven as far north as Cape Blanco in present-day Oregon, returned to Navidad on February 26.

At a tremendous cost in lives, Vizcaíno had carried out the orders of the viceroy, and the Condé de Monterey had only words of praise for the daring commander. Unfortunately, however, the viceroy was soon succeeded by a man who denigrated Vizcaíno's accomplishments and blocked all plans for utilization of the explorer's discoveries. Vizcaíno went on to spend several years searching for mythical islands of solid gold and silver somewhere off the coast of Japan and then died an old man in Mexico in about 1628.

The Glory Trail

Chance more than deliberate design finally brought about Spain's conquest of California. For a century and a half after Vizcaíno's expedition, the Spanish government showed little interest in the rugged and endless coastland to the north. Long and costly wars had diminished Spain's dreams of world empire.

At about the same time, the long line of settlements established by the Jesuits on the northern frontier of Mexico and in Baja California came to be looked upon as a liability and a drain on the royal coffers. Powerful and fiercely independent, the black-robed missionaries of the Society of Jesus had incurred the animosity of most European monarchs. But for Charles III, King of Spain, fear and hatred of the friars became an obsession. A bureaucratic tyrant, he selected a favorite among his coterie of civil servants, José de Gálvez, to improve the administration of New Spain. This "improvement" was to include not only expediting the flow of revenue to Madrid but also overseeing the total banishment of the Jesuits from Mexico.

To replace the Black Friars in the fourteen missions they had founded in Baja California, the Franciscans of the Apostolic College of San Fernando, in Mexico City, were chosen. The decision was based on the assumption that they would be more amenable to subordinating the interests of their order to those of their country. Appointed as father-president of the fourteen friars sent to the rim of Christendom was Father Junípero Serra.

Thus, in the spring of 1768, Gálvez and Serra converged upon the arid, barren land of Baja. Each was a man unique in his time. Together, they were destined to shape the future course of California history. If other men had been selected, it is quite possible that the Spanish occupation of Alta California would never have occurred.

Gálvez's orders from the Spanish government "to watch and guard the western coasts of California" did not even envision a land expedition into that forbidding land. And Serra's superiors had little reason to suspect aggressive adventurism from that humble servant of the Lord, who had always been so outwardly conforming. But in the heart of each man burned an all-consuming fire which, though fueled by different motivations, would blaze a path of empire for which Spain was ill-prepared.

Both men rose from inauspicious beginnings. Gálvez had begun his life as a penniless child of the petty nobility of Andalusia. From early youth, he had demonstrated both intelligence and a ruthless ambition. Sponsored by sympathetic clerics, he managed to acquire a good education, and a carefully calculated marriage to a Frenchwoman of influence boosted his career. Then, ingratiating himself with the court of Charles III, he rose to prominence. When, at 46, he received his royal appointment as visitor-general to New Spain, he had at last attained a position with the power to match his drive for wealth and status.

Since the early 1700s, rumors had been rife about the encroachment of foreign powers in Spanish Pacific waters. The intentions of the English, the Dutch, and even the Russians had become suspect, and discovery of the valuable sea otter had quickened competition for a coastline which Spain quixotically ignored and at the same time claimed to possess. The shrewd visitor-general knew how to make use of this situation to support his personal ambitions. He also knew how to make use of a determined and indefatigable man like Father Junípero Serra.

Junípero Serra, baptized Miquel Joseph, was born in 1713, the only son of humble farmers in the town of Petra, in Majorca. He was a promising boy and was allowed to attend school with the Franciscans until, at fifteen, he persuaded his parents that he was old enough to enter the service of the Church at the Franciscan headquarters in Palma. Nothing could dampen his exuberance and will to learn and succeed.

When at the time of his final vows Miguel was given the privilege of choosing a new name, he took that of Junípero, the name of the diminutive companion to Saint Francis. The day of his profession was one he never forgot. Kneeling with his fellow novices, he made the solemn promise to "become a Franciscan forever." Each year, for the rest of his life, he renewed his vows, saying "All good things came to me with it." He believed that his health improved and even that he grew taller. He finally attained the height of five feet and three inches!

Because of his brilliant scholastic record, Serra's superiors soon selected him to teach. It was in his philosophy classroom that he met two novitiates, Francisco Palóu and Juan Crespí, who were to join him as colleagues and inseparable friends in his lifelong task of bringing Christianity to the Indians of New Spain.

For the next nine years, the duties of priest and professor fully occupied Serra's time and attention, and he acquired a notable record in both. In his preaching assignments, particularly, he showed a marked talent for communicating with the simple farming folk and for putting abstract ideas into plain language.

At last, in 1749, his dream of being a missionary became a reality. He, Palóu, Crespí, and two others were selected to go to the College of San Fernando in Mexico City. Late in August, with a large missionary contingent, they embarked on the 99-day voyage across a turbulent Atlantic. Privations were inevitable on the small overcrowded sailing vessel, but Serra's felicitous combination of humor and asceticism stood him in good stead. If anyone complained of the scarcity of water, he would reply, "I have found a good remedy against feeling thirsty; and that is, to eat little, to talk less and so to save my saliva."

When the ship arrived at Vera Cruz, horses were waiting to carry the friars to their destination. The Franciscan rule forbidding them to ride had been waived. Serra insisted that he would walk and set out with another friar along the King's Highway of the New World, 270 arduous miles to Mexico City. The road stretched from sea level to an altitude of more than 7,000 feet, over tropical country and arid plains, across broad and often bridgeless rivers, and through the tangled mountain ranges of south-central Mexico. Begging their food and lodging, *por amor de Dios*, the two priests walked fifteen to twenty miles a day and made the journey in two weeks. In the course of their walk, Serra was stung in the leg by a virulent species of mosquito, called the *zancudo*, which left him with a swollen and open wound and a chronically painful and crippling infection.

Serra's reputation as a leader and teacher had preceded him to Mexico City. As a result, he was quickly assigned to the mountainous Sierra Gorda region north of Mexico City where primitive tribes of Pame Indians had defied repeated attempts by the Franciscan missions in the area to subdue them. Jubilant about his rigorous assignment, and despite the recurring pain in his leg, Serra walked the 200 miles to the mission at Jalpan in sixteen days. There he found a dilapidated, flea-ridden church and friary, built of cane and adobe, with thatched roofs. Everywhere were signs of misery and deprivation.

His first business was the saving of souls. He began by learning the Pame language, and soon he was able to preach to the Indians in their native tongue. Then his innate dramatic ability came into play.

The Lenten season offered an excellent opportunity to demonstrate the teachings of the Church. Daily, he led a procession carrying a huge cross in imitation of Christ and illustrating the Stations of the Cross. Every Saturday night, there was a splendid pageant, honoring the Virgin Mary, and in it the fascinated Indians carried lanterns and chanted the simple prayers they had learned. Crudely painted banners told the story of the sacred birth and sorrowful death. On Maundy Thursday, Serra symbolically washed the feet of twelve of the oldest Indians, then ate with them and explained the meaning of the ceremony. The descent from the cross on Good Friday was vividly acted out, with a lifesize figure of Christ. Serra spared no effort to make every aspect of the liturgy intelligible and intriguing to his neophytes.

The showmanship brought results. As childlike as they were savage, the Pames were irresistibly drawn to the scenes and to Serra's words. Nor did Serra slight the temporal needs of his flock. From his superior, he ordered livestock and farming implements. He planted corn and beans, and working side-by-side with the Indians in the fields, he taught them how to make each succeeding harvest more abundant.

When in his second year in Mexico, Serra was appointed president of the five Sierra Gorda missions, he developed a strict administrative procedure which was to serve him well many years later in the California missions. Every hour of the day was scheduled. At sunrise each morning, the Indians were summoned to prayer and instruction. All natives living in the mission community itself were expected to be present, and roll call, following Mass, checked for absenteeism. After this, adults were dismissed, the men to work on the communal farms and the women to spin and sew. Then the children were assembled for lessons in the dogma of the Church. Special instruction in the sacraments was held in the evening.

It is a tribute to Serra's charismatic personality that the Pames responded without reservation to this regime. The swarthy little man, with burning black eyes, who worked from dawn until dusk in torn habit and shabby sandals, won their hearts as much by his kindness and example as by his fervent preaching.

It soon became clear that formal tokens of esteem meant nothing to Serra. Once he had established a workable pattern for operation of the missions, he resigned as president. To his superior, he wrote with typical candor: "If it be considered an honor, it is time that someone else enjoy it. If it be a burden, it is time that someone else was given it to bear."

Before he ended his eight-year stint in the Sierra Gorda, he had transformed the missions into models of excellence. And when he was recalled to the College of San Fernando, he carried with him a block of sculptured marble which had been the principal idol of the Pame nation. It was a fitting tribute to his accomplishment.

Supposedly, his recall was for the purpose of sending him to the Apache missions, on the San Sabá River in Texas. Two missionaries recently had been murdered there by the fierce and unfriendly Indians. But harsh disappointment awaited him. No more missionaries were to be sent to the far north until the military had pacified the region. Ten frustrating years were to pass before the gifted missionary had another opportunity to utilize his hard-won experience.

For a man of Serra's temperament, Mexico City was intolerable. The fantastic riches, ostentation, and self-indulgence of the Spanish over-lords were deeply offensive to him. While the poor crowded against locked hospital gates, bejeweled women rode by in coaches lined with cloth of gold. Resplendent cavaliers, their mounts bedecked with silver and precious stones, galloped through streets where beggars scurried from their path. Cups of chocolate were served in the lavishly adorned cathedral, while on its steps hungry children patiently waited for a chance coin to be thrown.

Here were Christians more in need of his counsel than the heathen Indians. Using every ounce of forebearance at his command, he accepted the distasteful role of spiritual mentor to a people he could not help but despise. Always an electrifying preacher, he now augmented his words with acts. "Repent and do penance!" his voice thundered from the pulpit as he beat his bare chest with a stone or lashed his shoulders with a chain. To illustrate the pains of hell, he held a burning taper to his skin until the stench of scorched flesh filled the cathedral. These displays of violence did not alienate his worldly congregation. They flocked to see and hear him.

Several months of the year, Serra was sent to far-off places in south and central Mexico, where he could preach to simple farming folk and Indians. This was the work he loved. Despite the sore on his leg, which had become a chronic ulcer, he gladly walked the long tortuous miles through an untamed wilderness. Palóu, who usually accompanied him, estimates that they covered 2,000 miles in seven years.

An ascetic austerity became an even larger part of his way of life. He ate sparingly, never commenting on the food set before him. Restricting himself to four hours of sleep, he devoted the rest of the night to prayer. Next to his skin, he wore a sackcloth of bristles or a coat woven together with broken pieces of wire. These were his means of keeping his body subject to his will, and to the will of God.

This was the caliber of the man who, early in July 1767, suddenly received a summons to return from a remote Indian village to Mexico City. With heavy heart, the lame friar, now almost 55, obeyed the order. Little did he know that the long apprenticeship of patient prayer and waiting was over. The call to California had come.

4

Journey of the Flame

Junípero Serra was elated when he heard the news that he was to take over the Jesuit missions in Baja California. Crowning his great joy was the fact that his dear friends Palóu and Crespí were among those who accompanied him on the 600-mile trek to San Blas, a western port across from the Baja peninsula. When they finally reached Loreto on the coast of Baja, Captain Gaspar de Portolá, the newly appointed governor of Baja California, came forth to escort them into the frontier outpost that was mother mission, presidio, and capital of the California peninsula.

Visitor-General José de Gálvez was already en route from Mexico City with a plan that would consolidate the northwestern frontier and extend it into Alta California. He had devised the scheme as a way to advance his personal prestige and to earn material rewards from a grateful king. The fact that occupation of Alta California was neither necessary nor practical did not deflect him from his goal.

Furthermore, circumstances had played into his hands. As he approached San Blas, he was overtaken by a courier carrying dispatches from the viceroy of New Spain. Word had reached the Spanish court that Russia was moving southward from Alaska and might be expected to occupy the port of Monterey. In the interests of maintaining security, the viceroy urged that a maritime expedition be sent to the port and that Gálvez exercise his judgment concerning additional measures which might be taken. Here was the justification that Gálvez needed for carrying out the program he had already planned.

On May 16, 1768, he held a council meeting at San Blas in which he outlined his program. Arrangements were to be made at once for the occupation of San Diego and Monterey. Expeditions would leave, both by land and sea, from Baja California in the following year. Colonization of Alta California would be accomplished through the traditional Spanish system of transforming the natives Indians into Christians and colonists. At each of the northern ports, a presidio and a mission would be established. The missionaries had the responsibility of converting and training the Indians; the military garrison would reinforce their authority and provide protection. The cross and the sword moved forward together.

Gálvez now turned to enlisting the support of Father Junípero Serra, whom he had personally selected to head the religious mission. Skillfully he stressed the glorious opportunity the expedition would give for spreading Christianity among the heathen; northern California would be conquered for God as well as Charles III. Serra's response was predictable. The preparation of a lifetime had led to this moment. He proclaimed the great news with the ringing of bells and the celebration of a mass of thanksgiving.

Both men had much to do in the months preceding the start of the expedition. For Serra there was the task of installing and providing for his friars in the fourteen missions strung along 500 miles of barren peninsula. Gálvez had the immediate job of converting the small and shallow harbor of San Blas into a supply depot for the Californias and of outfitting the three vessels that were to comprise the sea part of the expedition.

The ships, all hastily constructed, arrived at the peninsula port of La Paz in a leaky condition and had to be careened for repairs. Determined that his project not be delayed, Gálvez threw himself into a frenzy of activity, personally scraping hulls and boxing supplies. Meanwhile, the garrison at Loreto was sent to gather horses and mules, tools and provisions, and an assortment of church vestments and vessels from the already impoverished Baja missions. By New Year's Day, 1769, preparations for the expedition had been completed. Captain Portolá, the governor of Baja, volunteered to be its commander. Portolá, an unmarried professional soldier in his middle years, had seen long and distinguished service with the Spanish army in Italy and Portugal. He harbored grave doubts about the practicality of the visitor-general's project; but he secretly hoped that by rendering some extraordinary service to the Spanish government, he might gain a release from his duties and be allowed to leave a country he abhorred. For him, his appointment as governor had been equivalent to banishment.

Following Gálvez's instructions, the expedition was divided into five parts—three ships and two land contingents. First to depart for San Diego were the ships *San Carlos* and *San Antonio*. The former sailed on January 9th, carrying an able crew of 23 sailors and 25 crack Catalan volunteers, all reassigned from recent duty in Sonora. The *San Antonio* sailed on February 15th, with a crew of 26 and two friars. The *San José*, heavily loaded with supplies, was held up for several more months by a series of accidents.

Slightly more than a month later, on Good Friday, the first of the expedition's land divisions was assembled at Mission Santa María, northernmost of the Baja mission chain. Captain Fernando Rivera y Moncada, veteran of a quarter century of experience in Baja California, was in command. With him were 25 *soldados de cuero*, or leather-jacket troops, from the presidio at Loreto. Tough, hard-bitten soldiers of the frontier, they derived their name from the sleeveless leather coat, made of deerskin seven layers thick, which they wore as protection against Indian arrows. Also in the party were Fray Juan Crespí, several muleteers, and 42 Christian Indians, who would act as interpreters and perform the menial tasks of the expedition.

On the 24th of March, the pack train of 180 mules began to move, but the cattle, collected to stock the new settlements, were so debilitated by the arid journey to Santa María that they had to be left behind. The loss of this important source of food supply, along with the delayed sailing of the *San José*, was a harbinger of problems the future would hold for the Gálvez expedition.

The second contingent of the land expedition did not get under way for almost two months. One reason was Father Serra's health. When Portolá saw the swollen and suppurating sores on the friar's leg and foot, he begged Serra to let Palóu take his place. Black eyes blazing, Serra spoke harshly: "I have lived with this condition for almost twenty years. I trust in God to give me the strength I need. The sting of a mosquito cannot keep me from reaching Monterey."

Still Portolá was deeply concerned. He wrote to Gálvez, pointing out that Serra's illness could seriously impede the progress of the expedition. Then he rode to the Mission San Xavier, where Palóu was stationed, and pled with him to dissuade Serra from making the almost impossible attempt. Having obtained Palóu's promise, Portolá then journeyed to Santa María to join his men and await Palóu's arrival.

On Easter Tuesday, the indomitable Junípero Serra left Loreto, riding a broken-down mule. He carried no clothing other than what was on his back and only a little bread and cheese for provisions. When he reached San Xavier that evening, he abruptly rejected Palóu's proposals that he give up the expedition. A month later, after the aging padre and his tired burro had completed the hard trail to Santa María, 200 miles away, Serra arrived to find the Portolá expedition assembled and waiting. Portolá gave up hope of leaving Serra behind. The man was now in fact a part of the expedition. Furthermore, Gálvez's reply to Portolá's request had been terse and as stubborn as Father Serra's actions: "I rejoice that Reverend Father Junípero Serra is traveling with the expedition and praise the mighty confidence he has that he will recover."

The expedition left for San Diego on May 15th. Within less than twenty miles, Serra's condition had worsened to the extent that he could not rise from his improvised bed. This time Portolá took a direct and firmer position, but to no avail. Serra's response was equally direct and firm: "Even though I should die on the way, I shall never turn back."

Portolá ordered that a stretcher be prepared so that the ailing friar could be carried along the trail by the Christian Indians, but Serra refused. He would not allow himself to become a burden. Instead, he called one of the muleteers to his side and requested that the man apply the same remedy to his ulcerated leg as he used to ease the sores of the pack animals. The muleteer complied, making a poultice of heated tallow and crushed herbs; and, miraculously, the crude medication gave Serra relief. He was able to resume the trek, and the expedition moved on. It was still about 300 miles to San Diego.

On July 1, 41 days later, the large and beautiful harbor burst into view. On the sparkling blue bay , the *San Carlos* and *San Antonio* rode at anchor. The tents of the first division of the land expedition led by Captain Rivera were stretched out in proper formation. All seemed well until the expedition drew closer and found that the bayside camp was little more than a series of hospital tents! Rivera reported to Portolá that when he had arrived with his land expedition on May 14th, he had found only sixteen men alive out of the original 90 comprising the sea expedition. The *San Carlos* had suffered a horrendous journey of over three months, fighting fierce headwinds that blew it 200 leagues off course. As a result of a diet soon reduced to salt meat and soggy biscuits, almost everyone aboard had fallen ill with scurvy. Those on the *San Antonio*, whose voyage lasted 55 days, were also afflicted, and all medicines and fresh food had now been consumed. Rivera had not been able to bring any relief to the destitute sailors, since his own men had been put on half-rations.

Around the campfire that night, Portolá summarized the situation as he saw it. He did not feel that the misfortunes that had overtaken the ships were sufficient excuse for not continuing the expedition. All of his men were in good health. He had a pack train still laden with provisions. And the *San José* would surely arrive any day with supplies for those left behind. He was most concerned about the weather. He knew that there were mountains before Monterey and he did not wish to risk snow in the mountain passages.

He ordered the *San Antonio* back to San Blas immediately, to carry a report to the visitor-general and to bring supplies and reinforcements in case something was amiss with the *San José*. Then after his men

were well-rested, two weeks later, on July 14th, Portolá bade Father
Serra farewell and marched northward with his expedition. Father Serra
had willingly agreed to remain behind and care for the invalids, for
at least the first of his two objectives had been achieved—a settlement
had been started at San Diego. Father Crespí accompanied the column
of soldiers, mules, and Indian workers and kept a careful diary of the
journey so that Father Serra could be well-informed.

Next to nothing was known about the country that lay ahead. Knowledge of the interior of Alta California was limited to what had been
visible from the sea. The only guides available to the expedition were
crude charts based on Vizcaíno's explorations and sailing directions written for the pilots of the Manila galleons by a navigator named Cabrera
Bueno. Even this information was, of course, far from exact, and the
latitudes given were often incorrect. The expedition averaged only four
to eight miles a day.

The expedition kept fairly close to the coast because of the mountains
that rose to the east but sufficiently inland to find pools of fresh water.
The weather was warm and sunny except for early morning fog. After
the arid country of Baja California, the explorers were delighted by
this land, lush with fruits and flowers. And each day the countryside
seemed to become more verdant and pleasing. Great numbers of Indians
came forth to meet the Spaniards. Though somewhat alarming in appearance, being naked and painted from head to foot in a variety of colors,
the natives were exceedingly peaceable and friendly. They brought
presents of fish, nets, and seeds, and in return Portolá distributed glass
beads.

Four days after leaving San Diego, the expedition reached a large
and lovely valley in which some day the Mission San Luis Rey would
be built. Then on July 23rd, they were at the future site of San Juan
Capistrano. Continuing their march along the foothills, they came to
a wide river where they experienced the first of a succession of sharp
earthquakes. For this reason, they named the river *Rio de los Temblores*.
It was later to be called the Santa Ana River.

On the second day of August, they found themselves in the midst
of a spacious valley, well-grown with cottonwood and alder and laced
by a beautiful river. As it was the anniversary of the festival of Our
Lady the Queen of the Angels of Porciúncula, Crespí named the river
in honor of the sacred celebration. Twelve years later, the pueblo of
Los Angeles would be founded near the spot where they camped.

By the middle of the month, they were on the coast of the Santa
Barbara Channel, which they followed westward along the arching shore-

line. This was the country of the Chumash Indians, an especially hospitable people who impressed the explorers with their accomplishments as well as their friendliness. The natives lived in clusters of houses, slept on bedsteads, wore fur capes, and excelled in a multitude of crafts, including construction of svelte and sturdy canoes. In exchange for glass beads, they offered otter-skins, intricately woven baskets, and hand-carved wooden bowls. As the expedition proceeded through the area, a lively competition developed among the numerous villages, each striving to excel in feasts and festivities for the visitors.

After the expedition passed Point Conception, there was an abrupt change in both the physical and social climate. Strong, chill winds blew from the north and the terrain became barren and rocky. Indian villages were few and widely separated, the natives reserved and less affluent. Then on September 1, sand dunes forced the explorers to leave the coast and climb over the high and rugged inland hills. They camped just west of what is now Santa Maria and then moved on the following morning to about present-day Pismo Beach.

There, Portolá ordered a halt for two nights and a day. Both the men and animals badly needed a rest, and scouts had been sent out to try to find a way through the rugged mountains that loomed ahead. Reports from the reconnaissance were not encouraging. Enormous sand dunes lay along the shore. Inland, a labyrinth of estuaries and marshes blocked passage. In some places, the mountains appeared to plunge abruptly into the sea. The scouts had been unable to approach even the foot of the range.

Portolá made the unfortunate choice of continuing along the coast. Had the expedition followed San Luis Obispo Creek to the northeast, they would have been on the route of today's Highway 101. Instead they tried to proceed along a course that would remain impassable for another 150 years, until Highway 1 was carved out of the rocky cliffs.

They spent most of the month of September in the tangled web of the Santa Lucia Mountains. On the 7th of September, they encountered a troop of bears and several soldiers mounted on mules had the temerity to pursue the grizzlies. They succeeded in killing one of the fierce animals with nine bullet wounds, but their mounts were maimed, and they barely escaped with their lives. Some of the men ate the flesh and claimed it tasted good.

Slowly the expedition trudged on, progressing only two to three hours a day. Provisions began to run low, and a number of the men were showing signs of scurvy. They passed the great, rounded rock at Morro Bay and followed a canyon for about six miles to the top of some low hills to the northwest. From this point they saw what looked like a river. Instantly, a joyous shout burst forth from the soldiers—the *Rio del Carmelo* at last! Here was the river they had been ordered to claim in the name of the king. But when they were closer, they realized that it was merely a stream, Santa Rosa Creek near today's Cambria.

Even the usually ebullient Crespí echoed the dampened spirits of the company in his diary. For three days they plodded along broken coastline, across what is now the Hearst ranch, until they found themselves in a canyon beyond which it was impossible to advance. They were at the mouth of San Carpoforo Creek. The date was September 13th.

Portolá ordered a two-day halt, and Captain Rivera was sent out with eight scouts to find an opening through the mountains. The following day, they returned to report that picks and bars would have to be used to prepare a path. The job was done by nightfall, and the following morning the expedition began the tortuous climb along the steep sides of San Carpoforo Canyon. Picking their way over its densely wooded, fog-drenched walls they progressed only one league that day. On the next morning, Sunday, fervent prayers were said at mass before they resumed their trek, step by step and very slowly up the steep grade.

Another halt of two days had to be called while soldiers and Indians cleared a trail over a still higher ridge. Then, at last, the expedition reached the summit of the Santa Lucias. In all directions, multi-layered ranges of mountains seemed to march into infinity. It was a scene of great beauty, but to the weary and worried travelers it brought mainly thoughts of despair. The cold at night had begun to be severe. Many soldiers now suffered from scurvy and were unable to work, increasing the toil of those still on their feet. And there was little pasture for the animals in the rugged, high country.

Hacking their way through bramble and brush, the expedition proceeded northeastward until they came to the Nacimiento River, where they camped for two days. Here there was a village of about 60 friendly Indians, who brought pine nuts to the grateful Spaniards. Scouts sent to reconnoiter returned with the first good news the explorers had heard in weeks. After pushing forward fourteen leagues along a wide river, they had seen the sea. This time they were sure the river must be the Carmelo. Actually, it was the Salinas River that the scouts had found.

The next day the expedition was in the Jolon Valley. Hopes rising with every step, the soldiers and padres worked their way out through a narrow canyon. Soon they looked down a long and fertile stretch of land, its river banks lined with poplar, willow, and oak. They were

near present-day King City. For four days they advanced along the Salinas
River until, on the morning of October 1, they came to where the river
emptied into the Pacific Ocean. Portolá unrolled the charts of Vizcaíno
and the galleon navigator Cabrera Bueno. They compared the pictured
shoreline with what they saw. There was something wrong!

The *Punta de Pinos* lay to the south, not to the north as indicated
on the maps. The latitude given by Cabrera Bueno did not agree with
where they were. And where was Vizcaíno's well-protected bay? They
saw nothing but a large, oval-shaped, open roadstead. Portolá and his
officers were confused and disheartened. If this was the *Rio del Carmelo*,
then it could not be the Bay of Monterey. Furthermore, there was no
sign of the *San José*, which was to have met them with fresh supplies.

Captain Rivera took a few soldiers southward along the coast, but
came back four days later completely discouraged. They had seen only
a very small bay and a rivulet of water emptying out of the mountains.
It occurred to no one that they had located the Carmel River.

The expedition had been on the road 83 days. Their situation was
desperate. Provisions were reduced to 50 sacks of flour, twelve of meat,
and four of vegetables, and it was imperative that they rendezvous with
the *San José*. Portolá called a meeting of his officers to decide what
to do.

It was difficult to arrive at agreement. Some were convinced that
in their wide swing through the mountains they had missed the harbor.
Others proposed further exploration northward. Still others considered
that with seventeen men sick and eight disabled, they should return
immediately to San Diego. Portolá finally made his decision. They would
continue the march northward as far as humanly possible.

Painfully, the expedition moved on. The only sign of human habitation was an abandoned Indian village and an enormous dead bird, stuffed
with straw. They named the stream, beside which the bird lay, the *Rio
del Pajaro*. They were leaving the boundaries of what someday would
be Monterey County.

Because of the serious condition of the sick, the column could seldom
advance more than a couple of miles a day. When the afflicted men
fell from their mules, limbs swollen and rigid, they were strapped to
tijeras, wooden frames that were lashed to the animals. The mules themselves were so thin and weak that they could scarcely stand. Still, Portolá
doggedly ordered the march to proceed.

By the middle of October, the disconsolate group was in the Santa
Cruz mountains, struggling through strange forests of towering red trees,
which they thought were cedars. And then the rains came. Having no

tents, the expedition was drenched by torrential downpours and tortured by wet, sleepless nights. Soon a new scourge set in to exhaust the strength of the men and break their spirit. Everybody succumbed to an epidemic of diarrhea.

Portolá feared that the journey would now be brought to an abrupt end. But, miraculously, the diarrhea seemed to ease the symptoms of scurvy. Many of the men recovered the use of their limbs and were again able to ride without support. This was considered to be a good omen.

Now October was drawing to a close and the weather worsened, with more rain and a chilling cold. Provisions were down to a few sacks of flour, and the men were subsisting on a daily ration of five tortillas. Then, on the last day of the month, the expedition sighted the *Punta de los Reyes* and the Farallones, which were recognizable from Bueno's charts. It was no longer possible to doubt that they had passed the port of Monterey.

But Portolá was not yet ready to turn back. He sent a group ahead to explore the region and resolve what he called "the perplexity of the incredulous." They returned to say that they had encountered natives, who by ambiguous signs had indicated that a port lay ahead with a vessel anchored in it. Once again the explorers persuaded themselves that the *San José* awaited them. The whole company plodded on.

On November 4th, from the top of a ridge, Portolá saw the immense bay and magnificent estuary, stretching to the southeast. However, there was no sign of a ship. For five days, scouts skirted the shores of San Francisco Bay. They reported that swampland and marshes would make passage around it extremely difficult. Besides the country beyond was devoid of pasture, having been burned off by natives who were both fierce and unfriendly.

A council of officers was again convened. This time Portolá had to yield to the inevitable. With a heavy heart, he ordered the expedition to return to San Diego. More than 500 miles of rugged trail had to be retraced.

The long march began November 11th. Seventeen days later they reached the site of the future city of Monterey. Portolá decided to gamble a few days in a last attempt to locate the great harbor. Camp was made south of the Carmel River, near the mouth of San José Creek, and a small scouting party was sent to explore the precipitous seaward fringe of the Santa Lucias.

Winter was closing in on the explorers. The starving men appeased their hunger with pelicans and sea gulls. A gift of pinole and seeds, brought by a band of inquisitive Indians from the Carmel Valley, was eagerly devoured. Two muleteers received permission to go hunting in the mountains and promptly deserted.

On December 4th, the exhausted scouts staggered into camp. No harbor had been found, and so threatening had been the terrain that they were thankful to escape with their lives. For the first time, real dissension struck the camp. Crazed by suffering, some of the men were afraid to move on, still clinging to the hope that the *San José* would appear with relief. Others were of the opinion that the expedition should be divided, part to remain where they were and the rest to return to San Diego. Snow had begun to cover the adjacent hills, and bone-chilling storms blew in from the sea. Realizing that they must get through the mountains before the passes were blocked, Portolá ordered an immediate retreat.

On December 10th, a large cross was built and erected on the place where they had camped. On it they inscribed the words "Dig at the foot and you will find a letter"; then in a bottle they buried a report of their fruitless search and fervent hope that they might reach San Diego safely. They then retraced their steps to what they had not recognized as Monterey Bay, and, having erected a second cross with the same messages, they resumed the journey southward.

They followed a route as close to the one on which they had come as snow would permit. On the 21st, they emerged from the mountains at San Carpoforo Creek. Here they encountered one of the muleteers who had deserted. He declared his only intention had been to persevere until he found the much sought-after harbor. But on this whole section of coast, not only were there no indications of a port, there were not even inlets! Portolá took what pleasure he could from the report; it was additional proof that the port did not exist.

Now each day, in order to keep alive, one of the weak old mules was killed and roasted in a fire made in a hole in the ground. The rank-tasting flesh was nauseating and merely added to the miseries of the men. As the year 1769 drew to a close, the expedition was mired in mud west of what would be Santa Maria.

As last, they rounded Point Conception. The weather improved, and friendly natives again plied them with food. Heartened by the warmer climate and a more nourishing diet, the men quickened their pace. On January 24th, the expedition arrived at San Diego. They had been on the road over six months and had traveled over a thousand miles.

5

Strangers in the Land

The situation at San Diego was desperate. Neither the *San Antonio* nor the *San José* had appeared with supplies. Scurvy had claimed the lives of more than a third of the men in the rude camp, and an Indian attack in August had resulted in six additional deaths. Many of the men were almost naked, having traded their garments for fish and fowl occasionally brought by natives who coveted anything made of cloth.

Portolá ordered Captain Rivera and forty of his men to march on into Baja California in order to bring up the cattle that had been left there as well as to obtain any other provisions he could from the peninsula's impoverished missions. Four weeks went by, and each day the shortage of food became more acute. On March 10th, Portolá announced that if no relief came by the 19th, the feast of St. Joseph, the expedition's patron, the settlement at San Diego would be abandoned.

Serra responded with his customary combination of fervent faith and practicality. He made it clear that he would remain if Portolá marched south with his soldiers. He persuaded Crespí to do the same. At the same time, he convinced the captain of the *San Carlos* that he should remain in San Diego harbor with his ship until one of the relief vessels came. If the ships did not come, of course, Serra and Crespí would have a way to get back to Mexico. Realistic arrangements having been made, Serra proposed a novena in honor of St. Joseph, which would end on the deadline set by Portolá.

The morning of the last day of grace dawned crisp and clear. After celebrating mass, Serra walked to the vantage point of Presidio Hill, from which he could see for miles out to sea. Patiently, he waited and prayed. The sun rose in the high arc of the sky and it was afternoon. Still there was no sign of a ship. Then, at three o'clock in the afternoon, he saw the faint outline of sails on the far horizon.

Joyously, he gave Portolá the great news, interrupting the soldier's final preparations to leave. But the ship did not enter the harbor. Instead, it slowly disappeared to the north. Still, Serra insisted that it was a sign that their prayers had been answered. Portolá agreed to wait a few more days.

On March 23rd, the *San Antonio* sailed into the bay. She had been proceeding to Monterey when the need for fresh water had necessitated a landing on the coast of the Santa Barbara Channel. There, the natives, using unmistakable signs, told the ship's captain of men mounted on horses who had passed through going north and then had returned again on their way south. Convinced that Portolá's expedition had been forced to turn back, the ship had returned to San Diego.

Now with food supplies from the *San Antonio* to secure the San Diego settlement, Portolá resolved to accomplish his assignment at Monterey. Father Serra also made a resolution. This time he would not be content with a secondhand report. On Easter morning, April 16, 1770, Serra embarked on the *San Antonio*, while on the following day, Portolá, Father Crespí, and the land expedition began the long march.

There were only twenty soldiers in Portolá's company, but among them were Manuel Butrón, destined to play a unique role in California history, Juan Bautista Alvarado, whose grandson would someday be governor, and José María Soberanes, who would found a long and distinguished line of Monterey rancheros.

Following the same route they had taken the year before, the expedition arrived at the Bay of Monterey on May 24th. Around the cross they had erected near the shore, they found a heap of clams, some meat and sardines, and several feather-topped arrows stuck in the ground—mute evidence that the natives held this strange wooden symbol in awe. Camp was made on Carmel Bay, near the mouth of San José Creek, on the spot where they had stayed the previous December. But there was no longer any doubt about the whereabouts of the harbor so glowingly described by Vizcaíno, though Portolá grumbled that Vizcaíno's report on the harbor was grossly exaggerated.

At dusk on the last day of May, the *San Antonio* arrived at Monterey. It anchored beyond Point Pinos and waited for a pre-arranged signal from the land. High on a hilltop above Carmel Bay, three fires were lighted to indicate that the land expedition had already reached the rendezvous. The ship answered with a salvo from its cannon. Early the next morning, Portolá and Father Crespí rode across what would come to be called Carmel Hill to meet a boat from the *San Antonio*. A happy meeting ensued with Father Serra, and over lunch, plans were made for the founding of Mission San Carlos Borromeo.

Sunday, June 3rd dawned in a roseate aura under a tender blue sky. With the clangor of bells suspended from the branches of the mighty oak where Vizcaíno and his Carmelite friars had said mass more than a century and a half before, the ship's crew, the men of the overland expedition, the officers, and the priests assembled around the tree. Then Father Serra, vested in alb, cincture, and stole, knelt and intoned the hymn of the day. A huge cross, prepared beforehand, was blessed and planted in the ground. Next, the standards of the king of Spain were set up to the deafening roar of musket and cannon fire, which frightened away a group of curious Indians who had gathered nearby. Solemnly, Father Serra sprinkled the adjoining beach with holy water; then he approached the table which served as an altar and chanted the high mass.

After the ceremonies of the church were concluded, Portolá stepped forward to take formal possession of the land in the name of Charles III. The troops stood at attention while the royal flag was unfurled and saluted. Continuing the ritual prescribed, Portolá pulled up a handful of grass, broke off a couple of twigs from the venerable oak, and threw stones and earth in the four directions of the compass. Once again the guns thundered and the bells rang out, accompanied by shouts of "Viva! Long live the faith! Long live the king!"

The formalities were over. Everyone sat down under the shade of trees near the shore to eat food brought from the galley of the *San Antonio*. The mission and presidio of Monterey had been founded.

Construction of a stockade began immediately. Miguel Costansó, an army engineer and cosmographer who had sailed with the *San Antonio*, chose a stretch of level land on an inlet now know as El Estero. He marked off a rectangular plot approximately bounded by today's Fremont, Abrego, Webster, and Estero Streets, and then camp was moved from Carmel Bay to the new site. Supplies were landed from the *San Antonio*, and every man in the expedition, including seamen and padres, worked on the construction of Costansó's palisade to enclose the area.

The enclosure was built of poles cut from the nearby pine forest. These were driven into the ground close together, then filled with branches and smeared with mud inside and out. Rooms with sloping sod roofs and dirt floors—the storerooms, barracks, and quarters for the officers and friars—were roughly formed around the inside of the enclosure. Small cannon were mounted on the parapet.

The first phase of Costansó's building program was completed within thirty days. Serra and Crespí, who had been living aboard the *San Antonio*, moved into the crude facility, and the joyful Serra converted one of the lean-to rooms into a temporary church. Several religious celebrations were held during the latter part of June, with as much pomp and ceremony as could be mustered. Then, on July 9th, a farewell mass was sung preparatory to the departure of the *San Antonio*, and on it, Costansó and Gaspar de Portolá. The patient and courageous commander had at last discharged his responsibility, although he still had serious doubts about the practicality of settling Alta California. In a personal letter to a friend, he wrote, "If Russia wants California, they deserve to have it. It is impossible to send aid to Monterey by sea or land, except at the sacrifice of huge sums of money and thousands of men." He was finally permitted to return to the Spain he missed so intensely, and he died there in the mid-1780s.

Lieutenant Pedro Fages, a career officer and a veteran of both land expeditions, was left in command at Monterey. For almost a year there would be no communication with the outside world. With him were only eighteen soldiers and a food supply from the *San Antonio* that was either putrid or weevil-infested and largely unfit to eat. Fages proved to be a strict disciplinarian. With a zeal approaching Serra's zest for saving souls, he pushed for completion of Costansó's presidio plan, which was considerably more elaborate than the sheds so far erected. It specified a 150-foot square plaza enclosed by adobe walls and a solid bank of single-story buildings. These included a chapel and sacristy, several warehouses and workshops, quarters for various levels of the military and religious, as well as dormitories for the Indian neophytes. On the periphery were the kitchens and privies.

The soldiers were put to work as carpenters and masons, and Lieutenant Fages set a goal for each week. Men caught resting or stopping to roll a cigarette were severely reprimanded. On Sundays they were expected to clean their weapons, wash and mend their clothes, and bring in a weekly supply of wood and water. And as the food supply dwindled, the role of farmer was also thrust upon them. Using a primitive plow made of two pieces of timber, four acres of land were planted in wheat, beans, barley, and rice. The fall brought heavy rains, and the soldiers took their turns plodding through the mud. Amid all of this activity, Fages was a careful and relentless supervisor, and his methods brought results. Within a year, construction of the presidio was complete but for the new chapel.

Father Serra's progress was slower. One problem was that the natives had been frightened away by the noisy demonstrations accompanying the founding of Monterey. But gradually the Christian Indians brought with the expedition from Baja were able to establish friendly relations with the inhabitants of two nearby *rancherias,* who began bringing gifts of deer and antelope to the presidio. Still they resisted conversion to the Christian faith which required complete separation from the pagan community. Children presented for baptism had to live at the mission under the supervision of the padres. It was a difficult program that Serra prescribed, and it was not until December that Father Serra was allowed to baptize the first native child, a five-year-old boy.

In May, the *San Antonio* returned with good tidings. Aboard were ample provisions, several workmen and mechanics, and Franciscan friars for the founding of five more missions. There was also a letter from the viceroy granting Serra's request to move the Mission San Carlos Borromeo to the *Rio Carmelo.* Serra was elated, for the new location had better soil, an adequate supply of fresh water, and closer proximity to a large Indian population.

The energetic padre lost no time. On July 8th, Serra was in Carmel Valley selecting a site. The very next morning he left, with two friars and a pack train, for the Valley of the Oaks, in the Santa Lucia Mountains, to found the Mission San Antonio de Padua. By the end of July, temporary shelters and an improvised chapel had been established at San Antonio; and on Christmas Eve, the new facilities of the Carmel Mission were activated with solemn services.

Carmel Mission consisted of a cluster of buildings built of mud-plastered poles and sod-covered roofs, enclosed in a stockade of rough-hewn logs that could not be secured because of a lack of nails. But Father Serra was content. Each day a group of Indians gathered, attracted by curiosity and the tiny bowls of porridge Serra dispensed. Before long, he began to learn their language and taught them the sign of the cross and the greeting *"Amar a Dios."*

Meanwhile Fages sailed for San Diego and returned with some of the cattle that Rivera had driven up from Baja California. Essential as breeding stock, these animals were not slaughtered for food but, instead, became the ancestors of the great herds that in the next century would roam the ranchos of Monterey.

When the supply ship from Mexico did not appear in the spring of 1772, a crisis developed both in Monterey and in San Diego. Few crops had been planted, and the rainfall was light. Serra sent a pack train of flour to the relief of San Diego, and as a result of his generosity, rations at Monterey were soon reduced to milk, a few scraggly vegetables, and wild game brought in by the natives. In a desperate measure, Fages led a hunt for grizzly bear north of present-day San Luis Obispo. Enough meat was obtained, cut into strips, and salted to stave off starvation at Monterey. But Serra realized that, if the missions were to survive and grow, a dependable means of supply had to be established.

Late in the fall, the padre left for Mexico City to plead for assistance from the new viceroy, Antonio de Bucareli. His hidden agenda included a request that one of Fages' subordinates, Sergeant Ortega, be assigned to replace Fages as military commandant of Alta California. A multitude of differences between the two strong-willed men had festered into a full-blown feud. Serra insisted that Fages should have no control over the activities of the friars. Fages contended that as he had responsibility for their safety, he must also have authority over their actions. The principal issue involved was Serra's right to found additional missions. The viceroy considered Serra's petition and then replaced Fages. However, the tough and hard-bitten soldier, Captain Rivera, was selected over the friar's choice of Ortega.

Coincidentally, the viceroy also received a petition at about the same time from Juan Bautista de Anza, the captain of a frontier presidio in Arizona, requesting permission to explore the possibility of a land route from Sonora to Monterey. Born into the outpost aristocracy, the 37-year-old Anza had enlisted at the age of eighteen. Both his father and grandfather had seen long and distinguished military service along the northern frontier, and Anza himself was a renowned Indian fighter and an unusually able officer. He also had cherished the dream of finding a practical route to Alta California since early boyhood and had attempted twice before to interest officials in such a venture.

Now he had the invaluable support of Father Serra, and in September 1773, authorization finally was given for the expedition, which Anza was to carry out at his own expense. When he left the presidio at Tubac, north of present-day Nogales, on January 8, 1774, he had a party of 34 men. Ferried across the Colorado River in the tule rafts of the friendly Yuma Indians, the expedition struck out across the great desert waste. Unfortunately, the men became lost in a sea of shifting sand dunes, and after ten days of weary wandering, they were forced to retrace their steps to Yuma. They then took a new route southward to circle the dunes. Turning west in the region of the present Mexican boundary, they traversed what someday would be called the Imperial and Borrego Valleys and crossed the mountains by way of the Royal Pass of San Carlos. They reached the Mission San Gabriel late in March, and on April 18th, 1774, they arrived in Monterey—the goal of their 1,000-mile journey.

When Anza arrived, Father Crespí and Father Palóu, who had been in residence at Carmel since November 1773, could not even offer him a cup of chocolate. The settlement at Monterey had suffered great hard-ship during the months of Serra's excursion to Mexico City. Whereas the supply ship had been late in 1772, the following year it failed to appear at all. Father Crespí, who was in charge of agriculture at the Carmel Mission, had planted some wheat and a small amount of beans and corn. But frost had ruined the vegetables and the grain he had grown had to be saved for seed. Thus for eight months, the new community had subsisted on milk and a thin gruel made from chick-peas and beans. Still, the two friars did their best to welcome the explorers, and Anza was given lodging at the mission.

On May 9th, the frigate, *Santiago*, reached Monterey with abundant provisions; and for the first time in almost two years, the soldiers feasted on ham and wine, tortillas and chocolate. To add to the excitement, the *Santiago* had brought among its passengers the settlement's first Mexican women. The new settlers included a physician, José Joaquín Dávila, and his wife and son; Fernando Antonio Chamarro, a blacksmith, and his wife and two daughters, one eighteen and the other twenty; and another settler, his sister and his wife and young children. Altogether there were three maidens available for marriage. Family life had been introduced into the Monterey presidio.

Two days later, Father Serra returned from Mexico, having come by land from San Diego; and with the food, the new settlers, and the good friar's high spirits, optimism crackled in the air of the tiny settlement. Before the month was over, three of the Catalonian soldiers married Carmeleño Indian women, who had been baptized. One was 46-year-old Manuel Butrón, who took for his bride the fifteen-year-old Margarita María.

The arrival of women and the three intermarriages had a salutary effect upon the Indians, who had been convinced until then that the Spaniards must be the offspring of the mules that carried them. Others of the natives, who had reason to be more sophisticated, were of the opinion that the white men had come only "to seek their convenience" among them. Now, the number of baptisms increased markedly, and Indians from distant *rancherias* began to appear at the mission. The chief of the *ranchería* of Ichxenta, in the Carmel Valley, presented not only his four-year-old son but himself for baptism. Joyously, Serra per-formed the sacred rites, giving the child his own name and bestowing upon the 50-year-old Chief Tatlun the name of Antonio María Bucareli. It was a period of grace for Serra.

When Captain Rivera set out from Mexico to replace Fages as commander at Monterey, he brought with him a group of soldiers and their families. Some 51 new settlers, including women and children, arrived in Monterey in October 1774. Among the soldiers was Ignacio Vicente Ferrer Vallejo, then 26 years old and a bachelor. Born of a prominent Spanish family in Jalisco, Mexico, Vallejo was educated for the priesthood but chose to enlist in the military, where he acquired a reputation as a fiercely independent, unmanageable, and remarkably able soldier.

Spurred mainly by Serra's enthusiasm, the government in Mexico City showed a continuing interest in keeping Alta California's embryo settlements alive. Since one of the ways to insure this was permanent colonization the viceroy, Antonio de Bucareli, authorized Rivera to assign plots of land to worthy soldiers. Thus, in November 1775, Manuel Butrón requested a 130-foot parcel near the Carmel Mission; and with Father Serra's permission, it was granted, making Butrón the first landowner in California.

Bucareli also pushed ahead plans for recruiting more families into the province. Anza, who had been rewarded with the rank of lieutenant colonel for blazing the desert trail to Monterey, was empowered to assemble and conduct a second expedition of settlers, this time at government expense, along his new land route. Thirty soldier-colonists and four civilian settlers, with their wives and children, were to be led by Anza from the Nogales area to Monterey, and from there, to the new presidio and mission to be founded near San Francisco Bay. The colonists came from poverty-stricken families in Sinaloa. It is probable that only their impoverished circumstances, along with the government's promise to outfit them and pay all their expenses, could have persuaded them to take the dangerous, 1,000-mile journey into that unknown land. On October 23, 1775, the caravan of 240 men, women, and children left Mexico. Among them were the Bernals, the Berryessas, and the Castros—families that were to play important roles in the history of Monterey.

The Anza caravan arrived at Monterey on the evening of March 10th in a driving rainstorm. For the cold, wet, and exhausted settlers, the presidio must have been a dismal sight. Only the church and the quarters for officers and friars were of adobe. The rest of the buildings were of pole and mud construction with sod roofs and black ribbons of earth oozing down their sides. The plaza was a filthy quagmire, and in it they were told to set up their tents and stay!

Even Anza spent the first night in a water-logged storeroom. After that he was housed at the Carmel Mission, where he suffered an attack of appendicitis so severe that he was confined to bed for a week. Impa-

tient with physician Don José Dávila's inability to help him, Anza resorted to an ancient herb remedy and recovered sufficiently to proceed
with a small party to San Francisco Bay for the selection of the mission
and presidio sites. When he returned to Monterey prepared to lead his
group on northward, Rivera, burdened with supply problems after an
Indian uprising in San Diego, and apparently resentful of Anza's promo-
tion to a higher rank than his, refused to authorize the new settlement.

Deeply discouraged, Anza decided to return to Sonora, leaving his
lieutenant, José Joaquín Moraga, in charge of the Anza colonists. The
group was disconsolate on April 14th, the day of his departure; all hope
of finding a haven in this strange land seemed to be fading. But once
Anza was out of the way, the mercurial Rivera surprised everyone by
ordering Moraga to proceed with the settlement of San Francisco. Thus,
on a bright sunny day in June, the caravan marched northward in a
huge cloud of dust, and the San Francisco presidio came into being.

A third of Anza's colonists chose to remain in Monterey. Among
them was Ana Joséfa Castro, the seventeen-year-old daughter of Joaquín
Ysidro Castro and his wife María Martina who, having seen better days
in their youth, were seeking a more promising life for their eight children.
In May, Ana Joséfa had married the handsome young soldier José María
Soberanes, and they had moved to the Carmel Mission, where José was
a member of the guard. Life held few hardships that summer for the
newlyweds and their compatriots. There were good crops of grain and
vegetables, the spring run of salmon in the Carmel River had been
plentiful, and Ana Joséfa, now pregnant, developed a great fondness
for the wild strawberries that grew along the trail to Monterey.

The following February, Monterey was named the capital of both
Baja and Alta California. The new governor, Felipe de Neve, took up
residence at the Monterey presidio, and the 66-year-old Rivera was
demoted to lieutenant governor and sent back to Loreto. Though Rivera
had continually infuriated Serra, the friar was sorry to see the irascible
old veteran go. Rivera had participated with Serra in the founding of
four new missions in Alta California, so that there were now a total
of eight, with Santa Clara de Asís the newest.

Governor Neve had been instructed to initiate a new kind of settlement in the northern territory, which would serve as an agricultural
base for the presidios. The first of these pueblos was San José, on the
Guadalupe River, near the Santa Clara mission. Fourteen soldiers and
their families were transferred from Monterey and San Francisco to start
the experiment. Joaquín Ysidro Castro, from San Francisco, was one
of the men who toiled to erect rude huts and plant some seed at San

José before the November rains came. On November 19th, just a few days after their arrival there, Señora Castro gave birth to their ninth and last child.

The next few years were difficult ones for Serra. There were few new converts and many runaways among the Indians, and a series of plagues, which probably were smallpox, had decimated the small Christianized group that remained. Then on the first of January, 1782, his loyal and humble friend and colleague Juan Crespí died. An added burden for Serra was his lack of rapport with Governor Neve. The energetic governor made marked improvements in the Monterey presidio, converting the log and earth construction into stone and adobe, but he had little interest in founding more missions. Also, he replaced some of the Franciscan authority over the Christian Indians with a limited form of self-government through native *alcaldes,* and he refused to round up Indian fugitives from the missions, who Serra felt had broken the contract they made at baptism. The weary and frustrated father-president of the California missions was not sorry when, in September 1782, Neve was recalled, even though it was an earlier combatant, Pedro Fages, who replaced him.

In any case, Serra's struggle against uncooperative and disinterested administrators was drawing to a close. Painful chest tumors were added to the suffering of his small and enfeebled body, and on the afternoon of August 28, 1784, he died quietly in his sleep. Until the last moments of his life, he had kept his physical needs subjugated to an indomitable will.

Fifty-four years had passed since the ecstatic youth first donned the Franciscan habit in Majorca. For him, the glory had never faded and he had served his calling well. He left his beloved mission system in excellent economic condition, and despite the strictness of his regime, the missions Indians flocked to the church where his body lay, bearing bouquets of flowers and weeping inconsolably. Soldiers and sailors solemnly filed past the coffin, surreptitiously snipping pieces of Serra's habit and even some of his sparse hair to be worn as protection against evil. Then to the tolling of bells and the booming of a salute from the guns of the presidio, Junípero Serra was interred beside his friend, Juan Crespí, in the sanctuary near the altar of the mission church.

Serra was immediately succeeded by Father Palóu, but within a year he left for the College of San Fernando in Mexico City and turned the office over to Fermín Francisco de Lasuén. Father Lasuén was a quietly efficient and exceedingly capable administrator, who had seen long service in both Baja and Alta California. For another eighteen years he guided the destiny of the missions, doubling the number he had inherited.

The second administration of Pedro Fages brought the new capital its first official scandal. While in Mexico, Fages had married a beautiful, fiery-tempered young woman who was less than half his age. Eulalia de Callis, reared in a high-ranking and wealthy Catalonian family, was most reluctant to join her husband at his new assignment in the crude frontier settlement of Monterey, and only after several months of importunate letters was he able to persuade her. Then he hurried to Loreto to meet her and, accompanied by a guard of soldiers, escorted her and their three-year-old son up the coast of California. One of the soldiers was Marcario Castro, destined to have the distinction of being the grandfather of General José Castro.

The journey, which took six months, was a triumphant procession of sorts and certainly the first "social" event in California. Doña Eulalia was given a regal reception at every small settlement en route, but she was deeply shocked by the conditions she saw, especially the nakedness of the natives. Impulsively, she gave away her own clothes and those of her husband until she had almost reduced them to a similar state.

She looked upon the cramped and barren adobe, which served as the gubernatorial residence within the presidio walls, as an insult. But she was five months pregnant when they arrived, and so she endured her fate until her daughter was born in August. Then she announced that she was returning to civilization in Mexico City. Don Pedro refused to allow her to leave. She retaliated by barring her bedroom door and abjuring all public appearances. Soon the gossip that the governor could not control his wife had spread up and down the coast.

When Fages remained adamant, Doña Eulalia resorted to more stringent measures. She bribed one of her Indian maidservants to seduce him and, though the plot did not succeed, she loudly proclaimed in the presidio plaza that he had been unfaithful and that she would seek a divorce. At about that time, Fages had to travel south on official business and decided to leave his hysterical wife in the care of the mission fathers at Carmel; but when the escort of soldiers came to conduct her to the Carmel Mission, she locked herself in a room with her two children. The long-suffering Fages broke down the door and threatened to tie and take her by force. She went then, but made the missionaries pay for her humiliation by indulging in wild outbreaks even in the church itself until, finally, the friars threatened to chain and flog her.

An apparent reconciliation was effected in the stormy marriage when

Fages returned six months later, for the following May, Doña Eulalia
gave birth to a daughter. Still, unbeknown to her husband, she was writing
letters to government officials in Guadalajara requesting that Fages be
recalled because of ill health. Only after her baby died, eight days after
it was born, did *la Gobernadora* come to her senses. She made a humble
public confession of her conspiracies, and, henceforth, peace reigned
in the house of the governor.

Life was very dull for the first lady after that. Amusements were
limited to singing and dancing, watching the soldiers drill in the presidio
plaza, and attending *novilladas,* a kind of amateur bullfight. She enjoyed
a bright interlude of excitement when the French nobleman Comte de
La Pérouse visited Monterey in 1786 on a global voyage of scientific
exploration. His two ships were the first alien vessels allowed to anchor
in Monterey Bay. For ten days, the settlement was in a happy furore
and Doña Eulalia put on entertainments as elaborate as the meager
resources of the province would permit.

In 1790, the lady's long exile was at last over. Her husband asked
to be relieved of his office, and she and their son returned to Mexico
City. Fages, for whom the fires of love were now less urgent, lingered
on another year, awaiting his successor.

During this period, Spain initiated a highly advantageous fur trade
between Monterey and Canton. The Orientals greatly prized the rich
glossy fur of the otter, which flourished in seemingly inexhaustible
numbers along the California coast. In exchange, the Chinese offered
quicksilver, which was needed by the Mexican mining industry. At first,
the mission Indians were trained to hunt the sea otter and paid with
a few glass beads or a piece of brightly colored cloth. Price of the
pelts soared, however, as the demand increased, and, by 1790, a skin
brought the equivalent of $120.

Four times between 1791 and 1794, the even tenor of days at the
Monterey presidio was again enlivened by visitations from official expeditions. The first was that of Alejandro Malaspina, sent by Spain to
explore the northwest coast. The other visits were made by Captain
George Vancouver, who was in charge of a British scientific and diplomatic mission. Artists with the expeditions made numerous sketches of the
presidio and mission, which were to prove invaluable to historians of
the future. But for the *pobladores,* the new settlers, the sojourns were
made memorable by the festivities that attended them.

The Vallejos, the Soberanes, the Berryessas, Bernals, and Alvarados
joined with the other residents of the Monterey area to enjoy contests
of horsemanship, bear and bull fights, the *meriendas,* and the brilliant

displays of firewords brought from China. Sixty-year-old Joaquín Ysidro Castro and his wife and children journeyed from San José for the festivities, but they also had more personal reasons for the long trip. The elder Castros were eager to see more of their new daughter-in-law María Gabriela Berryessa, whom their son Francisco had just married. And they always looked forward to visiting again with Ana Joséfa, her husband José María Soberanes, and their five young children. The Soberanes were now stationed in Salinas Valley at the isolated new Mission Nuestra Señora de la Soledad along with Marcario Castro and his family and Ignacio Vallejo and his fifteen-year-old bride María Antonia Isabela. Vallejo had waited a long time for the happy communal life that he found with his wife at Soledad mission, for he had contracted for María Antonia Lugo's hand in marriage when he assisted at her birth in 1776.

In 1795, when for the first time land grants of some size were made available to deserving settlers, Soberanes and his father-in-law Joaquín Castro both retired from the military service and jointly requested a land concession. They were given the 7,726-acre Rancho Buena Vista, located on the west side of the Salinas River, not far from present-day Spreckels. The two families worked together, building an adobe house, planting crops, and raising a small herd of cattle. Then, without warning, the mission padres demanded that the land be returned to them. Actually, the land still belonged to the Church, at least in theory; for the early rancheros like Soberanes were given only provisional concessions, which amounted to little more than permits to occupy and run cattle on the land. Soberanes appealed to the governor; Joaquín Castro was an old man and gravely ill with pneumonia. Where could they move him?

The governor gave them a reprieve but when old Castro died in 1802, and when the following year Soberanes succumbed to the plague, the widowed Ana Joséfa realized that it would be impossible to keep their land. The eldest of her three sons, Feliciano, was still only fifteen. Sorrowfully, she told her mother, María Martina Castro, that it would be best now for her to live with Francisco Castro in Monterey.

Then, Ana Joséfa stayed a few more months at Rancho Buena Vista until her daughter María Joséfa had been securely married to the master of a frigate. The girl had given birth to a child in October 1802, much to the chagrin of her parents, and had refused to name its father. The wedding was held in the new stone church at the Carmel Mission; then, with that business taken care of, Señora Soberanes and the rest of her family moved to Monterey, where Feliciano enlisted as a presidio soldier. The beautiful Rancho Buena Vista was abandoned, and with it, for the time being, the Soberanes/Castro dream of becoming landowners.

Ignacio Vallejo was also finding life in the colony difficult. Throughout his military career he had been shifted from one location and assignment to another, with slight recognition for his accomplishments. Now, he was very embittered that despite his bravery in the Indian campaigns, the highest rank he had been given was that of sergeant. In 1809, he was living at the Monterey presidio with a family of eight children, the youngest the two-year-old Mariano de Guadalupe.

Life was hard for all inhabitants of Monterey at the turn of the century. For years, Spain had been embroiled in wars with France, followed by revolutionary upheaval in Latin America. She had neither time nor money for California. Supply ships and salaries for soldiers, always sporadic, soon ceased to come at all, and the land route, pioneered by Anza, had been cut off by an Indian uprising at Yuma. Only the missions were economically self-sustaining and able to supply provisions to the presidios in return for worthless drafts on the royal treasury.

Conditions in the Monterey presidio itself were primitive. Over 50 buildings were crowded inside the quadrangle that comprised an area only 300 yards long and 250 yards wide, and the damp, crowded, and unsanitary living conditions took a frightening toll both in lives and in morale. Timorously, a few families asked permission of the governor to build outside the presidio walls. It was considered to be a dangerous move, since with the wars of independence in the Spanish colonies, Argentinean revolutionaries had been harassing the Spanish ports of South America. Monterey, with Mexico still loyal to the crown, was expected to be a likely target, and houses on the mesa would be extremely vulnerable.

Corporal Manuel Boronda, who had retired from San Francisco to Monterey, was among the first to take the risk. The adobe he constructed, within shouting shouting distance of the presidio chapel, still stands on Boronda Lane, off present-day Fremont Street. It was a long, low three-room house, with thatched roof and dirt floor. But what luxury after the presidio houses!

The feared attack on the port by privateers occurred less than a year after the Boronda adobe was completed. On the evening of November 20, 1818, two vessels, commanded by a Frenchman, Hippolyte de Bouchard, but sailing under the flag of Buenos Aires, appeared in Monterey Bay. Their combined crews totaled 360 men.

To oppose this force, 24 cavalrymen, under *alférez* (ensign) José Mariano Estrada, were stationed at the fort, located across the mesa to the west of the presidio. Below them on the landing beach, near what eventually became the Custom House, Corporal José de Jesús Valejo, the son of Ignacio, had eleven artillerymen to serve three guns. The small company put up a spirited defense but were soon outnumbered and were forced to retreat to the Salinas Valley, where the townspeople had been evacuated at first sight of the ships.

Bouchard's vandals remained in Monterey for almost a week, looting and burning. The colony's slender supplies were pillaged and most of the buildings were severely damaged. Governor Pablo Vicente de Solá ordered that reconstruction begin at once, but it was many months before the families of the presidio had their simple homes restored.

In 1816, Ana Joséfa Castro de Soberanes had remarried. One of the three sons with whom she had been left was dead, and Feliciano and Mariano de Jesús had families of their own. The latter had wed the Vallejos' eldest daughter, María Isidora, and her sister, the widowed Joséfa María Vallejo de Alvarado was now married to José Raimundo Estrada, brother of the alférez. Joséfa María had left her son from the previous marriage, the young Juan Bautista Alvarado, to be raised by the elder Vallejos. The tyrannical old Don Ignacio was a harsh disciplinarian. Frequently, as punishment for small transgressions, Juan Bautista was forced to eat his meals kneeling before a stool in a corner.

On the morning of April 11, 1822, a great crowd gathered in the presidio plaza to hear the governor's proclamation. Mexico had declared itself independent of Spain! The pioneers who had toiled to build a colony for the glory of God and the king of Spain undoubtedly listened with mixed feelings. For the last time the familiar crimson and gold colors were lowered, and the new red, white, and green banner of Mexico, bearing an eagle and a snake, was raised in its place. The presidio guns thundered a salute, and the townspeople recited the oath of allegiance. Half a century of Spanish rule in Alta California had come to an end.

CHAPTER

6

Advent of the Entrepreneur

In June, 1822, William Hartnell stood on the deck of a brig as it glided past the awesome seaside mountains toward Monterey. He had just come from a cordial reception at San Diego, but the hurdle of an audience with the governor of the California territory still lay ahead.

When the steep mountain fastness gave way to a rocky, pine-clad shoreline of incredible beauty, Hartnell had reached the country where he hoped to make his fortune. Conversations with sea captains in Lima had convinced him of the rich opportunities in Monterey that awaited the right approach.

At age 24, after a quiet boyhood in Lancashire, a year at the College of Commerce in Bremen, and, with the death of his father, immigration to Chile and a job as bookkeeper in a Santiago import-export agency, Hartnell was eager to become more than a clerk. He was affable, gifted with languages, and adaptable—*modo corriente* was the phrase his associates used to describe him, meaning willing to please and to take things as he found them. He soon became known as Don Guillermo Arnel to a coterie of warm companions; and when his boss, John Begg, decided to move the company offices to Lima, Peru, he asked Hartnell to go along.

Hoping to make more money, Hartnell had agreed; but he was disappointed in his new assignment. He had taken on long hours and hard work, with no share in the company profits and little chance of advancement. But just as his situation was becoming hopeless, he was rescued by a co-worker, the Scotsman Hugh McCulloch, who suggested that they go into partnership and establish a firm to trade along the fabled coast of California. Mr. Begg was persuaded to let them operate as agents of John Begg and Company on a profit-sharing basis, and Hartnell and McCulloch set sail with a variety of tempting merchandise secured below—everything from combs, buttons, and shawls to cocoa, cooking utensils, and cloth.

It had been only a matter of months since the Mexican government had opened the ports of San Diego and Monterey to foreign trade, so the young British nationals were not at all certain that the governor would be receptive. On the other hand, they were fairly certain that they would be the first traders to arrive upon the scene, which could be a very important advantage. As the ship rounded Point Pinos, the sparkling, sapphire-blue bay of Monterey burst into view. Above it, a gentle rolling mesa, mantled in emerald green, swept to the crown of pine-covered hills, dark against an incredibly blue sky. To the east on the great arc of the bay rose the presidio buildings, a large quadrangle with an imposing chapel dome towering high above the walled-in enclosure. In the protected curve of the bay to the south was the anchorage, and above it the fort. In between the presidio and the fort, a few houses, with bright red roofs and white walls, were scattered over the grassy plain.

A boat was lowered to take Hartnell and McCulloch into the narrow finger of the landing cove, where they were met by a uniformed horseman. The soldier was unprepossessing in his shabby blue uniform, with tattered red cuffs and collar and broad-brimmed black hat. Hartnell apprised him of their business, and within minutes, the soldier had effortlessly lassoed a couple of horses grazing nearby so that the partners could ride to the governor's quarters inside the presidio walls. In the *sala* of his unpretentious adobe residence, Governor Pablo Vicente de Solá, looking like a stern patriarch with his massive head, broad shoulders, and bushy white beard, greeted the young traders.

After chocolate had been served in small silver cups, he listened to Hartnell's presentation of the terms of the proposed contract. The firm would agree to take all hides available for the next three years, at the equivalent in merchandise of one dollar per hide. This would be in exchange for supplies the province desperately needed.

Solá was impressed. A meeting was arranged with the *presidente* of the missions, Father Mariano Payeras, and "Macala y Arnel," as the traders soon came to be called, were a success. On June 17, 1822, Padre Payeras dispatched a communique to each mission, stating his belief that the terms of the proposed contractual agreement were most advantageous and warmly recommending the merchants.

Immediately, Hartnell sent out a follow-up letter promising to "do everything possible to merit your approval and friendship" and signed "your humble servants who kiss your hands," and a strong, supportive note went from Governor Solá to the three presidio *comandantes* outside of Monterey. The groundwork laid, Hartnell and McCulloch prepared to visit the missions and obtain signatures from the padres in charge. But before leaving Monterey, they made a point of becoming well-acquainted with some of the important residents and landholders.

Most were present at the regular Sunday evening gatherings in the governor's *sala*. The Spanish trader Estéban Munrás had been a resident of Monterey for only two years, but he had already acquired considerable status and owned one of the few adobe houses outside the presidio walls. The Soberanes family was usually represented in the governor's *sala* by the brothers, Feliciano and Mariano de Jesús, sons of Ana Joséfa Castro and the late José María Soberanes. Both soldiers at the presidio, the Soberanes brothers were trying to get the governor to look with favor upon their request for a land concession. The brothers, now married and with growing families to support, keenly resented their loss of the beautiful Buena Vista, which now belonged to José Mariano Estrada.

Estrada was another of Monterey's leading citizens. He had come to Monterey in 1806 as a cadet and had led the fight against Bouchard. With his son, Santiago, he had just acquired the 7,726 acres of fertile land near the Salinas River and was pleading with the governor to let him have several thousand additional acres adjoining the Buena Vista. Another grantee with whom Hartnell became acquainted was José Joaquín de la Torre, who had been given the 6,916-acre Rancho Bolsa del Potrero y Moro Cojo, north of the Salinas River and south of the Tembladera. After 21 years of service in the presidio company and a severe paralytic stroke which left him unable to carry out his duties, Torre had humbly petitioned the governor for a piece of land on which he could support his wife and seven sons.

Such petitions were the routine procedure under Mexican law for obtaining title to land. Authority to grant land was vested in the governor, and the individual who wished to acquire a particular piece of property would direct the petition to him. The petition included information about the person's religion, citizenship, and occupation, as well as a careful description and a map of the land he wished. The graphic delineations, or *diseños*, of the land were primitive works of art. Carried out in pencil, pen and ink, and watercolor, these quaintly charming maps reflected a wonderful variety of cartographic technique.

If the governor was inclined to grant the petition, it was referred to a local magistrate for processing. This involved checking its accuracy, preparing an official title paper, and performing the act of juridical possession. The latter was a ceremony for which the prospective owner and all his neighbors gathered on the land. Then they established a corner of the rancho and marked it with a pile of stones. Next, two mounted men, or *cordeleros*, measured off the boundaries of the property by means of a length of rawhide cord tied between two poles. The magistrate kept count of the number of *cordeles* and adjudicated any disputes between the owner and his neighbors on the spot.

When the place of beginning had been reached, the magistrate formally indicated to the grantee his possession of the land. The ranchero could then act out the fact of his ownership. By pulling up clumps of grass, breaking off branches of trees, and throwing rocks in the four cardinal directions, he demonstrated that he could do things to the land that would not be permitted to another. On this amazing procedure was based the validity of all private land claims at the time of American occupation. Often, of course, steps were omitted, papers were mislaid by carefree *Californios*, or the same piece of property was granted several times to different individuals by casually indifferent governors. These claims became easy prey for the more practical *Americanos* who descended on the land a few decades later.

By late June, Hartnell and McCulloch were ready to start their journeys on the mission trail. McCulloch traveled south and Hartnell took the northern territory. On the basis of what they had seen, the partners on their return agreed that they would need stations along the coast to collect and take hides aboard ship but that it would be best to make Monterey their headquarters. More cosmopolitan than San Diego, Monterey offered the advantages of social intercourse and contact with the outside world.

The fledgling firm had just established itself when, without warning, it received a harsh blow. One morning, a Boston ship dropped anchor in the bay of Monterey, and a new trader came ashore. William Gale was a tough, aggressive New Englander who, twelve years before, had whetted his appetite for California trade while sailing under contract to Russia for sea-otter and seal skins. Determined to return and pluck the golden goose for himself, he had induced Bryant and Sturgis of Boston to participate in a business venture, the far-reaching results of which they could not have anticipated. An assorted cargo of notions and foodstuffs had been assembled on the *Sachem* and, with Gale as supercargo and part owner, the vessel had set sail around the Horn.

The Yankee trader lacked the finesse of Hartnell, but he was possessed of enormous energy and knew how to drive a bargain. His first step in undercutting "Macala y Arnel" was to offer twice their price for hides. Inevitably there were some, even among the padres, who went for the better deal. Then Gale managed to ingratiate himself with the Californians. His appearance and mannerisms were a source of great amusement to them. They nicknamed him *Cuatro Ojos* (four eyes) because of his great, staring eyes, magnified by thick spectacles. Others called him *Cambalache* (barter), referring to the zeal with which he haggled over a sale. His desregard for grammar and his broken Spanish only added to his popularity.

There was no question that Hartnell and McCulloch had stiff competition on their hands. But they still held some trump cards. The new governor, Luis Arguello, was most amicably disposed towards them and granted them permission to "trade in all the ports of California and also in all the landfalls and bays near the missions." This was an unusually liberal interpretation of Mexican law, which had opened only San Diego and Monterey to foreign vessels. In addition, he agreed to allow them to build any needed warehouses, stores, or residences at Monterey.

Besides the governor's favor, Hartnell and McCulloch had the advantage of knowing precisely the type of goods the padres wanted. Their first consignment of merchandise had been a broadside approach. Now, before Gale had time to get acquainted with the market, they sent off orders to Lima for such articles as thermometers, religious images, gold thread for embroidering altar pieces, musical instruments, sacred music, and "diamonds to cut with."

The charm of Hartnell's personality put him on an intimate basis with both the Franciscan fathers and the first families of Monterey, and this, too, had been good for business. From the beginning, Hartnell had enlisted the friendship of Estéban Munrás, the Estradas, and the Soberanes brothers. Soon he also became acquainted with the elderly and powerful Ignacio Vallejo, resident of the Monterey area since 1774. Young Mariano, one of Vallejo's thirteen children, worked in Hartnell's store, as did Juan Bautista Alvarado.

It didn't take Hartnell long to learn the intricate interrelationships between the pioneer Monterey families; and before he had been in California a year, he had also gained entree to the prominent de la Guerra family of Santa Barbara. Don José de la Guerra y Noriega was the wealthiest, most cultivated, and most influential man in the province. Attracted at once to Hartnell by the cultural interests they shared, he made the Englishman welcome at *la casa de la Guerra,* a mecca for distinguished visitors from all over the world. It was in this setting that Hartnell met the lovely Teresa de la Guerra, then only thirteen, whom he was to marry three years later.

In 1823, more competition for "Macala y Arnel" arrived in the person of Captain Roger Cooper. But perhaps because of a similarity in background, he and Hartnell were from the beginning *simpatico.* Born on Alderney Island, off the coast of Britain, Cooper had come to Massachusetts as a boy with his mother. An injury in his youth had caused his left hand to be deformed, and before long, this defect was to earn him the name *Juan el Manco* (the Maimed). He began his mercantile career in California by selling his ship, the *Rover*, to Governor Arguello but continuing to command her on trading voyages under government contract.

By 1824, two more men who were to become prominent in the business and political affairs of the capital had arrived. The Yankee trading ship the *Panther* brought a young Spanish Basque, José Amesti, who decided to stay and become a merchant. Possibly his decision was influenced by Prudenciana Vallejo, elder sister to Mariano, since Amesti married her before the year was out. Then, in September, the Scotsman David Spence came at the request of Hartnell.

Hartnell had been appalled at the waste and unsanitary conditions resulting from the annual, springtime slaughtering of cattle. Stripped of hides and fat for tallow, the carcasses were left to rot on the ground. The stench was overpowering and the air filled with carrion crows, swarming over the putrid flesh. He wrote to McCulloch, now handling their business in Lima, and suggested that the firm might embark on a venture of salting beef for shipment to Peru. David Spence was his choice for the employee to manage the operation.

Though not well-educated, David Spence was a hardworking, canny businessman. He brought several expert salters and coopers with him from Lima. and the venture was soon under way. However, it proved to be expensive and unprofitable; salt had to be imported, since the local variety was unsuitable, and there was little market for the beef. Still, Spence quickly became indispensable to Hartnell. His common sense, versatility, and good-natured attitude made him an ideal manager of the Monterey office during Hartnell's frequent absences on business.

With his many competitors, and particularly with William Gale, who lost no opportunity to discredit the "Macala y Arnel" operation, Hartnell had increasing business difficulties after his auspicious beginning. Misunderstandings had developed with the parent company in Lima, and rumors were rife that the partners planned to close out their business as soon as the three-year mission contract had expired. Perhaps most damaging of all was Hartnell's drinking problem, which was interfering with his work. Then, briefly, the clouds lifted. He was persuaded by a friar to go into a retreat at the Mission San Luis Obispo. The week of prayer and self-examination had a salutary effect. Shortly afterwards, Hartnell was baptized in the Catholic faith, and a few months later he married his beloved Teresa.

Being a member of the influential de la Guerra family opened up new business opportunities. In addition, some of his friends among the pioneer families had achieved a certain amount of security and influence. The doughty Sergeant Ignacio Vallejo was now the owner of the Rancho Bolsa de San Cayetano in the Pajaro Valley. The 8,866-acre grant was the first property owned by the Vallejos in California, and on it stood a two-story adobe which would come to be called the "Casa Materna," or mother house, of the family that would someday be famous.

Feliciano and Mariano Soberanes were also living on a land grant, provisionally given them in 1823, which was located not far from Rancho Buena Vista. They named their new land Rancho de Nuestra Señora de la Carmen, but, before long, it came to be called El Alisal for the lush groves of alder trees that grew along the river.

A nearby neighbor was José Tiburcio Castro, son of Macario and father of the young José, who had built an adobe on the Rancho Sauzal and was asking that the governor grant him the 10,242 acres. And north of Monterey, José Tiburcio's brother Simeon Castro had been given the Rancho Bolsa del Moro Cojo, which eventually would comprise better than 30,000 acres.

These new landowners helped Hartnell, but the advent of a new governor, combined with a worldwide depression, once again brought his firm into a crisis. A new governor, José María Echeandía, was sent from Mexico to replace the easygoing *hijo del pais*, Don Luis Arguello, who had been accused of granting too many favors to his friends, notable among them Hartnell. Echeandía ordered that foreign trade be restricted to the ports of Monterey and San Diego and that heavy duties be levied. The higher tariff coupled with the expense of transporting hides over great distances and the inroads being made by the Yankee traders bid fair to wreck "Macala y Arnel." Unfortunately Hartnell's *modo corriente* no longer worked its magic in the tough, competitive situation that had developed in California. Willaim Gale was still his worst adversary. But even his friend Cooper, who had been baptized Juan Bautista Roger and married Mariano Vallejo's younger sister Encarnacion, was becoming a serious rival in trade.

In 1827, another blow came with the resignation of David Spence. He was courting José Mariano Estrada's daughter Adelaide. Since an elder Estrada daughter, Joséfa, was married to the rich Peruvian trader Juan Malarín, a resident of Monterey for two years, there was the possibility that the prospective brothers-in-law would go into partnership and open a general store.

The following year, the firm of McCulloch, Hartnell and Company had to be dissolved. Hugh McCulloch, busy with his own affairs in Lima, did not care, and John Begg, who had financed the company, wanted only to get his money out. Accumulated losses for the firm totaled over $29,000. Hartnell agreed to assume responsibility for debts owed in California—over $18,000! And so the pioneer entrepreneur William Hartnell, who had arrived in an unexploited country, created a demand for foreign commodities, and made trade a part of mission life, was left burdened with a difficult obligation. To make matters worse, the thunderheads of political upheaval were massed along the horizon and all Californians were in the path of the storm.

7

A *Period of Political Turbulence*

On the night of November 13, 1829, Mariano Vallejo was entertaining his childhood friends Juan Bautista Alvarado and José Castro, in his quarters at the presidio. Vallejo, now 21, was the most impressive of the three. Tall, with curly dark hair, a determined chin, and intelligent and penetrating eyes, he had been appointed *alférez* (ensign) of the San Francisco company but was still stationed in Monterey. Shorter and somewhat stocky, with a fair complexion and light hair, Alvarado, a year younger than Vallejo, was now secretary to the *diputacion*, or legislative assembly. Castro, at nineteen, was obviously the youngest and, lean and uneasy-eyed, the least attractive. He held a position with the *ayuntamiento* (town council).

Their card game had ended about two o'clock, and the young men were retired for the night. Suddenly, the silence was broken by a clamor at the door. Vallejo demanded to know the cause of the disturbance.

A low urgent voice replied that a message from the governor must be delivered at once. Drowsy and annoyed, young Vallejo growled that it could wait until morning. Instantly, there was a crashing assault at the door and a crowd of soldiers burst into the room. Their leader announced that the garrison was in revolt and, without giving the astonished youths time to dress, hustled them off to the *calabozo*.

As other government officials were brought into the rude prison, it was learned that Joaquín Solís, an ex-convict banished from Mexico, had incited the ragged and half-starved soldiers to rebel. He had the support of Commissioner Herrera, who for months had not had funds with which to pay the troops. This was the start of the series of revolutions and counterrevolutions that were to continue until the American occupation.

Herrera had high hopes of enlisting financial aid for the revolution from the foreign businessmen of Monterey, who resented Governor Echeandía's rigid trade restrictions. A meeting was held in Herrera's home at which Hartnell, Spence, and Cooper were present, as well as a newcomer, Abel Stearns, who was in Cooper's employ. Herrera read a list of the soldiers' grievances to which his guests responded sympathetically. They then fixed their signatures to an official statement to be circulated to all presidios and pueblos, and several hundred pesos were collected for the cause.

Governor Echeandía, who had established his gubernatorial headquarters in San Diego because of a hypochondriacal fear that the damp climate of Monterey would be injurious to his health, sent out a circular letter from the southern presidio, calling on all citizens to lay down their arms. Then, he marched north with troops to meet Solís's ragamuffin army. The forces converged in Santa Barbara where, after two days of bloodless confrontation, the rebels were dispersed.

Echeandía was unduly vindictive in his punishment of the instigators of the revolt, and since the reasons for the rebellion had been valid, many people were estranged by his actions. Thus when the governor arrived in Monterey, he found the capital seething with unrest. The businessmen of the community were especially outraged at the ever-increasing instances of violence and vandalism by Solís's defeated men. They felt their property endangered by the lawlessness let loose in the region. There were mutterings among the younger *hijos del país*, like Juan Bautista Alvarado, that the only solution to an impossible situation was the appointment of a new governor.

The wily incumbent governor then hit upon a scheme that held promise of giving him a popularity he had never enjoyed. Aided and abetted by the fiery radical José María Padrés, he developed a plan for transferring control of mission lands from the Church to civil administrators. The newly created positions of power could then be parceled out to *paisanos* willing to support him. The program was mantled in a cloak of idealism and philanthropy—at last, the Indians were to be freed from bondage and given some of the land that was rightfully theirs.

The bill for secularization of the missions was presented to the summer session of the *diputacion*, and amidst ringing oratory about the tyranny of the missionaries and the crimes committed against defenseless Christian Indians, it passed by a substantial majority. Undoubtedly, the motives of those who voted for the measure were mixed. Without question there was justification for some of the accusations against the mission system, but there was also real resentment of the prosperity the missions possessed.

The original design for the missions in California had provided that after ten years they would be converted to civilian towns and the missionaries would then be transferred to new frontier outposts. This did not happen. Instead, the missions soon became the economic mainstay of the whole province. Soldiers, ill-paid and practically without the necessities of life, envied the relative riches of the padres, and second-generation colonists, with little opportunity for financial security, hungrily eyed the mission lands. Land grants were scarce; in 1830, only 50 private ranches were held in all of Alta California, of which seven were in the Monterey area. On the other hand, vast stretches of coast and a goodly portion of the inland country belonged to the Church.

Echeandía's legislation was sent to Mexico City for approval, but he issued a proclamation putting the plan into effect without waiting for sanction from the central government. José Castro and Juan Bautista Alvarado were among those who benefited at once, being appointed administrators respectively of the Missions San Luis Obispo and San Miguel. It wasn't long, however, before word came that a replacement for Echeandía had been appointed and was en route from Mexico.

The replacement, Lieutenant Colonel Manuel Victoria, was a poor choice for governor at this sensitive moment in the politics of California. Harsh and overbearing, his convictions contrasted sharply with those of the *hijos del país*. There was much in his manner to indicate that he considered native Californians to be an inferior group of country bumpkins. His first official act was to issue a decree declaring secularization illegal, and his opening speech in Monterey was a call for the restoration of law and order—"The government must be obeyed and our institutions respected." Summary exile was the punishment meted out to those who persisted in carrying out the secularization program. But Victoria's worst offense was a refusal to convene the *diputacion*. When repeated appeals to call the legislative assembly into session resulted in a manifesto suspending that body, several members, including Vallejo and Alvarado, petitioned the central government in Mexico for protection against the tyranny of the new governor.

There were other law-abiding citizens, however, who championed his cause. Conspicuous among them were the businessmen, who felt he provided the security necessary for the orderly conduct of affairs. Men like Hartnell, Cooper, Spence, and Alfred Robinson, who had replaced the tempestuous William Gale as resident agent for the Boston firm of Bryant and Sturgis, favored Victoria's authoritarian approach. Their sentiments were echoed by old-line conservatives like Hartnell's father-in-law, José de la Guerra of Santa Barbara.

Gradually, the liberal element in California drifted south to gather in San Diego. Soon Echeandía, who was now popular among the radicals, slipped back from Baja California to join them. Together they plotted revolution, while Monterey remained the stronghold of Victoria.

Finally, late in November 1831, Governor Victoria marched southward with 30 veteran soldiers and engaged the rebels in battle on the outskirts of Los Angeles. When victory was seemingly assured, Victoria was severely wounded and his men deserted to the insurgents. The wounded officer was then forcibly transported to San Diego and put aboard a Yankee frigate bound for Mexico.

Great was the lamentation in the missions at the loss of their great good friend, but the fiery young *paisanos* rejoiced. The long-delayed meeting of the *diputacion* was immediately called in Los Angeles. Monterey, still dominated by the group of merchants staunchly opposed to revolution (it was bad for business), had chosen Captain Agustín Zamorano, ranking officer of the presidio and close friend of Hartnell, to carry on the legitimate chain of governmental administration.

Meanwhile, in Los Angeles, where the *diputacion* was in session, young Vallejo was instrumental in drawing up a document to the Mexican government, indicting Governor Victoria for his actions and defending the Californians. The legislative assembly then elected one of the radical leaders, Pío Pico, as temporary governor. Echeandía, who expected the honor himself, refused to administer the oath of office, whereupon Vallejo and Alvarado took matters into their own hands—the former climbing through a skylight to obtain the articles necessary for the ceremony and the latter presuming to perform the ceremony.

Before long, the political scene became even more chaotic. Pico was deposed by Echeandía, and Zamorano sent troops south to assert his authority. There was threat of civil war, followed by a compromise that split California into two sections, with Zamorano in control from Sonoma to Los Angeles and Echeandía in power south to San Diego. The bickering and bluster had something of the quality of comic opera, but responsible citizens were not amused.

A type of vigilante group developed in Monterey when Zamorano realized that he had little strength should there be a sudden uprising. As a last resort, Zamorano appealed to Hartnell to organize a voluntary police force, which could assist in protecting the lives and property of residents in and around the capital. Hartnell agreed, and the group, comprising about 50 men, became known as *La Compañia Extranjera,* because it included all the merchants in the community, who for the most part were foreigners.

In January 1833, another political change came in the person of Brevet Brigadier General José Figueroa, who replaced Zamorano in

Monterey. Having had a long and distinguished career as governor of
Sonora and Sinaloa, the 41-year-old General Figueroa knew how to
handle the troubled California situation. His first official act was to
grant anmesty to all who had taken part in any of the several rebellions.
This won his instant popularity, and all factions vied to extend him
a cordial welcome. Soon he was nicknamed *el Pacifico y Calmoso.*

Under the progressive and peaceful regime of Figueroa, Monterey
and the whole province enjoyed a period of prosperity. One reason for
the success of his rule was that the new governor was generous in the
granting of land concessions, bestowing four in his first year. Juan Malarín
was given the Rancho Guadalupe y Llanitos de los Correos, which
stretched for 8,859 acres on the west side of the Salinas River, opposite
today's towns of Chualar and Gonzales. José Armenta was granted the
Rancho Punta de Pinos, 2,667 acres including present-day Pacific Grove.
Graciano Manjares received the 2,212-acre Rancho Saucito on which the
Monterey Airport now stands. And the widowed Cristina Delgado was
given the 2,220-acre Rincon de las Salinas, "corner of the salt marshes,"
not far from the mouth of the Salinas River. Both she and her husband
had been Carmel Mission Indians.

In the following year, 1834, Figueroa bestowed another 50,000 acres
of land in five grants. Among them were the 26,581-acre Rancho los
Tularcitos, east of today's Carmel Valley Village, which was given to
Rafael Gomez, and the 8,949-acre Rancho El Sur, on the coast south
of the Little Sur River, which was granted to Juan Bautista Alvarado.
Doña Catalina Manzanelli, the wife of Munrás, received the 2,179-acre
Rancho Laguna Seca, east of Monterey, and for David Spence, now
a naturalized citizen and married to Adelaide Estrada, there was title
to the Rancho Encinal y Buena Esperanza, 13,391 acres adjacent to
his father-in-law's Buena Vista. Also in the valley of the Salinas, José
Tiburcio Castro was granted his claim to the Sauzal, and confirmation
was given to the Soberanes brothers for the Alisal grant. At the same
time, the governor gave official sanction to division of the Alisal rancho
between the Soberanes and Hartnell.

The division of El Alisal came about because, several years earlier,
William Hartnell had made an arrangement with the Soberanes brothers
permitting him to farm and pasture cattle on the beautiful Ranch. Soon
he longed to move, with his rapidly growing family, to the sunny valley,
but ranching on shares did not provide sufficient income to allow aban-
donment of his trading interests in Monterey.

His father-in-law, José de la Guerra, then suggested the perfect
solution. Hartnell had shown that he was a teacher at heart by voluntarily

tutoring the adolescent Vallejo and Alvarado. Don José de la Guerra therefore proposed to finance the purchase of a piece of land from the Soberanes so that Hartnell could open a boarding school at El Alisal. Governor Figueroa, who was an enthusiast for education, readily gave his support, ratifying the deed to the 2,971 acres. The Soberanes family retained almost twice that amount of acreage and continued to reside on their portion of the ranch. Feliciano Soberanes now had twelve children for whom to provide. His brother Mariano de Jesús had been a widower since 1830, when María Isidora died eleven days after the birth of their ninth child. Now Mariano lived alone with his seven sons, while his eighteen-year-old daughter, María Ignacia, stayed with her grandmother Vallejo in Monterey.

Juan Bautista Cooper, still a powerful force in the mercantile field, had also become a landowner. From the beginning, José Joaquín de la Torre had had difficulty holding on to the Rancho Bolsa del Potrero y Moro Cojo. Two years after receiving the grant, he was forced to cede a half of the property to an Irish seaman named John Mulligan in order to satisfy a debt. Then, in 1829, he sold his remaining portion to Cooper for $2,000. Now, Cooper had also picked up the Mulligan section for $826. It was a portent for the future. Foreigners were beginning to take their place in the ranks of California rancheros.

In 1833, the last of the great entrepreneurs arrived in Monterey. He was another Bostonian and the younger half-brother of Cooper. Thomas O. Larkin, born in Massachusetts, was orphaned at the age of fifteen. Thrown on his own resources, he moved south, where, with his keen aptitude for business, he became a storekeeper and office holder by the time he was twenty. When a severe illness forced Larkin to give up his store, Cooper suggested that he come to California.

Larkin landed at Yerba Buena, on San Francisco Bay. A small scattering of huts and adobe structures met his appraising eye, but the great harbor was almost empty. He quickly obtained work as a clerk but, disillusioned with the embryonic San Francisco, he moved on to Monterey, bustling center of trade. When Larkin arrived in the capital, it had grown to a town of about 30 houses, dotted around in an irregular pattern. The houses had a bandaged look, their south sides dressed with boards and brush to keep out the rain. None had chimneys, as there were no fireplaces, and cooking was done in tiny separate buildings. There were no streets, but paths that wound across the mesa had developed a semblance of lanes, since they had been widened by the heavy wheels of oxcarts. Plank bridges spanned the steep gullies, permitting the loaded *carretas* to pass along *Calle Principal* to the beach.

Californians, Larkin soon decided, were a naive, childlike people, whose philosophy was summed up in the oft repeated phrase, *"No se apure*—don't be in a hurry." They bought bad wine, made in Boston, when their country abounded in grapes. They cheerfully bartered hides valued at $2 for articles worth seventy-five cents. They also purchased boots at $4 made of these same hides, carried twice around the Horn. Indolence and ease hung in the air, like the ubiquitous coastal fog.

The men of Monterey seemed scarcely to move from one house to another without mounting a horse. The animals were exceedingly abundant and ran loose, dragging long leather ropes by which they were easily caught. Inside the crude adobe houses, with their hard-packed dirt floors, the women wore silk gowns and spangled satin shoes.

Larkin found that a dozen or more Englishmen and Americans, married to Californians, had all the trade of the province in their hands. And of these, representatives of Bryant and Sturgis, the Boston firm, led the field. Supersalesman that he was, Larkin knew that he could cut in on the lucrative game, so with $500 borrowed from his half-brother, he set up shop as trader and importer. Since business was slow at first, he went after it by recognizing the native love of color and sparkling trinkets and creating new markets with gaudy merchandise from Mazatlan and the Sandwich Islands. He also made himself popular with the *doñas* by ordering special dresses for them and promising delivery in twelve months.

Competition was rough but Larkin held his own, partly by virtue of his wits and personality and partly through the political influence he enjoyed as the half-brother of Cooper, who had married into the Vallejos. Then, he hit upon another lucrative financial scheme. The Sandwich Islands were the trade center for the Pacific, and traffic was brisk between there and the California coast. Several American firms, with headquarters at Honolulu, carried large stocks of merchandise from Boston and the Far East, which they wholesaled to Monterey merchants. The merchants in turn had to extend credit to the leading families of the Monterey area. The word of a *caballero* was his bond, and no questions were ever asked nor pressure applied. An open account might run for years. Gradually, Larkin acquired these delinquent accounts, so that his store became a clearing house for the notes and drafts of the other traders in the area. Since he then made a substantial service charge when he collected hides from the rancheros for these notes and drafts, he soon had improvised his own version of Wall Street in the dusty lanes of Monterey.

Possessed of a strong independence and Yankee pragmatism, Larkin did not hold California customs or even laws to be sacred. A case in point was his easy contempt for import duties, which sometimes ran as high as 100% of the cost of the cargo. Revenue officials often connived with traders to circumvent the outrageous tariffs imposed by the Mexican government, and Larkin quickly became an old hand at the practice. The bulk of one cargo from Honolulu, valued at $20,000, was unloaded during the night, and the following morning duty was paid on the remnant at a valuation of $1,100.

Most of Larkin's flauntings of convention were financial maneuvers, but in one case at least, romance was his motive. He alone, among all the entrepreneurs, held out against the attractions of California's lovely *señoritas*. En route from Boston, he had found a congenial companion in Rachel Holmes, an attractive young woman on her way to Hawaii to join her husband. When the ship anchored in Hilo harbor, it was learned that Mrs. Holmes had been widowed a few weeks before her arrival. Larkin resumed his voyage alone, but he did not forget the slender fair-haired Rachel, and in the autumn of 1833, she came to be his bride. They were married aboard ship, off the coast of Santa Barbara, by the United States Consul of Honolulu. There followed a brilliant fiesta on shore, attended by members of most of California's first families. Then, a few days later, *"la señora Yanqui"* was at home in Monterey.

Soon, a fine new house was constructed by the Larkins on a hillside overlooking the bay. The building, which reflected the colonial influence of the eastern seaboard, was the talk of the town. Two stories high, with glass windows, a center staircase, an upstairs fireplace, and redwood shingles for the roof, the Larkin home resembled its neighbors only in the adobe brick that was used for its construction.

Now the period of grace, brought by the capable Governor Figueroa, was drawing to a close. In the spring of 1834, Figueroa received two communications from the government in Mexico. The first ordered him to secularize all missions at once; the second informed him that his request for retirement had been honored. A relationship between the two dispatches was obvious. The new governor, José María Híjar, was to be accompanied by the radical Padrés, who had been exiled by Victoria. With them were to come 250 colonists, subsidized by the government in accord with a plan developed by Padrés. These people would have to have land.

Figueroa felt that immediate and total secularization would have disastrous effects, and for the brief time he had left in office, he decided to temporize with the problem of secularization. The decree that he issued provided for ten missions to be secularized in the current year, six more in 1835, and the remaining ones in 1836. One half of the mission property was to be distributed among the Christian Indians; the rest of the land to be placed under control of civil administrators. The four missions in the Monterey area were listed among the last to be converted to secular control.

Padrés and his assemblage of pioneers set sail from San Blas, with the new governor of California, but when they arrived in Monterey in September, they were confounded by the news that there had been a sudden upheaval in the central government and Híjar's appointment had been cancelled.

Based on the sentiments and friendship they had shared in the days of Echeandía, Padrés assumed he could count on the support of the young liberal Californians. He was dumbfounded when Vallejo and Alvarado refused their support. The picture had changed; why should they back Padrés, who had brought Mexican colonists to serve as mission administrators and to appropriate their properties? The *diputacion* voted that Figueroa continue as governor, and Padrés and Híjar were reduced to the role of directors of colonization, with a band of homeless *pobladores* on their hands. Unable to accept the situation, the two men fomented an uprising and were deported by Figueroa, who, despite increasing ill health, was making a last valiant attempt to keep order and peace in the province.

During the last year of his administration, the governor granted eight more land concessions, bringing to 27 the number of private land concessions in what would become Monterey County. José Ramon Estrada, son of José Mariano, received the 5,668-acre Rancho El Toro, ten miles east of Monterey. In the Carmel Valley, on the redwood mantled slopes of the Santa Lucias, the 8,814-acre San Francisquito was granted to Catalina Manzanelli de Munrás, and on the coast south of San José Creek, the 8,876-acre San José y Sur Chiquito was given to Teodoro Gonzales. Doña Catalina's husband, Estéban, also was not neglected, receiving the 19,979-acre Rancho San Vicente, across the river from the lands of the Soledad Mission.

On September 29, 1835, Governor Figueroa died of an apoplectic stroke. His demise initiated a decade of chaos unprecedented even in California's turbulent past. According to provision made by Figueroa, José Castro and Nicolas Gutiérrez took over temporary conduct of governmental affairs. But a new governor, Colonel Mariano Chico, was already appointed by the Mexican government and en route from Mexico City.

Disturbing rumors preceded him. The worst of these was the report that he would move the capital to Los Angeles. Monterey was in an uproar. Hartnell was instrumental in drafting an immediate protest to the central government. Among the arguments advanced were that "Monterey has decent buildings for government uses . . . mild climate, fertile soil . . . " and "here women, plants, and useful animals are very productive." The document ended on a plaintive note: "Monterey has done no wrong to be deprived of its honor."

Despite their misgivings, the residents of Monterey welcomed Governor Chico with a gala ball. With the wizened, bespectacled governor was a glamorous young woman whom he introduced as his niece. The *doñas*, who set the rules of social propriety, exchanged knowing looks and were noticeably cool to both in their greetings. Influential men of the province soon were antagonized by Chico for quite different reasons.

Chico made a personal vendetta of the wrongs he felt his friend Victoria had suffered. He struck out against foreign merchants for their monopoly of trade and railed against the evils of secularization. Indiscriminate arrests of prominent citizens fanned the flames of resentment. Then, an incident occurred which united the men and women of Monterey in righteous indignation.

At a theatrical performance in the presidio plaza, the Governor arrived accompanied not only by his "niece," whom everyone knew was his mistress, but also by her friend, a scandalous lady who had once been arrested for adultery. Many of the *doñas* left at once. The *alcalde*, Ramon Estrada, responded more subtly. He sent for the adulterer—the man who had compromised Chico's lady's ladyfriend—and gave him a seat of honor next to him. Chico flew into a rage. The next day he ordered Estrada removed from office as mayor. Residents of Monterey were outraged, and a threatening mob gathered outside the Governor's house. Not noted for his courage, Chico departed for Mexico.

Once again Gutiérrez took over as acting governor. But his days were also numbered. A devotee of wine and women, with a fondness for Indian girls, his morals were considered no better than those of Chico. An even more damaging likeness to Chico was his highhanded behavior.

The young Californians, briefly held in check by the beneficent administration of Figueroa, were now totally fed up with officials whose allegiance was to Mexico. They felt it was time to choose a governor from their own ranks, one who understood the needs of their country. Juan Bautista Alvarado took the lead in this popular movement.

The genial Alvarado was now 27, fair-haired and good-looking, and the recently elected president of the *diputacion*. Possessed of much practical ability in addition to being a smooth politician, Alvarado was a favorite with all classes of *paisanos* and he also enjoyed the support of the foreign merchants. His single evident weakness was a strong fondness for drink. But being the nephew and close friend of Mariano Vallejo protected him from scandalmongers (although Vallejo was only a year older than Alvarado, he was also Alvarado's uncle, since old Ignacio Vallejo's daughter was the mother of Juan Bautista).

The talk about rebellion turned into action as a result of two foolish moves made by Gutiérrez. The first was a threat to dissolve the *diputacion*. The second was the issuance of an order for Alvarado's arrest, following a quarrel about enforcement of tariff regulations. When Alvarado's arrest was ordered, the assembly, composed of freedom-loving *hijos del país*, fled from Monterey to San Juan Bautista, where their revolutionary headquarters was established.

It was decided that Alvarado must travel at once to Sonoma, where Mariano Vallejo was stationed as *comandante* of the northern frontier. En route, Alvarado stopped to see a Tennessee backwoodsman named Isaac Graham, a resident of Natividad, who had established a distillery there. A wild and reckless fellow, with a reputation as a crack-shot and hater of Mexican soldiers, Graham readily agreed to round up a band of his cronies to fight with the rebels.

Alvarado was not as successful with Vallejo. To his astonishment, his best friend counseled caution. Vallejo was now a man of property and position. He enjoyed a free hand on the frontier. He had a family for whom to provide. No longer was he the adventurous youth with everything to gain and nothing to lose. He would be unable to cooperate with the revolutionists.

Despite the stand Vallejo had taken, Alvarado used his uncle's name anyway as the leader of the movement. With José Castro's assistance, he assembled a force of about seventy-five men, armed with lances and a few old muskets. Mainstay of the insurrection was the contingent provided by Graham, made up mostly of deserters from Yankee ships and a sprinkling of fur trappers.

On the evening of November 3, 1836, the rebels advanced on Monterey. Castro devised several clever ruses to convince the presidio garrison that he had a strong army at his command. Small groups were deployed on the hills, fires were kindled, and trumpets and drums were sounded from the widely separated spots. The fort fell without resistance.

Residents of Monterey were terrified at the sight of Graham's bearded roughnecks, but the foreign merchants were, to a man, in sympathy with the rebellion, expecting that Alvarado would favor their commercial interests. Foreign ships anchored in the harbor went so far as to provide ammunition to the insurgents. Soon soldiers from the presidio began deserting to the enemy, and a demand was sent to the besieged governor for surrender within two hours.

Contemptuous of Graham, the *gringo* in the fantastic fur cap, Gutiér-rez did not deign to answer. At the precise time that the specified period of grace was up, a shot was sent from the cannon monted on the fort. It crashed through the roof of the governor's house. The presidio quickly capitulated and the governor, mustering what dignity he could, departed for Mexico.

The very next day the *diputacion*, chaired by José Castro, declared California a free and sovereign state. Alvarado was elected governor and Vallejo was appointed *comandante general,* despite the fact that he had not participated in the revolution. At last, the *hijos del pais* had their own man in the gubernatorial seat. Great was the rejoicing in Monterey

But even as the crowds in Monterey acclaimed Alvarado and the new government, the forces of counterrevolution were gathering in the south. The ensuing five years of rule, over an increasingly fragmented California, were destined to be stormy. They would transform the ebullient and idealistic young man into a prematurely middle-aged alcoholic.

8

Two Cultures Co-exist

From the first days of his term as governor, Alvarado was beset by problems. His genial, charismatic personality was better suited to the pyrotechnics of a political campaign than to the grinding pressures of everyday administration. He also found that political victory had its price. Graham and his mercenaries clamored for their rewards. However, since he was strapped by inadequate revenues and unable to give land to non-citizens, the governor was helpless to meet their demands.

To compound his difficulties, the rift with tío Mariano Vallejo once again widened. Vallejo had the heart of a soldier and placed great emphasis on military discipline. He was shocked at the informality and familiarity which the affable Alvarado allowed. It was unthinkable for a governor to be addressed as "Juanito," for example. Vallejo also felt that it was urgent to strengthen the military defenses of the province. The Monterey presidio, especially, was in ruins after being pillaged by residents to obtain building material for their houses. But where was Alvarado to get funds? There was not even enough money to pay the troops.

The strain upon Alvarado's mercurial temperament began to show. Although he had two fine adobe houses in Monterey, he spent increasingly long periods with his friend Feliciano Soberanes at Rancho El Alisal. Frequently, he was away from his office for weeks at a time, turning his duties over to Manuel Casarin Jimeno, the brother-in-law of William Hartnell. Jimeno, who was officially Alvarado's secretary of state, disliked Vallejo intensely and added fuel to the growing feud between the governor and his uncle.

Twice Vallejo came to Monterey to reason with Alvarado, but he was informed that the governor was out of town and too ill to be bothered. In a dramatic move to illustrate the urgent need for a military reorganization, Vallejo then arranged for his good friend Solano, chief of the Suisun Indians, to visit Monterey accompanied by a hundred of his tribesmen. The giant Indian, his six-foot seven-inch frame clothed in the dress of a Spaniard, rode through the placid streets of the town, while behind him, mounted on fine horses, his warriors followed, wearing elaborate costumes fashioned of feathers and carrying lances and bows and arrows. Frightened women barred the windows and stout-hearted *caballeros* reined in their horses to make way for the entourage. But Alvarado was absent at the time and Vallejo obtained no satisfaction for his efforts.

By midsummer of 1839, the 30-year-old governor was drinking heavily. His personal life held almost as many problems as his besieged public office. For some years he had kept a mistress, more or less in secret. She was Raimunda Castillo, daughter of the town pharmacist and bloodletter. An astonishingly beautiful young woman, Raimunda was apparently devoted to Alvarado and had given him three daughters. Now, the governor felt the time had come for him to assume a mantle of respectability. Perhaps a deep-seated insecurity prevented him from marrying the woman upon whom he had brought the taint of scandal. Or he may have hoped that his marriage could bring needed political support. In any case he chose for his bride a girl he had apparently never met, the 25-year-old María Martina Castro, daughter of Francisco Castro and María Gabriela Berryessa.

Elaborate preparations were made for the August 24th wedding at the Santa Clara Mission. There Martina awaited her bridegroom, surrounded by a huge assemblage of family and friends. But on the fateful morning it was not Juan Bautista, but his half-brother, José Antonio Estrada, who appeared at the church. Estrada stumbled through the message he had been instructed to give: the governor had been unavoidably detained by official business, and José Antonio had been sent to act as proxy in the ceremony. The Soberanes brothers, Martina's cousins, knew better. They had seen the governor the day before, and he was in no condition to attend a wedding.

Eight days later, the bride came to Monterey and the newlyweds met. When Alvarado saw Martina, he was dismayed. Later he remarked that though she was a lovely girl, she was neither the one in the picture he had been shown nor the one of his dreams. What Martina thought of the fat and flabby Juan Bautista, with pouches of dissipation under his eyes, is not known. But the festivities lasted for a week.

Early in 1840, Graham's gang of *rifleros* began to harass Alvarado more blatantly and strained his patience to the breaking point. They strutted through his chambers and accosted him on the streets, calling out "Ho! Bautista, come here! I want to speak to you." Members of the "bandit gang" also began to openly toast the new Republic of Texas, with cheers of "California next!" And it did not contribute to Alvarado's peace of mind to find a human skull hanging from the halyard of the flagstaff outside his door. Both the governor and his friend, José Castro, became alarmed for their personal safety as well as that of the province.

Matters came to a head when the governor received a message from Padre Suarez del Real, warning him that Graham and his followers planned to seize Monterey and cast off Mexican sovereignty. The plot had been revealed to him in the confessional by a foreigner on the point of death. Instantly, Alvarado went into action, since he had grounds for getting at the nest of troublemakers, who had been buzzing around his head like horseflies.

In the middle of the night, on April 7th, Castro and a *cuadrilla* of men descended upon the Graham saloon at Natividad, arresting the ringleaders of the projected insurrection. Following those arrests, there ensued a wholesale roundup of all foreigners not married to *hijas del pais* or engaged in approved occupations. On April 23rd, 46 aliens, including Isaac Graham, were shipped to Mexico to stand trial, and Alvarado was temporarily free of his tormentors.

Still he had ample reason for continuing concern. The chaotic condition of the government, combined with an ever increasing number of *extranjeros* in positions of influence, could lead to acquisition of the province by a foreign power. Men like Larkin were working subtly to practice the "Texas game" by publicizing the attractions of California in eastern newspapers. And in 1841, the first organized American group penetrated California for the purpose of settlement, when the Bidwell–Bartleson party crossed the Sierra. They were the vanguard of a different breed of men who were ready to take aggressive action to bring about American conquest. Vallejo, who had supported Alvarado in the Graham affair, now felt the need for more drastic measures. He petitioned the Mexican government to send a new governor, accompanied by a strong force of well-trained troops and a contingent of colonists, to counteract foreign immigration.

During the last two years of his governorship, a disillusioned and disheartened Alvarado did what he could for his countrymen. He had an elaborate, two-story government building erected in the center of Monterey to house the officers of the garrison. *El Cuartel*, as it was called, cost $4,000, a staggering sum for an impoverished treasury. With an equally lavish hand, Alvarado stepped up the giving away of land, with the Soberanes family, close relatives of his wife, receiving a lion's share.

In 1840, for example, Mariano de Jesús Soberanes asked Alvarado for a grant of land in the name of his two eldest sons, José Mariano and Juan José Antonio. The following year title was issued to the 13,346-acre Rancho San Bernardo, southernmost of the ranchos along the Salinas River in Monterey County. Today's San Ardo stands on the long narrow tract. For himself, Mariano de Jesús requested a large tract along the San Antonio River. Since he had been administrator of the San Antonio Mission since 1835 and had "commenced works of much importance and placed 947 head of cattle on the land," he petitioned for a just portion of the mission lands.

Alvarado gave him the 8,900-acre Rancho Los Ojitos, "little springs," adjoining the southern tip of Rancho Milpitas ("little gardens") on which the mission stood. Rancho Milpitas itself had been granted, in 1838, to Ignacio Pastor, a San Antonio Mission Indian. It was said to comprise three leagues, but the boundaries were indefinite.

Soberanes occupied the larger of two adobes already standing on the Los Ojitos. It was a substantial two-story building that remained in good repair for more than a century. Two years later, the 50-year-old Mariano de Jesús married Raimunda Castillo, once the mistress of Alvarado. She bore him five children, and they lived out their days together in the beautiful wind-swept valley of the oaks.

The governor's generosity also extended to Feliciano Soberanes. In January 1841, Alvarado purchased the El Alisal and took up permanent residence in Feliciano's adobe, where he and Martina were already living most of the time. That same year, he appointed Feliciano administrator of the Soledad Mission and awarded him the 21,884-acre Rancho San Lorenzo on the east side of the Salinas River. It adjoined the Rancho San Bernabe at the point where today's King City is located. Then, Feliciano petitioned for a land grant for his eldest daughter, María Joséfa.

The young woman was married to William Brenner Richardson, an emigrant from Maryland, nicknamed "William the Red" because of his bright-colored hair. She was granted the 8,794-acre Rancho Los Coches, to the east of the Mission Soledad, and on it she pastured the 300 head of cattle given her by her father. The next year, Richardson built a two-room adobe on the property and planted a row of black locust trees from seeds sent him from Boston. Later, as their family increased, he added more rooms and an upper story. Both the trees and house are still standing, and the building is a State Historical Monument.

Other *hijos del país* who benefited from Alvarado's largess were Juan Malarín, the Espinosas, Gabriel and Joaquín de la Torre, sons of the old soldier, two of the young Borondas, and Rafael Estrada, son of José Mariano. José Manuel Boronda's grant was the 6,625-acre Rancho Los Laureles in the Carmel Valley. In the Salinas Valley, Malarín received the 8,890-acre Rancho Chualar, for which the present-day town is named. Estrada was granted the 8,875-acre Rancho San Lucas, slightly to the southwest of the city of that name. And Joaquín de la Torre was given the 16,523-acre Rancho Arroyo Seco, adjoining Los Coches on the south.

Altogether Alvarado bestowed 28 land grants during his term of office, totaling over a quarter of a million acres of land. Most of the Salinas Valley and all of the Carmel Valley were occupied by private land concessions. Then, on August 25, 1842, the last of the governors to be sent by Mexico, Brigadier General Manuel Micheltorena, arrived in California. Willingly, Alvarado turned over the last vestiges of responsibility. He had been cloistered and inactive at El Alisal for almost a year. Some say the government treasury held the equivalent of 25 cents at the time Micheltorena assumed office.

Micheltorena did not provide the strong administration which Vallejo had hoped for when he petitioned Mexico to send a governor. Courteous and friendly, he was well-liked personally; but his army of 300 *cholos* made his regime unacceptable from the start. More brigands than soldiers, they had been recruited from the prisons of Mexico with the promise of pardon if they would enlist for service in California. As the government had no funds with which to pay them, they foraged for food and stole from the residents.

Two months after the official change in governors, while Micheltorena was still lingering in Los Angeles, Larkin glanced out of an upstairs window of his house and saw two American warships anchored in the bay. Soon a small boat came ashore with a message demanding surrender of the capital. In the absence of the governor, the demand was accepted by the *comandante*, Captain Mariano Silva. Arrangements were made for the formal surrender to take place the following morning at nine o'clock.

On October 20, 1842, the townspeople were horrified to see a large force landing below the fort. Resistance was impossible, as the garrison numbered only 29 regular soldiers and 25 untrained recruits, while the American contingent comprised 150 men. With the Stars and Stripes flying and a band playing the national air, the Americans marched through the streets of Monterey to *El Cuartel*, where a proclamation was read to the populace. Commodore Thomas ap Catesby Jones, commander of the United States Squadron in the Pacific, informed them that the United States and Mexico were at war and he had been ordered to take possession of the department of California. The Mexican flag was lowered and that of the United States raised, as the guns of the warships fired a salute.

The town was in an uproar. Late that afternoon, Commodore Jones met with Larkin and Hartnell, who inquired about the basis for the action he had taken. He explained that while at Callao, Peru, he had received a report that a state of war existed, and he was under instructions in such an eventuality to seize California before the British could do so. With a wry smile, Larkin showed him the latest communications from Mexico and the United States, which clearly showed that as of the moment no war existed between the two countries. The embarrassed commodore hastened to undo his mistake.

Twenty-four hours after capitulation of the capital, Monterey was restored to Mexico with appropriate ceremonies. The commodore and his officers called upon the Mexican officials to pay their respects, and the latter went aboard the American flagship where they were warmly welcomed and entertained. A letter of apology was dispatched to Michel- torena, still sojourning in Los Angeles, and the governor invited Jones to visit him there and held a fiesta in his honor. But all *Californios* did not so easily forget the humiliation of the American occupation, and the resultant outrage in Mexico City seriously affected future nego- tiations for peaceful cession of territory to the United States.

As American warships continued to patrol Pacific waters and the depredations of Micheltorena's army increased, tension tightened in Monterey. Pessimism spread among the rancheros. Men like the Estradas, the Castros, and the Soberanes knew that they might well lose the security they had so carefully built. Even Mariano Vallejo, the powerful lord of the North, was deeply concerned.

Still, business was booming and merchants prospered as never before. The arrival of a warship meant heavy purchases of supplies. Cash also flowed freely from the pockets of sailors on shore leave. The clever Larkin had cornered a considerable share of this very profitable trade, and out of his gains he contributed to civic improvements, building Monterey's first wharf and reconstructing the dilapidated Custom House. The government reimbursed him for neither project, but he recouped in other ways.

The refurbished Custom House became a center for gala social events. When a foreign warship anchored in the harbor, Larkin gave a *baile grande* for the officers, and they reciprocated with dances and parties on board. On the Fourth of July, the Larkins always celebrated with an elegant dinner party in their home. To emphasize the significance of the patriotic occasion, bumpers of imported champagne were provided. As all of the first families of Monterey were included in the roster of guests, no one criticized the Yankee festivities.

Talk of war and revolution continued to fill the air. Antagonism toward Micheltorena was augmented by rumors that he had arranged an alliance with the German–Swiss, John Sutter, who was as powerful in the Sacramento Valley as Vallejo was at Sonoma. Faced with debtor's prison after a business failure, Sutter had fled from Switzerland, arriving in Monterey in 1839. With the acquiescence of Alvarado, he had selected a huge tract on the Sacramento and, after becoming a naturalized citizen, received a land grant of eleven square leagues, which he named New Helvetia. Within its boundaries, he was in complete command, having been appointed by Alvarado as regional official representing the laws of the country. Now he was said to be training Indians to be used in warfare against *Californios*.

Alvarado's health was improved by a few years of tranquil family life at El Alisal, and once again, the fires of ambition were rekindled. He was also goaded with talk of revolution by his old friend, José Castro, whom Micheltorena had displaced as ranking military officer of the northern district. Perhaps to appease Alvarado, Governor Micheltorena gave him a grant of the 44,360-acre Rancho Las Mariposas in the foothills of the Sierra. But ten leagues of land in such a remote and inhospitable region did not temper Alvarado's ambitions.

The Castro adobe in San Juan Bautista became a rallying point for military revolt. Alvarado and Castro collected a force of 220 supporters in the territory north of Monterey, and by November 1844, the insurgents were ready to move. After a skirmish near San José, in which the rebels successfully opposed 150 of Micheltorena's *cholos*, the governor agreed to send his objectionable army back to Mexico. But word soon reached Alvarado that an especially obnoxious element of foreigners had come to Micheltorena's aid.

Isaac Graham and his followers, released from prison in Mexico, had returned to Monterey. Harboring a lasting animosity towards Alvarado and Castro, they had combined forces with Sutter's contingent of American immigrants and Indians to enlist with Micheltorena. It was obvious the governor would not now abandon the field. Alvarado and the insurgents marched to Southern California to rally support for their cause.

With silver-tongued oratory, Alvarado induced rancheros to join him. All the old charisma came into play. Hundreds of the finest saddle horses were collected, and large numbers of men were recruited. In Los Angeles, he was even able to enlist Pío Pico, long a jealous rival, by promising him the governorship. A group of prominent Americans also jumped aboard his bandwagon.

Residents of the Monterey area were happy to see Micheltorena's troops leave for the south. On their way to Los Angeles in pursuit of Alvarado, they had pillaged the stock of the Soledad Mission. Angrily Don Feliciano Soberanes, now a portly gentleman of 57, told his neighboring rancheros how they had rudely demanded 40 of his best horses, 50 head of cattle, as well as sheep and oxen. He had carefully procured a receipt from the army, certain the government would be made to pay!

On February 20th, the two opposing armies, each numbering about 400 men, met in the San Fernando Valley outside of Los Angeles. For two days, there was considerable exchange of gunfire, but casualties were confined to a couple of horses and a mule. Then Sutter's men, recognizing fellow Americans in Castro's army, decided to withdraw from the battle, declaring this was not their fight. As a result, Micheltorena capitulated and, taking his troops with him, left for Mexico via Monterey. The last thread of Mexico's tenuous control was now broken.

Pío Pico became the new governor and designated Los Angeles as the capital, since he had no influence farther north than Santa Barbara. General José Castro was acknowledged as military commandant with *de facto* control of the Monterey Custom House and, consequently, the treasury. Alvarado once again retreated to El Alisal. And Mariano Vallejo, who had taken no part in Alvarado's war, remained aloof in Sonoma. As the critical year of 1845 began, the government of California was hopelessly divided. That spring, across the continent in Washington, D.C., events were set in motion which would take advantage of the unstable situation.

CHAPTER

9

End of an Era

When news of Micheltorena's ouster reached the east coast of the United States, newspapers blazed with editorials calling for acquisition of California. The newly inaugurated president, James K. Polk, was an ardent expansionist, and he confided to Secretary of the Navy George Bancroft that to acquire the province was among his most cherished goals. But he preferred to do so peaceably. Accordingly, he sent John Slidell to Mexico with an offer of 40 million dollars for the purchase of Upper California and New Mexico. About the same time, in Washington, a young officer in the Army Corps of Engineers was preparing for a scientific expedition that would play a significant part in bringing California under dominion of the United States.

John Charles Fremont was the son-in-law of Senator Thomas Hart Benton, chairman of the powerful military affairs committee. Soon after marrying Benton's daughter, the brilliant and beautiful Jessie, Fremont had conducted two exploring expeditions in the far west, authorized by Congress at the prompting of the senator. Reports of these expeditions, written by Fremont in collaboration with his wife, became bestsellers and established the explorer as a national hero. Now Fremont, spurred by Jessie's ambitions as well as his own, was convinced that his third expedition to the Pacific coast should be organized for military as well as scientific purposes. Undoubtedly his idea was encouraged by Benton. But there is no evidence that either the War Department or President Polk concurred.

The President, having little confidence in Mexico's willingness to accept his purchase offer, put another and more subtle plan into operation. Secret instructions were dispatched to Thomas Larkin, who the prior year had been appointed United States consul for California. The instructions asked him to do precisely what he had been doing for sometime. Larkin had long been operating as a one-man publicity bureau to attract American immigrants to California. At the same time, he had worked guardedly among his friends and business associates to plant the notion of a need for change from the chaos of Mexican dominion. Finally, he made a point of promptly reporting to Washington every rumor of aggressive intentions on the part of the British. Most of these were completely imaginary.

The communication from the American Secretary of State, James Buchanan, was couched in more discreet terms, of course. Buchanan simply wished to warn Californians against the encroachment of foreign powers and to arouse a love of liberty "so natural to the American Continent." The United States would not intervene, but "should California assert and maintain her independence, we shall render her all the kind offices in our power as a sister Republic." And "if the People should desire to unite their destiny with ours, they would be received as brethren, whenever this can be done, without affording Mexico just cause for complaint."

The convoluted communication must have made Larkin chuckle. Well-versed in this kind of double talk, he plunged into his assignment with a suave mixture of enthusiasm and caution. He had every reason to anticipate success. The psychological setting for non-violent penetration was perfect, since almost everyone agreed that the present government was intolerable and Larkin enjoyed the confidence of most Californians as well as the foreign residents.

Then, in December of 1845, Fremont arrived in California with sixty armed men. For a month he camped at Sutter's Fort in the Sacramento Valley. Then, early in January, with a passport provided by Sutter, he proceeded alone to Monterey. Following the irregular pattern of streets, Fremont located the Larkin house. There the two men, so different in temperament but united by a single goal, conferred for several hours, and Fremont learned much about the divided and discontented state of the province. Later in the day, the consul took him to pay formal calls upon Commandant José Castro and other town officials.

With these men, Fremont assumed a deferential attitude. He stated that he was a scientist and not a soldier and that he had only civilians in his party. His mission was to make a survey of the briefest route from the east coast to the Pacific. He begged their indulgence to permit him to replenish his depleted supplies and spend the worst of the winter in the San Joaquin Valley. Suspicious but polite, José Castro acquiesced. Fremont tarried a few days at the Larkin house, buying provisions and meeting important residents of the area. Then he left to rejoin his men.

Larkin was apparently relieved to see Fremont leave, for there was too much danger of disturbing the delicate balance on which his plans depended. But a much worse situation was soon to develop. On the third day of March, William Hartnell was astonished to see a cavalcade of buckskin-clad men, wearing beaver hats and carrying long rifles, riding across his rancho. A moment later he opened the door to a bearded and long-haired individual, who upon closer inspection turned out to be John Fremont. The rough-looking fellow bore little resemblance to the gentleman he had talked with a couple of months earlier.

Hartnell knew there would be concern in Monterey about an armed encampment so close to the capital. Still he was too hospitable to refuse Fremont's request for permission to camp on his property. Besides he enjoyed the company of the American engineer, who was an engaging conversationalist. A few days later, however, the happy arrangement came to an end. Three of Fremont's men, who had been too long in the wilderness, went to the nearby house of Don Angel Castro, uncle of the commandant, and offered insult to his daughters. That same day a Mexican cavalry officer reined up before Fremont's tent and handed him written orders to leave California at once, under threat of arrest and forceable expulsion.

Fremont was outraged. The tone of the dispatch and the peremptory manner of the officer were an insult to himself and his country. He disregarded Hartnell's advice that he depart peacefully and, instead, moved his men to the slopes of Gavilán Peak, overlooking San Juan Bautista and the Salinas plain. There he raised the American flag and defied the Mexicans to eject him.

The horrified Larkin sent urgent messages, pleading with Fremont to leave. Arrogantly, the ambitious young officer replied that he was fortifying his position and would fight to the finish, "trusting to our country to avenge our deaths." Meanwhile José Castro issued a fiery proclamation, declaring that a band of robbers commanded by a captain of the American army was loose in the country and calling for volunteers "to lance the ulcer which would destroy our liberties." He assembled a force of 200 men at his headquarters in San Juan Bautista.

A showdown almost occurred. But Castro's language reflected more bombast than bravery; and before he could summon courage to attack, Larkin's counsels to Fremont finally prevailed. With the frivolous excuse that the falling down of their flagpole was a sign to break camp, Fremont set off for the Sacramento Valley. But he moved with deliberate slowness. Castro claimed full credit for having routed the *bandoleros*.

Much of Larkin's careful work had been destroyed. Influential rancheros like the Soberanes, the Estradas, and the Malaríns were deeply disturbed. The actions of the Americans were more compelling than the assurances of the smooth-talking Yankee Consul. Still Larkin commanded the respect of many members of the community, including the Mexican officials whom he had served for years in a mercantile capacity. He decided upon a bold diplomatic maneuver.

Late in March, he invited to his home a group of men representing diverse roles of leadership in the province. Over an ample supply of *aquardiente*, he launched a discussion of California's future. Among those present were the merchants, the military, and Mariano Vallejo, lord of the North. The heated debate was laced with fervid pronouncements. William Hartnell went on record as favoring a British protectorate, urging her advantages as a strong imperial nation. David Spence added that England would not sanction slavery, an abomination to any God-fearing man yet practiced by the United States. José Castro surprised everyone by declaring himself for annexation to France, for religious reasons. The young Mariano Soberanes sprang to his feet with the ringing words: *"California libre, soberana, y independiente!"* Alvarado supported him with a stirring speech. Larkin maintained a discreet silence.

Then, the dignified Don Mariano Vallejo stood and addressed the group. He spoke slowly and persuasively. California could not hope to maintain her independence, if left to her own resources. Only one course of action held promise for a stable and prosperous future. The government must immediately detach itself from Mexico and ask for admission to the great confederation known as the United States. An uproar of voices sought to interrupt him. But he continued, carefully explaining the constitution of the United States and how, under its provisions, California would have representation in Congress. For a moment following his presentation, the group was speechless. Suddenly, someone called for a vote and pandemonium broke loose. It increased in violence until the meeting adjourned without any agreement being reached. But Larkin was well-satisfied. Much had been accomplished toward his goal, for Vallejo's voice carried great weight.

During the month of April, John Fremont was in Oregon but within easy marching distance of any military activity that might develop. He still believed that war was imminent and that he might receive instructions from Washington to take decisive action. At Sutter's Fort, American settlers had gathered about him with loud praise and protestations of loyalty. Without difficulty he could raise an army equal to any the Californians would have.

As if conjured by the force of his anticipation, a messenger appeared at the Fremont camp in the person of Lieutenant Archibald Gillespie. An officer of the Marine Corps and a secret agent of the United States government, Gillespie had come via Vera Cruz and Mexico City disguised as a merchant traveling for his health. His orders were to cooperate in Larkin's plan of peaceful persuasion, and he brought Fremont a copy of Secretary Buchanan's dispatch to Larkin, some American newspapers, and letters from his wife Jessie and from Senator Benton.

Buchanan's instructions had not changed. Larkin was requested to be "discreet, cautious, and sleepless." He was told to warn the people of California against British and French aggression. He was to encourage them to become a separate nation and to promise them that once this had been accomplished they might look forward to annexation. Nothing in the communication could be construed as suggestion for the use of armed force.

But in the light of what Gillespie had seen and heard in his travels across Mexico, the evidence was overwhelming that Mexico and the United States hovered on the brink of war. The two officers convinced each other that the instructions were outdated. After all, they had been written the previous October. Fremont moved his men back to the Sacramento Valley.

It was May 1846. That month, President Polk had signed a declaration of war, based on a blood-letting incident over the Texas boundary. The news would not reach California until July, so, meanwhile in Monterey, Larkin still strove to carry out his mission. But the temper of the native Californians had changed. The past two years had brought a dramatic increase in the influx of American immigrants, and the newcomers were a rugged and hard-hitting lot. Mingled among them were reckless adventurers and malcontents, spoiling for a fight. Most looked upon Californians with condescension if not contempt, and the vast majority simply squatted on the lands of their choice, with complete disregard for Mexican laws and property rights. Word that Fremont had returned added to the atmosphere of uneasiness and mistrust.

A *junta* of military men was convened in Monterey by José Castro. The group concluded that Castro must assume full powers for both the military and civil government, a decision which further widened the rift between the northern and southern parts of the province. Following the meeting, Castro issued a proclamation, warning Americans that only Mexican citizens could be landowners and threatening to drive all aliens from the country.

Fantastic rumors flew among the settlers in the Sacramento and Napa Valleys. Some were certain that Castro intended to instigate an Indian uprising against them, and their alarm increased as Castro's men ranged the northern country from Monterey to Sonoma, raising troops and gathering supplies. Early in June, a group, led by the tall rawboned Ezekiel Merritt, took matters into their own hands. In a surprise move, they seized a herd of horses intended for Castro's militia.

Appetites whetted by the successful foray, the American settlers were ready for more action. Fremont decided the time was ripe for him to take advantage of the situation. He chose the outpost of Sonoma, where soldiers were no longer stationed, as the object of initial military attack. Thirty-three men, loosely organized under the leadership of Merritt, Robert Semple, and William Ide, were deployed to "capture" the village that was the home of General Vallejo. The dignified Don Mariano entertained the marauders with food and brandy, while he quietly negotiated surrender of the small store of munitions at the post. So great was his confidence in the American government that he willingly submitted to arrest and allowed himself to be transported to Sutter's Fort. There he had reason to reconsider, as he was imprisoned for two months and shabbily treated under direct orders from Fremont.

At Sonoma, William Ide, a former schoolteacher from Vermont, issued a flowery proclamation, declaring himself and his associates a republic. But even he was a bit timid about raising the Stars and Stripes, so a flag was fashioned. On a yard and a half of white cotton cloth, a large lone star and a grizzly bear were painted with pokeberry juice. Under these emblems, "California Republic" was lettered in black ink. And a broad strip of red flannel, made from a man's shirt, was sewn along the bottom of the cloth. Thus, the Bear Flag Revolt, destined to last less than a month, and the state flag of California, which flies to this day, came into being.

José Castro assembled about 50 men, under the command of Joaquín de la Torre and sent them to the relief of Sonoma. A brisk engagement ensued in which several *Californios* were killed or wounded and the entire contingent put to flight. Fremont arrived with reinforcements and pursued de la Torre's retreating troops. Only by good luck and an adroit ruse were they able to escape.

At last Larkin had to acknowledge the defeat of his plan for peaceful separation of California from Mexico. Hard on the news of activities in the north came a sealed dispatch from the commander-in-chief of the United States naval forces in the Pacific. It carried electrifying information. The fleet was coming!

Larkin had mixed feelings. War might well endanger the security and prosperity he had so painstakingly built. And he was basically a businessman and a pacifist. But he was also the United States consul, and he had new and grave responsibilities to meet. On July 2nd, his heart lifted with pride as he watched the Pacific squadron enter the bay. One by one they rounded Point Pinos with shortened sail. An officer from the flagship, *Savannah,* came ashore with a message. The commodore wished to salute the presidio, but there was no Mexican flag visible. Dressed in his official consular uniform, resplendent with gilt buttons and gold-fringed epaulets, Larkin went aboard to greet John Drake Sloat. He informed him that there was neither a flag nor powder with which to return the honor of a salute. It was the first of many conferences in which the consul apprised the naval commander of the sad state of affairs in the province.

Sloat, a sallow nervous man of 65, was hesitant about exceeding the authority given him by his orders. While in Mexican waters, he had received definite but still unofficial reports that the United States and Mexico were at war. His instructions were to seize the ports of California if hostilities had opened, but not to offend the inhabitants. Of course, Larkin continued to urge caution, and Sloat did not wish to repeat the mistake of Commodore Jones.

For five days the residents of Monterey were kept on tenterhooks. They knew they were defenseless. Castro had deserted the capital, taking his troops to join forces with Pío Pico in the south. Word had come that the despised *gringo* Fremont was celebrating with fireworks on the Fourth of July in the village of Sonoma, while the Vallejo women were virtual captives in their own home. Feliciano Soberanes was particularly worried about the 8,900-acre grant of Soledad Mission lands that he had just recently received from Pico in payment for the $800 claim he had made against the government for the depredations of Micheltorena's troops. What if the government fell to the Yankees?

Early on the morning of July 7th, the suspense ended. Concerned over Fremont's filibustering activities, and fearful that the British squadron was headed for Monterey, Sloat took action. Several officers were sent ashore with a formal demand for surrender of the port. Once again the old artillery captain Mariano Silva was left alone to face the inevitable. He could only reply that he had no authority to surrender the post and neither troops nor arms with which to resist.

At ten o'clock, 250 marines and seamen landed at the wharf and marched to the Custom House. There, Commodore Sloat's proclamation was read in both Spanish and English to a crowd of tight-lipped citizens. The words that fell upon their ears were carefully designed to be reassuring. "I declare to the inhabitants of California that, although I come in arms with a powerful force, I do not come among them as an enemy to California: on the contrary, I come as their best friend, as henceforth

California will be a portion of the United States, and its peaceful inhabitants will enjoy the same rights and privileges they now enjoy."

Certain advantages were also pointed out. All imports from the United States would now be duty free and those of foreign nations available at one quarter of what was paid under Mexican custom regulations. A marked increase in the value of real estate could be anticipated, and persons in rightful possession of land would have their titles guaranteed to them. Finally, no provisions, supplies, or other private property would be taken without compensation at fair prices.

To the thunder of a 21-gun salute, the American flag was raised. The troops gave three cheers; then accompanied by the martial music of a brass band, they marched across town and took possession of *El Cuartel*. The great day closed with a splendid dinner on the flagship, attended by Consul Larkin as guest of honor.

After the initial shock had worn off, most of the populace accepted the Yankees as likeable and permanent guests. Many private adobes were thrown open to entertain officers of the fleet, and the merchants were delighted with the increase in business from the sailors on shore leave. The *señoras* enjoyed the music of the military band as it paraded through the streets, and *señoritas* surreptitiously flirted with the handsome marines. Never had Monterey been more lively.

Still, six days after the fall of the capital, a group of prominent Californians met to protest American occupation and sign a resolution of loyalty to Mexico. Hartnell's brother-in-law, Pablo de la Guerra, pled with his countrymen to flee Monterey for the south, where Castro was in command of the resistance. When someone suggested that the protection of England be invoked, as the British navy was known to be hovering offshore, Rafael Estrada retorted bitterly, "California is lost to us. You propose only to seek another owner!"

Couriers carried the news of the occupation to San Francisco, Sutter's Fort, and Sonoma. Word reached Fremont in a moment of triumph. He had just merged the Bear Flaggers with his own forces into a company comprising over 200 men. Eagerly, he rode forth at the head of his California Battalion in response to Sloat's summons to Monterey. Not since the visitation of Chief Solano and his tribesmen had the townspeople of Monterey seen such a force in their small community. Two by two the swarthy, darkly bearded men rode through the deserted streets, battered hats pulled low over their long straggly hair. Clothed in buckskin smeared with blood and grime, they wore leather belts from which hung glittering bowie knives. The corps of grim-visaged men camped in the pine forest just outside of town.

The following day Fremont went aboard the *Savannah* to confer with Commodore Sloat. Anxiously, the elder officer asked under what instructions Fremont had taken up arms. "Solely on my own responsibility," was the proud reply. The timid commodore was shocked. He had hoped that any orders received by Fremont would justify his own action in taking Monterey, and he feared the effect Fremont's battalion would have upon his own attempts to conciliate the Californians. Perplexed, weary, and in poor health, he solved his problems by turning over his command to Commodore Robert F. Stockton, who had arrived a few days earlier. Stockton was a man of a different mold. Larkin saw him as a militant uncompromising executive who would brook no opposition to immediate and total conquest of California. The last, flickering hope of friendly acquisition was quenched.

Fremont and Stockton related at once. They planned an energetic land campaign into the south, where they would either take Castro prisoner or drive him and other recalcitrant officials from the province. The California Battalion was taken into the naval service and Fremont was made major in command. His men were reinforced by 80 marines, and the whole contingent sailed for San Diego, where they could cut off Castro's rear. From there they were to march to Los Angeles and join forces with an additional 360 of Stockton's men.

The people of Monterey were happy to see the ruffians depart. Once again tranquility was the order of the day. Walter Colton, chaplain berthed aboard the *Congress* and former professor and newspaper editor, was appointed the first American *alcalde*. Personable and intelligent, he soon became popular with all conditions of men, and his three-year administration was just and decorous, contributing immeasurably to the even temper of affairs in and around Monterey.

Among Colton's many accomplishments was publication of California's first newspaper. His partner in the venture was Robert Semple, dentist from Kentucky and former Bear Flagger. Standing almost seven feet tall, Semple cut a rugged figure in deerskin shirt and trousers and a coonskin cap complete with tail. Quick on the trigger, he was also an experienced typesetter and ready with a roughhewn rhetoric.

An ancient hand press, brought from Mexico in the 1830s by Agustín Zamorano, was found stored in *El Cuartel*. The type was rusty and mice had burrowed in the balls, but Semple scoured the letters and, with a jack-knife, cut a sheet of tin into rules and leads. A keg of ink was located near the press, but the only paper available was that used to roll cigars. Fortunately, a trading vessel had a small supply of foolscap on board, and this was procured.

On August 15, 1846, when the first sheet was pulled from the press, a great crowd was waiting. The paper, christened the *Californian*, consisted of four pages and carried news from all important military posts, the complete text of the declaration of war with Mexico, and an abstract of the debate over the war in the United States Senate. Set up in two columns, half of the paper was in English and the other, edited by William Hartnell, was in Spanish. The news sheet sold for twelve and a half cents and appeared every Saturday, filled with military proclamations, news items, and editorials. A year later, Semple became sole owner of the *Californian* and moved it to San Francisco.

Walter Colton's most enduring and remarkable achievement was the construction of a town hall. A commodious, two-story building, it was erected by prison labor at practically no cost. Such funds as were required came from the sale of town lots, fines on gamblers, and taxes on liquor shops. Built of white stone quarried from a neighboring hill, the edifice was graceful in style and ornamented with a portico. The lower floor housed schoolrooms. Above them was a hall, 70 feet by 30, for public assemblies. Named after its ingenious and resourceful creator, Colton Hall was without rival in the California of its time.

While the struggle for California was waged in the south, Monterey basked in peace and prosperity. Then in November 1846, Fremont and his boorish followers were back. He was now a lieutenant colonel in the army and in charge of the northern military district. With headquarters on the outskirts of Monterey, he deployed men to comb the region for horses and for newly arrived immigrants to swell his army in the southern campaign.

A group of *Californios* decided to teach the arrogant Yankee colonel a lesson. Among them was Manuel Castro, who had once driven Fremont and his freebooters from the area. Learning that the *Americano* foraging party of 60 settlers was bringing a herd of 300 horses from the Sacramento Valley through San Juan Bautista to Monterey, Castro and 150 men planned a surprise attack. A brief but sharp engagement occurred at Natividad, in which several Americans were killed or wounded. Castro's men suffered more severe losses and also failed to capture the horses. Forced to retreat, they departed for Los Angeles, but they recouped in a startling way. They had Thomas Larkin with them.

The previous day Larkin, on his way to San Francisco, had stopped at the Rancho Los Vergeles, southwest of San Juan Bautista. His whereabouts became known to the Californians, and at midnight he was roused from sleep and abducted to the Castro camp. He was treated with courtesy and consideration, but for two long and fretful months he was detained as a hostage.

It was a time of despair for the man who had labored so long to bring California under the flag of the United States. At the moment when triumph seemed assured, he was deprived of enacting his prestigious role. In addition, he was tortured by concern for his family, whom he had sent to San Francisco for safety at the beginning of the Bear Flag Revolt. At the time of his capture, he had been enroute to see his youngest child, who was dangerously ill. Not until the middle of January did he receive word that she had died.

Fremont and his army of 400 men moved out of Monterey on the day after the Battle of Natividad. In a driving rainstorm, over trails fetlock-deep in mud, the long lines of riflemen rode through the Salinas Valley. Cold and wet, they camped that night at Los Coches, the rancho of María Joséfa Soberanes de Richardson. Peremptorily, they took pack mules and provisions without recompense.

The next night they were sprawled over Rancho Los Ojitos in the valley of the oaks. Mariano de Jesús Soberanes and his family were held prisoners in their house. Cattle were slaughtered in sufficient number to provide ten pounds of meat per man; and when the marauders moved on, there was a herd of a hundred more in their train. Ashen with anger, Soberanes wrote out a claim for $20,000 of which he would never see more than a pittance.

As the year 1846 drew to a close, Monterey was beset by the inevitable results of a boom economy, a shortage of supplies, and inflation. Walter Colton found it so difficult to procure eggs that he purchased six hens at a dollar apiece. Flour sold for 25 dollars a barrel and scarcely could be obtained. Both farm hands and animals had been drafted by the military.

Meanwhile, news of the war in the south came in a slow trickle. The fastest and most reliable information was relayed, fantastically, from a pool formed by a large underground spring, located where Aguajito Canyon touches present-day Fremont Avenue. Women gathered there to do the community laundry while they gossiped, and there were always those in the group who had picked up tidbits of startling authenticity from roving Indians or other nomads. The capture of Los Angeles by Commodore Stockton was first announced from "Washerwoman's Bay," as was the final capitulation of the *Californios* to Colonel Fremont at Cahuenga Pass.

The surrender at Cahuenga, on January 13, 1847, ended organized resistance to the American occupation. Official intelligence of the surrender reached Monterey on January 30th. Residents of the area, who had left their homes to fight in a hopeless cause, began returning with a mixture of apprehension and relief. Larkin was released and back to cope with a flood of neglected matters both mercantile and consular. Soon he was aware that the new government was as difficult to deal with as the old.

General Stephen Kearny, who had brought an army by land to occupy California, assumed command of both military and civil affairs on orders of the Secretary of War. But Stockton still considered himself in charge and, before leaving the country, he appointed Fremont as military governor of California. Neither Fremont nor Kearny would acknowledge the authority of the other, and a bitter feud developed between the two. General Kearny set up his headquarters at Monterey and his residence in Larkin's house; but during the entire three months of the general's administration, Fremont continued to claim the powers of governor and repeatedly defied the orders of his superior officer. Finally, General Kearny's patience was at an end, and he took action to remove Fremont from the scene. He had him arrested for mutinous conduct and instigated his court martial in Washington.

Alcalde Colton saw Kearny as an amiable and forbearing leader, but, for a number of reasons, Consul Larkin favored Fremont—although publicly he maintained a neutral position. One problem was that Kearny had rejected Larkin's bill for $8,200, the alleged cost of building the Monterey wharf, which the Mexican government had never paid. Another point of contention was that Kearny also had brusquely rebuffed Larkin's proposal for an assembly to discuss creation of a representative government. To Larkin, Kearny appeared to be "iron-clad and inflexible."

Of course, at the time, Larkin was acting as agent for Fremont in an important business deal. He had been given a draft of $3,000 and was commissioned to purchase a tract of land near Mission San José, which had captured Fremont's fancy. Instead, he used the money to come to the aid of Juan Bautista Alvarado who, hounded by his creditors, was in desperate financial straits. Without his knowledge or consent, Fremont became owner of the Rancho Las Mariposas, which had belonged to Alvarado. News of the transaction reached Fremont when he was being held prisoner at Sutter's Fort, awaiting transport to Washington. He was outraged and demanded that Larkin return the purchase price. Yet within a few years, the vast acreage would acquire a valuation of ten million dollars and lead Alvarado to claim that Larkin had despoiled him of a fortune.

The discovery of gold in the foothills of the Sierra Nevada occurred nine days before the signing of the peace treaty, on February 2, 1848, which ended the Mexican-American War and ceded California to the United States. The news leaked out quickly enough but attracted little attention. Most people dismissed it as idle rumor. Then, late in May, the enormity of what the discovery meant suddenly took over people's minds. Overnight, gold fever reached epidemic proportions, and even the sleepy town of Monterey succumbed.

Colonel Richard Mason, under orders from Washington, had succeeded Kearny as military commander and ex-officio governor. He occupied a house in Monterey and maintained his headquarters at *El Cuartel*, assisted by Lieutenant Henry Halleck, whom he appointed secretary of state, and Lieutenant William Tecumseh Sherman, then a young officer. Mason was a capable man and, for a year, had managed to run the government on an even keel. But with the discovery of gold, his troops began deserting by the hundreds, and he found it almost impossible to maintain law and order. How could he hope to keep them when a soldier on a three-weeks furlough had found $1,500 worth of gold, more than his Army pay for five years!

Monterey had become a town of women, children, and men too old to be mobile. There were no servants and very little food. Colton complained that both he and the governor were reduced to grinding coffee, toasting herrings, and peeling onions in a smoking kitchen. He noted that ladies of the finest families had broomsticks in their jewelled hands.

Finally, in August 1848, news of the peace treaty with Mexico reached Monterey. The period of military occupation was over, and Colonel Mason knew that he no longer had legal authority to govern. Anxiously, he awaited word that a territorial government had been established to end the ambiguous and potentially dangerous situation. But Congress, deadlocked over the question of allowing slavery in the newly acquired territory, came to no agreement about legislation to replace the military regime.

Discharge of the New York Company of Volunteers reduced the military force in California to two companies of regulars, scarcely enough to guard the munitions depots at Monterey and San Francisco. Southern California was restless and sullen, the immigrant population in the north was impatient of *alcaldes* with absolute powers, a makeshift political structure derived from Mexico. The miners in the mountains improvised their own government and tolerated no other.

The situation was critical. Urgently Colonel Mason wrote to the adjutant-general about his predicament. But a whole continent separated the two men, and this meant a wait of at least six months for the exchange of messages. The long wet winter of 1848–49 went by without any outbreaks of violence, but in San Francisco and San Jose, now the largest towns in Northern California, meetings were held to discuss organization of a government. Out of these meetings came resolutions in favor of calling a state constitutional convention as soon as the rain-saturated roads were passable. Men who were not strangers to the political procedures of the United States were ready to take matters into their own hands.

Still, Governor Mason kept his faith that Congress would act. A new president, Zachary Taylor, had just been inaugurated, and Congress was once again in session. The steadfast soldier waited as February slid into March. The steamship *Oregon* arrived with dispatches and papers, but they brought no news that California had been given a legal government. Then, on April 12, 1849, the long wait was ended, not by congressional action but by the arrival of Brigadier General Bennett Riley. He came by appointment of the president to succeed Colonel Mason, who had asked that he be relieved. Less than two months later, Governor Riley himself issued the call for a constitutional convention.

Monterey

Watercolor of Monterey, in 1855, by James Alden. Corner of the Custom House at extreme left. Alvarado Street and Calle Principal are the two lanes discernible in center of the picture. The Pacific House stands in the right foreground. Painting was the gift of Mr. Alden's daughter, Sarah Alden Dorsey. Reproduction courtesy of the Monterey City Library.

98

The town house of Estéban Munrás was one of the first adobes built outside the presidio walls. Engaged in the mercantile business and married to the charming Catalina Manzanelli, Don Estéban offered warm hospitality to foreign merchants in the Monterey of the 1820s. This picture was probably taken in the 1880s, courtesy of the Monterey City Library.

El Cuartel was built by Governor Alvarado, in 1840, to house the officers of the garrison and government offices. Located on what is now Munras Avenue, just south of the present Jules Simoneau Plaza, it stood for about 70 years. Photograph from the Los Angeles Title Insurance and Trust Company, courtesy of the Monterey City Library.

A rear view of the Casa Soberanes about 1900. Built by José Rafael Papías Estrada, the adobe was sold around 1850 to Ezequiel Soberanes, son of Mariano de Jesús and María Isidora Vallejo de Soberanes. Later it was purchased by Jean Booth, who sold it to the William O'Donnells. It is now the property of the State of California and known as the House of the Blue Gate. Photograph was the gift of Harriet Coombs, courtesy of the Monterey City Library.

Governor Alvarado's town house still stands on Dutra Street in Monterey. In 1842, when Alvarado sold it to his secretary, Manuel Dutra de Vargas, for 100 silver dollars, the adobe had three rooms and a tile roof. Photograph, taken in the 1880s, courtesy of the Monterey City Library.

Colton Hall was built by Walter Colton, first American *alcalde*. Completed in time to house the Constitutional Convention in September, 1849, it was constructed of stone quarried from a neighboring hill and erected by prison labor. Such funds as were required came from the sale of town lots, fines on gamblers, and taxes on liquor shops. Photograph taken in 1897, from the Adam Clark Vroman Collection, courtesy of William Webb.

The Manuel Casarin Jimeno adobe was a favorite gathering place for influential delegates to the Constitutional Convention. Doña Augusta Jimeno was noted for her charm and wit.

Adjacent to the adobe was the convent of St. Catherine of Sienna which housed a school. Photograph by William Morgan. Amelie Elkinton Collection.

The Washington Hotel, at the corner
of Pearl and Washington Streets,
was the finest hostelry in Monterey
at the time of the Constitutional
Convention. Its owner, Alberto
Trescony, rented it for $1,200
a month to a former private in the
New York Company of Volunteers.
Originally the adobe residence of
Eugenio Montenegro, it was greatly
enlarged and became the scene of
gambling and boisterous merriment.
Photograph taken in 1906.
Amelie Elkinton Collection.

General Mariano Guadalupe Vallejo,
Comandante of the northern frontier at
Sonoma, was held political prisoner at
Sutter's Fort during the American
occupation. Still the greathearted
hidalgo continued to support the
cause of the United States and was a
delegate to the Constitutional
Convention. Amelie Elkinton Collection.

David Jacks, who settled in Monterey
in 1850, was one of its most influential and controversial citizens.
At one time, he owned 60,000 acres
in Monterey County with portions of
as many as 10 land grants in his
possession. Photograph from
Monterey Urban Renewal Collection.

Looking north on Alvarado Street. This photograph was probably taken at a later date than given on the picture. The Custom House can be seen in the center background at the end of the street. The two-story building with balcony, in the foreground to the left, is the Juan Malarín adobe. In 1879, Doctor Heintz, son-in-law of Madame Girardin lived in this adobe and Robert Louis Stevenson was taken there to recuperate from pneumonia. Picture courtesy of the Monterey City Library.

Señorita Rosanna Leese's boarding house on Calle Principal, next door to the Larkin House. This was where Robert Louis Stevenson first stayed after arriving in Monterey on August 31, 1879. Photograph courtesy of the Monterey City Library.

Pearl and Tyler Streets in 1875. The building to the right was José Castro's town house. In a walled-in area back of it was the pit where bull and bear fights were held. The two-story building in the center background is the Cooper House. The small building in front of it was Jules Simoneau's restaurant. The buildings to the left were torn down to extend Tyler Street southward. Amelie Elkinton Collection.

The French Hotel on Houston Street, now preserved by the State of California as the Stevenson House because the author lived there during part of his stay in Monterey. The man in front of the horse cart is Jules Simoneau. Mayo Hayes O'Donnell Library Collection.

Señorita María Ygnacia Bonifacio, who lived
with her mother, Carmen Pinto de Bonifacio,
in the adobe on Alvarado Street where Fanny
Vandegrift Osbourne stayed. Alberto Trescony's
children were reared by Señorita Bonifacio
after the death of his wife. María Ygnacia,
who never married, was left alone in the old
adobe during the last years of her life.
Photograph courtesy of the Monterey City Library.

(Top and bottom right)
The Hampton House, called the Pacific
Ocean House in 1889, is the two-story
building in the center foreground. To the
right, beyond the vacant space, is the
Pacific House. Back of it can be seen the
long roof of the First Theatre. In the upper
right hand corner are the Doud House and
the cluster of buildings which were part
of the David Jacks property.

Monterey
in the 1880s.

The Southern Pacific Railroad depot is in
the foreground. In the upper left hand corner
is the Washington Hotel. The large house
inside the wall in the right hand corner
is the Osio adobe on Alvarado Street.
Above it Colton Hall can be seen. Watkins'
Photographs, courtesy of the Bancroft Library.

(*Right top*)

Monterey in 1881. Photograph by Charles W. J. Johnson, taken from the roof of the Pacheco adobe. The long adobe building in the background on the left was the town house of William Hartnell, who died in 1854. In the center is *El Cuartel*. Colton Hall can be seen on a rise back of it. Amelie Elkinton Collection.

(*Right bottom*)

Looking south on Alvarado Street in 1885. In the left foreground is the Custom House. On the right side of the street is Oliver's Curio store. The tiny building in the center of the picture is the shell store of Mrs. Thomas G. Lambert. Captain Lambert, who was the master of a whaling ship, established a lumber mill in Monterey. He was the great-uncle of the Carmel Valley rancher, Bill Lambert. Photograph by William L. Morgan. Mayo Hayes O'Donnell Library Collection.

The St. Charles Hotel was originally the José Mariano Estrada adobe. In September, 1879, it was described as a rambling two-story adobe with "many rooms, bad cooking, and one bathroom." By the end of that year, the third story was added. Later the hotel was called the Everett House, and in 1902 it belonged to a Mr. Casper who advertised "first class meals at 25 cents." Amelie Elkinton Collection.

Cattle drive
along dirt road
near Monterey in 1901.
Photograph courtesy
Monterey City Library.

The second Del Monte Hotel, May, 1912. Rebuilt after a disastrous fire in 1887, it was internationally famous as the "Queen of American Watering Places." Fire again destroyed the huge establishment in 1924, after which it was reconstructed on an even larger scale. It is now the United States Naval Postgraduate School. Photograph by S. L. Slevin, courtesy of the Bancroft Library.

A large carry-all met guests at the Del Monte station, a quarter of a mile from the Del Monte Hotel.

Photograph by S. L. Slevin, 1925, courtesy of the Bancroft Library.

10

Monterey Has its Finest Hour

Governor Riley was an experienced soldier with a great deal of common sense. Though he had no actual authority to call a constitutional convention, he recognized the necessity of the action for the preservation of the peace as well as his own position. But he was concerned about how the proclamation would be received, especially by the native Californians. Could a conquered people be expected to be enthusiastic over framing a new government in an unknown language?

There was also uncertainty about the miners in their nomadic camps. Would they take the trouble to identify boundaries of voting districts, let alone spend time away from their diggings to dabble in politics? As it developed, the citizens of San Francisco offered the strongest resistance, refusing to acknowledge Governor Riley's right to call the convention but finally going along as a matter of expediency.

Fast-riding couriers carried copies of Governor Riley's proclamation to all parts of the territory. August 1 was the date set for election of delegates, and the convention would convene in Monterey on the first day of September.

But because of the great distances over which the population was scattered, it was difficult for the government to influence public opinion. Little help could be had from the press, as there were only two small weekly papers, the *California Star* and the *Californian*, and their circulation was limited. Thus, in the sweltering days of July, General Riley journeyed to the foothills of the Sierra to talk with the miners. He wanted to become acquainted with the people and their problems and to explain the purposes of the convention. The effort paid dividends, doing away with the prejudice many had entertained against his military administration.

Another visitor to the mines that summer was Thomas Butler King, personal emissary of President Taylor, sent to urge the miners to take an interest in the forthcoming elections. The president could only lend unofficial support, as California's governmental status lay entirely within the province of Congress, but personally he was in favor of the convention.

On the steamer that brought King from Panama, there were two other noteworthy passengers. One was Jessie Benton Fremont, en route to join her husband in San Francisco. Separated from the service as a result of his court-martial, Fremont was engaged in a fourth exploring expedition. The other passenger of note was William Gwin of Tennessee, who came to California with the avowed purpose of becoming one of its first United States senators. Within the year, he and John Fremont would draw lots for the long versus the short senatorial term.

Governor Riley was much encouraged by the success of the August elections. Still, there was anxiety about whether the delegates would make the long and arduous trip required of many to attend the convention. In the drowsy days of Monterey's summer, there was little to indicate that momentous questions were about to be settled in the placid town. Fog-misted streets were almost deserted, since most of the men were away at the mines. The rancheros quietly went about their business, demonstrating slight interest in the impending event. Only one of them had been elected as a delegate. He was Jacinto Rodríguez, whose father was grantee of the Rancho Bolsa del Pajaro, site of present-day Watsonville.

Thomas Larkin and Henry Halleck, still California secretary of state, had also been elected as delegates, and they directed the preparations for the convention. School was suspended at Colton Hall, and the large second-story chamber was made ready for the sessions. Carpenters built a railing across the middle of the hall to divide spectators from members. A rostrum was erected, over which hung two American flags and a local artist's conception of George Washington. Although there were neither hotels nor restaurants, all was deemed to be in readiness.

At last, the day arrived. Fog blanketed the bay, and delegates who came by ship were unable to land. Others were simply delayed. Only ten delegates were present for the opening session, and two of these were Larkin and Halleck. Without a quorum, the meeting adjourned until Monday, September 3rd.

For two and a half weeks, delegates continued to drift into Monterey. Finally there were 48 members, of whom ten were from southern districts and 38 from the north, an index to the distribution of population in California at the time. San Francisco and Sacramento led the field with eight delegates each; San Jose had seven; San Joaquin and Monterey, six each; Los Angeles, five; Sonoma, three; San Diego and San Luis Obispo, two each; and Santa Barbara only one.

The delegates were, for the most part, young men, about half being under 35 years. Overwhelmingly, they were *Americanos.* Among the eight *Californios* at the convention were the distinguished Mariano Guadalupe Vallejo and Pablo de la Guerra, brother-in-law of William Hartnell. There were fourteen lawyers, eleven farmers, and seven merchants. Exclusive of the native born, the delegates' residence in California ranged from twenty years for the prominent Angeleno, Abel Stearns, to three months for William Gwin, delegate from San Francisco.

The convention opened with an inspiring message from Governor Riley, reminding the members that the stability of the state structure would depend upon the foundation they established. Organization was completed on the second day, and to the surprise of some, Robert Semple, delegate from Sonoma, was elected president.

A hush fell upon the assemblage when the elongated frontiersman was escorted to his seat of honor by Mariano Vallejo and John Sutter. Don Mariano was handsome in appearance and elegantly dressed in the embroidered clothes of the *Californio;* the ruddy Sutter was immaculate in an elaborately adorned uniform. They made a most impressive pair as, with great dignity, the Spaniard and the Swiss moved forward beside the tall gaunt Kentuckian. Many who were present remembered when Vallejo and Sutter were sovereigns of rival kingdoms. And few would forget that Vallejo had once been the prisoner of Semple and Sutter.

In his opening address, Semple spoke with a roughhewn grandiloquence, urging as motto for the convention "Justice, Industry, and Economy." Despite his simplicity and lack of experience, he made a good chairman, though there were those who would have preferred the smooth and canny ex-congressman, Gwin, who almost defeated Semple for the post. Four long tables had been installed for the delegates. At one of these, the eight *Californios* sat in a group with their interpreter William Hartnell. Hartnell—Don Guillermo—the first of the *extranjeros,* was now 51. Still one of the best loved and most respected men in California, he had been affectionately nicknamed *pestana blanca* for the white frosting on the lashes and brow of one eye. Always immediately to his right sat the great-hearted *hidalgo* Vallejo, who despite all that had happened to him at the hands of the Yankees, remained the self-styled "foremost friend of the Americans."

First issue before the delegates was the question of whether the new government should be that of a state or a territory. Gwin introduced the motion for a state structure. After all, he could not become a senator from a territory. The vote was 28 to 8 in favor of his motion. All those opposed were either from the southern districts or native rancheros, who knew that financial support for a state government would come largely from taxation on their large land holdings while the administrative expenses of a territory would have come from federal funds. Jacinto Rodríguez of Monterey cast his vote along with his fellow landowners; of the *Californios*, only Vallejo favored statehood.

The next question of critical importance before the convention was that of slavery. It was quickly decided by unanimous vote: "Neither slavery nor involuntary servitude, unless for the punishment of crimes, shall ever be tolerated in this state." But before the clause was adopted, Morton McCarver, a stern and hardened pioneer turned miner, was on his feet with an amendment—"Nor shall the introduction of free Negroes under indentures or otherwise be allowed."

A short debate followed relative to the propriety of combining the two propositions into a single section, and McCarver temporarily withdrew the measure. Twice more he introduced it as the convention's work progressed, and the second time it was adopted. Many delegates felt that owners of slaves would bring them to California, granting their freedom on condition that they work in the mines as indentured servants. The miners wished to prevent at all costs such competition in the garnering of gold; other members of the assembly were simply opposed to an influx of blacks on any basis, proclaiming that free Negroes were "idle in their habits, difficult to govern, thriftless and uneducated." Finally, the convention reversed itself again and defeated the McCarver measure by a vote of 31 to 8. The sentiment that prevailed, however, was that of expediency, not humanitarianism. The overriding consideration was that no obstacle should be put in the path of California's admission into the Union and there was concern that Congress would consider the McCarver amendment in violation of the federal constitution.

Not so amicably settled was the matter of suffrage. When the vote was granted only to white male citizens, the injustice to *Californios* was obvious. Many native Californians had some admixture of Indian ancestry, and the peace treaty had specifically provided that former Mexican citizens of California had the right to become American citizens. At least one prominent *Californio*, sitting as a delegate in the convention, was denied the vote by this provision. An amendment was introduced by Pablo de la Guerra giving the state legislature power by a two-thirds vote to extend the suffrage to Indians or their descendants, but it was an inadequate compromise, mainly designed to prevent Congress from considering the proposed constitution in violation of the treaty with Mexico.

Towards the end of September, the convention undertook to resolve its most difficult issue—the question of the eastern boundary. No definite limits had been established under Mexico. On the map used in the negotiation of terms ending the war, California had included not only the present area of Nevada, but the bulk of Utah and Arizona as well. The convention's boundary committee, on which Sutter, de la Guerra, and Rodríguez served, recommended inclusion of most of the Nevada territory. Gwin and Henry Halleck argued for a still larger state, extending to the Great Salt Lake. Robert Semple, with a substantial following, maintained that the logical line was formed by the Sierra Nevada and the Colorado River.

The most tumultuous debates of the sessions centered about these divergent proposals. Repeatedly, the convention changed its mind. Delegates rushed out of the room. Some moved for adjournment. Several times the convention almost dissolved. But throughout the fight and the fury, most of the members were primarily concerned about the effect California's size would have upon its chance for admission to the Union. Accordingly, they voted for the boundaries of the state as they presently exist.

It is remarkable that these men, with such varied background, experience, and orientation, were able to hammer out successfully a state constitution. Many of the questions they were called upon to settle had been stumbling blocks for years in the proceedings of the Congress of the United States. And although relatively few of the members were familiar with legislative procedures and some had for years known only mining camps or mountain wilderness, the courtesies of debate were never crassly violated, nor did a minority ever fail to acquiesce to the vote of the majority.

Undoubtedly, many an issue was maneuvered to the edge of compromise outside the convention hall. Delegates were entertained in the homes of prominent residents. Thomas Larkin was a generous host. In addition to more elaborate affairs, he made it a point to have at least one delegate come to lunch and another to dinner every day.

The home of Dōna Augusta Jimeno, sister of Pablo de la Guerra, was also a favorite gathering place for influential convention members, both American and Californian. At first Dōna Augusta, whose husband frequently had acted as governor under Alvarado, was bitterly opposed to the American occupation. Known for her pungent speech, she had once remarked that she would delight to have the ears of the officers of the United States squadron for a necklace. But at the time of the convention, she made them welcome in her house with great warmth and hospitality, and after she was widowed, she became the wife of an American officer, Dr. James Ord.

Another captivating hostess during the days of the convention was Jessie Fremont. Following a brief stay in San Francisco, she and John had rented a portion of the Castro adobe in Monterey. Though they had only two large rooms, the Fremonts furnished them comfortably with such items as satin-cushioned bamboo couches and bearskin rugs. Before the big living-room fireplace or in the spacious patio, around a long table made of rough planks, many informal star-chamber meetings of delegates were held. Fremont was not a delegate, but used his influence privately, particularly in behalf of free-soil principles, and the scintillating Jessie knew how to create an atmosphere in which his ideas could be manipulated to a favorable conclusion. Once the slavery question had been settled in the convention, however, Fremont became less intent on the proceedings and devoted his time to the Rancho Mariposas. The land that he had so summarily tried to reject was now pouring forth fantastic riches. Regularly, 100-pound buckskin bags of gold, worth about $25,000 each, were brought for safekeeping to the Fremont quarters in Monterey. Certainly, the excitement of politics could not compete.

The highly esteemed Feliciano Soberanes, white-haired at the age of 61, was forgiving if not forgetful of the past. Though his sons so recently had fought against the *Americanos,* the doors of his beautiful new adobe in Monterey, located at the corner of present-day Franklin and Pierce Streets, were opened wide to the delegates for receptions and *bailes.* With its magnificent parlor and other high-ceilinged capacious rooms, it was considered by some to be the showplace of Monterey. Later, in 1889, the adobe was converted into a luxurious hotel, called the *Alta Vista.*

Liveliest entertainment was enjoyed at the Casa Abrego, for in it was that rarity among musical instruments in the far west, a piano. Don José Abrego, a prosperous merchant, had imported his prized possession, one of three in all of California, at a cost of $600. Many an evening of relaxation was provided the delegates, dancing the quadrille and the polka, in the spacious parlor over which the lovely Doña Joséfa Estrada de Abrego, the step-sister of ex-Governor Alvarado, presided.

Not so felicitous were the day-to-day living arrangements of the delegates, at least not when they first arrived. Many were forced to bed down on blankets under the pines, as there were no hotels. Some were offered sleeping accommodations in the upper story of *El Cuartel,* but their pallets of straw were so infested by fleas that the men soon took refuge in the woods. (An especially zestful account of this peculiar torment was given by Bayard Taylor, correspondent for the New York *Tribune,* in his colorful book *Eldorado.*)

At the beginning of the convention, there was also only one restaurant, called *Fonda de la Union.* It consisted of two small rooms, smudged and smoky, in which meals were served, and a third adjoining billiard-room. The menu was modest: beef boiled or roasted with red peppers, stew, cucumbers and corn, and unlimited quantities of execrable coffee. Cost of a dinner usually ran around $1. Located across the street from *El Cuartel,* the place reaped a fortune, but competitors soon sprang up to split the business.

By the first of October, four hotels had been established. The best of these was the Washington Hotel, part of which was once the home of Eugenio Montenegro and his wife, María Juana, the fifth child of Mariano de Jesús Soberanes. It now belonged to Alberto Trescony, an Italian tinsmith who had arrived penniless in Monterey seven years earlier and had already amassed a fortune of $50,000, which he was rapidly augmenting. He rented the hotel to a former private in the New York Company of Volunteers for $1,200 a month, and the ex-private rented the rooms in the converted building, at Pearl and Houston Streets, at $200 a month, with board at $12 per week. The rates were not considered exorbitant.

Unprecedented prosperity flooded Monterey, a contagion caught from the gold fever engulfing San Francisco. Real estate prices soared, and speculators flourished. A lot 75 by 25 feet, with a small frame store on it, sold for $5,000. A one-story house on the outskirts of town, with a lot 50 by 75 feet, was held at $6,000. Men like Larkin knew how to make the most of the boom.

While the convention was still in session, another son-in-law of Senator Thomas Hart Benton arrived on a momentous mission. William Carey Jones, a young lawyer married to Jessie Fremont's sister, had been appointed by the United States government to make a comprehensive study and report of land claims under Spanish and Mexican law. His work would be the basis for all federal legislation governing the rights of *Californios* to hold title to their land grants. Earlier in the year, under orders from Governor Mason, Henry Halleck had made a similar report; but his report was less comprehensive and his point of view regarding the legality of Mexican land grants was less liberal than Jones'. The fact that brother-in-law Fremont's claim to the Rancho Mariposas was at stake may well have influenced Jones' generous attitude.

After six weeks of intensive effort, the convention was ready to adjourn. Members voted themselves exceedingly generous compensation: $16 for each day served and $16 for every mile traveled. This was paid out of the Civil Fund, an accumulation of revenue taxes received at the several ports. Since these funds were principally in silver, members staggered through the streets with heavy bags slung over their shoulders, and the little Irish boy, who acted as page, was almost pressed down under the weight of his wages. Other payments were on a similar scale. J. Ross Browne was granted $10,000 for printing his detailed reports of the convention proceedings—1,000 copies in English and 250 copies in Spanish. And $1,000 was voted for engraving the design of the state seal.

On October 12th, the morning session was short, as the assembly hall had to be made ready for a gala ball celebrating the close of the convention. It was to be held in honor of the citizens of Monterey, who had given so lavishly of their hospitality. Each delegate contributed $25 toward the expense, and a sum in excess of $1,000 was collected. The floor was cleared of tables; the rostrum and railing removed. Fragrant boughs of young pines decorated the walls and the glow of many candles shone from the three simple chandeliers. At eight o'clock, the guests began to gather.

The orchestra, consisting of two guitars and two violins, played a lilting waltz. Beautiful dark-haired *señoritas*, in rainbow-hued satins and silks, made whirling ribbons of radiance amidst the more somber garb of the Americans. Stately *doñas*, elegant in gowns of rich brocade, sat on the sidelines as was their custom. Gentlemen in full dress, with gleaming white kid gloves, mingled with miners who had hastily assembled what finery they could. One man paid 50 dollars to rent a pair of patent-leather shoes.

General Riley was present, resplendent in dress uniform and yellow sash, and the courtly Mariano Vallejo, attired in blue velvet trimmed with gold lace, moved through the measures of the *contradanza*. Pablo de la Guerra made a superb director of the dance. They were all there on that dazzling autumn evening: the Soberanes and the Castros, the Estradas and the Malaríns, all the first families of the proud capital of California. It was a night to remember. Yankees and *Californios*, conquerors and conquered, they danced away the hours in gay camaraderie. At midnight, an elaborate supper was served, complete with the finest wines and liquors, but it was well past three o'clock in the morning before the ball was over.

A few hours later, the delegates assembled to perform their final duty—the signing of the constitution. There was a slight delay, as Lieutenant Hamilton had not quite finished engrossing the document on parchment. A messenger brought word that although he had written day and night and had a lame and swollen hand, he was still working on it. The sympathetic crowd, made mellow by their night of revelry, voted him the sum of $500 for his outstanding service and adjourned for lunch.

At one o'clock, they reconvened. Robert Semple, weak from a bout with typhoid fever, took the chair. Then, one by one, the delegates moved forward to affix their signatures to the historic document. As the first salute boomed forth from the guns of the fort, John Sutter sprang to his feet. Waving his arm as if swinging a sword, he exclaimed: "Gentlemen, this is the happiest day of my life. It makes me glad to hear those cannon. They remind me of the time when I was a soldier. Yes, I am glad to hear them—this is a great day for California!" Then, he sank back into his seat, tears streaming from his eyes, and tumultuous cheers resounded through the room.

As the signing continued, gun followed gun, the roar of cannon reverberating around the bay. When the 31st shot was fired, proclaiming the birth of a new state, a glad cry rang out—"That's for California!"

An enormously difficult undertaking had been accomplished. Soon Monterey would celebrate its eightieth birthday. It had witnessed many a stirring event since Spain sent the first settlers to its isolated shores. But this had been its finest hour. The foundation for a great state had been securely laid.

11

The Old Pacific Capital

Like a swiftly lowered curtain, quiet settled over Monterey following the constitutional convention. The delegates departed, and once again the narrow, sandy streets were empty except for townspeople moving unhurriedly about their affairs. The halcyon days of political prestige and commercial expansion were over.

Henceforth the rising star of San Francisco would attract enterpreneurs eager to cash in on the boom of the gold rush. Even Thomas Larkin moved his residence and center of business operations to the budding city by the Golden Gate. And when the first state legislature met, on December 15, 1849, it was in San Jose. Monterey was no longer the capital of California.

Early in 1850, one man, David Jacks, chose to leave the bursting bonanza of San Francisco for what had become the charming but somnolent backwater village of Monterey. Why he did so is one of the many mysteries of the man, but for his choice he was well-rewarded. He became the most influential and controversial character in the drama of the city's ensuing 40 years.

Born in Scotland to devout Presbyterian parents, David Jacks dreamed of entering the ministry. Then, the death of his father brought a sudden end to the cherished goal. Unwilling to burden his widowed mother with the expense of his education, he set forth in 1841, at the age of nineteen, to earn his way in America.

For seven years, he worked in New York as a clerk in a large mercantile establishment that supplied wagons and harnesses to the army. Then, in 1848, when eastern newspapers began flaunting enticing accounts of fortunes to be made in California, Jacks became intrigued. He invested his meagre savings of $1,400 in revolvers, surmising they would bring a good price on the West Coast, and accepted a civilian job with the army which took him to the land of promise.

Within 48 hours of his arrival in San Francisco, the guns were sold for $4,000. This was indeed the land of opportunity! Before long, he also discovered that he could lend his small cache of capital at two percent per month; and living thriftily on his $100 monthly salary as inspector at the Custom House, he quickly accumulated a tidy sum. He briefly considered going to the goldfields but decided not to take the risk. Instead, after business had brought him to Monterey in January of 1850, he returned there to stay a few months later.

His first employer was Joseph Boston, proprietor of a general store in the Casa del Oro on Olivier Street. Jacks, who had never found it easy to make friends, idolized the kindly Mr. Boston and happily accepted the invitation to board in the Boston home, at the upper end of Van Buren Street. Fascinated with the beautiful location overlooking the bay, he made up his mind that someday it would be his.

Jacks' next job was with James McKinley, a fellow Scotsman, who had a grocery and drygoods store in Monterey. With savings and a salary of $2,000 a year, he had enough money to buy a few acres in Carmel Valley, where he experimented with growing potatoes, beans, and barley. Inexperience and naivety in marketing his produce made the venture unprofitable. At one point, he was forced to sell a herd of hogs for $50 after he had paid $3,000 for them. Unquestionably, his talent lay in finance rather than farming.

David Jacks was now 34 years old and had been away from home for fifteen years. Longing to see his mother and sister, he abruptly departed for a twelve-month trip to Scotland. The year was 1856. By the time he returned, the stage was set for a notorious land deal that would make this quiet man Monterey's wealthiest and most maligned citizen.

Three years earlier, the City of Monterey had retained Delos Ashley, an attorney, to secure patent to its old pueblo lands. Under Spanish and Mexican law, each pueblo and presidio was entitled to at least four square leagues of land, and the grant to Monterey had been 29,698.53 acres. Since such pueblo claims were covered in the congressional act of 1851, governing settlement of private land claims in California, Ashley was hired to appear before the United States Land Commission in San Francisco, to obtain title confirmation for the Monterey lands. This he did and submitted his fee of $991.50. But there were no funds in the city treasury with which to pay him.

However, the year after the land title was confirmed in 1856, the California legislature passed an amendment to the city charter of Monterey, authorizing its trustees to sell any or all of the city's lands necessary in order to pay the expenses of securing title to them. No one seemed to know who had instigated this legislative action, but early in 1859, a plot became apparent.

Few people noticed the obscure item in the Santa Cruz *Sentinel*, announcing an auction to be held on February 9th, at five o'clock in the evening, on the steps of Colton Hall. But news of the event that took place there spread like wildfire. All of the city lands of Monterey were actioned off for $1,002.50! And the sole bidders on this historic occasion were Delos Ashley and David Jacks. To these two men the city's board of trustees delivered a conveyance of title for almost 30,000 acres of land surrounding Monterey and a goodly portion of the town itself. In addition, Ashley received from the proceeds of the auction the $991.50 owed him, plus $11 for legal costs.

The extent to which Jacks was responsible for the maneuver that brought this deal about is uncertain, for he was abroad at the time of the legislative act that authorized the land sale. Nevertheless, for his complicity in the sale, he earned a condemnation that outlasted his lifetime. Ashley was unable to stand for long the criticism heaped upon himself and his partner. In 1868, he sold his interest in the former city lands to Jacks for $500 and left town.

Twice, the citizens of Monterey tried to regain their lands. In 1866, a new board of trustees declared the action of their predecessors to be illegal. But State Assemblyman Mathew Ireland, a business associate of Jacks, introduced a successful bill which retroactively ratified all land sales made by the City of Monterey after February 8, 1859.

Again, in 1877, the people of Monterey were sufficiently aroused to bring suit against Jacks for recovery of their lands. Ironically, Robert Forbes, hired to represent the city in the court action, was promised 15,000 acres of the city's lands as compensation if he won the case. Forbes based his plea on the claim that the state legislature did not have the right to authorize the sale. Superior Court Judge Dorn ruled against the city as did the Supreme Court of California. The case was carried on to the United States Supreme Court, which also upheld the sale to Mr. Jacks.

It is germane to note that six years before the infamous auction, at least part of Monterey's city lands were sold to a Daniel Murphy in satisfaction of three judgments issued in his favor. Therefore, the action for which David Jacks was vilified was not without precedent. An interesting sidelight is that Jacks acquired this piece of land as well. Murphy lost the property through tax delinquency, and a portion of it was picked up by William La Porte, who gave Jacks a quitclaim on the land in return for $400.

In the midst of this controversy, David Jacks maintained a very successful banking business without the formality of a bank. Many of the rancheras were in trouble because of an alternating series of droughts and floods, as well as the crippling expense of defending their land claims before the Land Commission. Some mortgaged their property to Jacks at two percent per month, the going rate at the time, and foreclosures reached frightening proportions. Jacks also became involved in buying up tax delinquent tracts, on which it was then possible to clear title after waiting only six months. Though deeply religious and scrupulously conscientious about staying within the letter of the law, Jacks remained a hardheaded and shrewd businessman. Jacks also became very rich. In 1861, he married the soft-spoken María Cristina Romie, daughter of a German emigrant who came to Monterey via Mexico, and they had seven children. They lived in the old Boston house on Van Buren Street, where Jacks had boarded as a youth, dreaming that someday it would be his.

At the time David Jacks acquired its city lands in 1859, Monterey had become little more than a bankrupt village with but one industry, shore whaling. This difficult and dangerous occupation was begun in Monterey in 1854, when Captain Davenport formed a whaling company of twelve men, of whom only four were experienced. The following spring, seventeen Portuguese whalers organized the group that came to be called the "Old Company," and by 1861, there were four companies operating in Monterey Bay. The Carmel Company, fourth to be organized, moved to Point Lobos in 1862.

Both the Humpback and the California Gray Whale were abundant off the shores of Monterey at certain times of the year. The best season for hunting the Humpback was between September and December, when, moving southward, the animals came into the bay in search of food. The California Grays migrated from the Bering Sea to their breeding grounds on the coast of Baja California in November. On their return trip in the spring, when they were accompanied by their young, they were particularly easy hunting; for once a calf was struck, the cow would never desert her offspring.

At first, the methods of the whaling industry were primitive, using only hand harpoons and lances as had the Norsemen of the Middle Ages. Soon, however, bomb-lances and harpoons were introduced. The boats went out at dawn, cruising under sail as they searched for their prey.

When the telltale column of mist was sighted, they approached swiftly, then peaked their oars and propelled by paddles as they drew near the animal. At a distance of 40 yards the harpoon gun was fired, projecting a spear that was attached by a long line to the boat. Struck, the whale ran out to sea, dragging the boat with it.

Often, this was a desperate moment. If the whale sounded deeply, the line had to be cut or the boat would be pulled under. Usually, the injured animal wearied quickly and surfaced for air. A new danger arose, then, as the boat hauled up close enough to kill the creature by shooting two or three bomb-lances into a vital part. The huge mammals, which averaged 45 feet in length and 30 in circumference, often thrashed about and with their ponderous flukes upset and splintered the small boats.

The mammoth prize was towed to the try works on the beach below the presidio. This was a crude shack comprising a washroom, drying room, and cooper's shop. Outside were huge vats of planking which held the blubber as it was stripped from the carcass, and next to these were enormous kettles, set in a rude furnace formed of rocks and clay, in which the whale fat was rendered into oil. Thick black clouds of smoke, the stench overpowering, rose from these steaming pots.

The Whaling Station was the headquarters of the "Old Company," and Captain Davenport's group operated out of the Jack Swan adobe, now known as California's First Theatre. For several years, each company produced around a thousand barrels of oil annually. By the late 1870s, however, shore whaling became sporadic and contributed little to the support of Monterey. The slaughtering of females and their young had led inevitably to a scarcity of the animals. At the same time, the demand for whale oil had decreased as mineral oil began to be used for light and lubrication.

At this point, Monterey was still in an unstable condition both politically and economically. It had already lost its status as a city by action of the legislature in 1853, only two years after it was first incorporated. Since then, subsequent attempts at reincorporation had been unsuccessful. Now, in an election held in November of 1872, it also lost its position as county seat to Salinas. Never had the fortunes of the once proud capital been so low. Bereft of its city lands, its treasury empty and its businesses stagnant, the town was called the "Sleepy Hollow of California."

Meanwhile, the Salinas Valley was prospering. In large measure, this was due to the Southern Pacific Railroad, which had been extended from San Jose to Soledad in 1872. The agricultural interests of the valley had fought hard for this new rail line, which provided their products with an outlet to San Francisco and, from there, to the rest of the country via the recently constructed transcontinental railroad.

Before long, however, the Salinans became disillusioned. The Central Pacific Railroad, which controlled the Southern Pacific, held a transportation monopoly and was free to charge the highest rates the traffic would bear. The rising freight rates took too deep a bite out of the profits of the valley ranchers. Thus, in 1874, a movement was initiated to break the Southern Pacific's stranglehold. It was led by Carlisle Abbott of Salinas and David Jacks. Their plan was to provide a narrow-gauge railroad between Salinas City and Monterey, where the agricultural freight could then be shipped by steamship to San Francisco. It was estimated that the grain growers of Salinas Valley would save not less than $200,000 a year, while Monterey would be transformed into a thriving seaport.

On February 26, 1874, the Monterey and Salinas Valley Railroad was chartered, with 72 stockholders and a capital stock of community subscriptions totaling $300,000. David Jacks borrowed $75,000 on his ranchos and invested a third of it in the company. The balance of the money he loaned to stockholders who were unable to pay for their subscriptions. Construction of the nineteen mile three-foot-gauge track began in April and was completed by October.

From the beginning, the railroad was beset by financial problems. Twice, a pile trestle and bridge were washed out by floods, necessitating expensive reconstruction. A suspicious fire in the Monterey engine house severely damaged two locomotives and destroyed a passenger coach. Then, the final blow came from the powerful Southern Pacific. It reduced its freight rates to the point where the narrow-gauge could no longer compete, and the fickle farmers transferred their business. The end came on December 22, 1879; the Monterey and Salinas Valley Railroad was sold under foreclosures to the Central Pacific.

David Jacks, along with many other investors, suffered heavy losses, but the short-lived little railroad had accomplished a great deal. The Southern Pacific immediately began construction of a standard-gauge track from its main line at Castroville to Monterey. Not only did this center attention on the old capital, but it aroused interest in the whole area from Charles Crocker, one of the principal owners of the Central and Southern Pacific Railroads. A new era was about to begin for the Monterey Peninsula.

During the mellow autumn days of 1879, when Monterey's *dolce-far-niente* period was drawing to a close, the community was visited by a sensitive and prescient new observer. Robert Louis Stevenson arrived on August 31, a passenger on the narrow-gauge railroad. He was 29 years old, broke, and desperately ill. His seedy blue serge suit hung loosely on his shrunken body, and the joints of his spidery limbs made sharp corners under his coat. Out of the finely-chiseled oval face shone great brown eyes, made more brilliant by a high fever. Stevenson had traveled 6,000 miles to be with his beloved Fanny.

Born to upper-middle-class parents in Edinburgh, he had been educated both as an engineer and an attorney. But he wanted only to write. He turned his back on a promising career, alienated his father, and "dropped out." While vagabonding about the French countryside, he met Fanny Vandegrift Osbourne, an Oakland, California, woman, estranged from her husband and living abroad with her two children. Ten years older than Stevenson, Fanny Osbourne had a swarthy gypsy beauty, with clear-cut cameo features, curly black hair, and glittering golden eyes. Volatile and often emotionally unstable, she was capable of irresistible charm and possessed a keen intelligence. They were instantly attracted to each other, and two years passed while the lovers continued their liaison in Paris.

Then Fanny's husband cut off her allowance, and she was forced to return to him. A desolate Stevenson was subsisting on a hundred pounds a year provided by his father; but when he received word from Fanny that she was ill, he borrowed enough money to travel emigrant-style and took off for California. Fanny was staying in Monterey, once again separated from but supported by her husband.

Now Stevenson set out to find her in the straggling town. Hiring a dray cart, he rode up Alvarado Street, a narrow lane paved with sea-sand and deeply rent by fissures. Short sections of wooden sidewalk tilted high above the roadway, and at the corners, old Spanish cannon were stuck upright as hitching posts. He stopped at the Sanchez saloon for a swig of brandy, then walked a block beyond, to the two-story, red-tiled Bonifacio adobe, where he had been told Mrs. Osbourne had an apartment. Seconds later, they were in each other's arms.

Later in the evening, Joe Strong, a young artist who was courting Fanny's daughter, took Stevenson to the boarding house of Rosanna Leese, which stood on Calle Principal, next door to the Larkin House which had been purchased by her father. Señorita Leese, a granddaughter of the Vallejos, was horrified to see the eczema on Stevenson's hands, and before long, she evicted him and burned the bedding he had used. In the four months he remained in Monterey, he was to move often as a result of one of his illnesses.

Meanwhile, Louis drove himself to write in the bare chilly room.

By October 8, he had completed half of *The Amateur Emigrant*, based on the agonizing adventures of his trip. He also tossed off a suspense-filled short story entitled *The Pavilion on the Links* and started a novelette. To his London agent he wrote, "At times I get terribly frightened about my work. . . . I must make money for myself and my sick one."

In the walled garden opening out of her apartment, Fanny was convalescing from a nervous disorder. Every afternoon, amidst the masses of cloth-of-gold and Castilian roses, she, her children Isobel and Lloyd, and her sister Nellie gathered to hear Stevenson read his morning's work. He was very attentive to their criticism.

His evenings were spent at the restaurant of Jules Simoneau, "a dear and kind old man" who often fed the impecunious Stevenson free of charge. The establishment, a small steamy room back of a combination barber shop and bar, was located in the area of the plaza which now bears Simoneau's name. A jovial crowd assembled there nightly, including the artists Julian Rix and Jules Tavernier, who decorated the walls with their drawings, and Crevole Bronson, editor of *The Monterey Californian*, the town's weekly newspaper for which Stevenson wrote articles. His salary of two dollars a week was secretly donated by Simoneau and his customers. They were very fond of the writer, who, despite his personal problems, never failed to be entertaining and full of fun.

When a *cascarón* ball was held at the Bagby Opera House on Alvarado Street, Stevenson escorted Fanny, elegant in a garnet velvet gown. Young Isobel Osbourne and Fanny's sister Nellie both wore Spanish dresses of red and yellow silk trimmed in black lace, which they borrowed from Señorita Bonifacio, their landlady's daughter. As the fandango began, gallant gentlemen and sparkling *señoritas* broke *cascarónes* over each other's heads as tokens of admiration and flirtation. The eggshells had been emptied of their contents and filled with finely cut pieces of paper immersed in perfume. One contained gold dust, and the lady honored with the golden *cascarón* became *La Favorita*.

After the ball was over, the sound of tinkling guitars and deep melodious voices rose under darkened adobe windows as *caballeros* sang their lilting love songs. For the privilege of this serenading, the young men had applied for a permit from the city and had paid over a dollar for it. The ordinance read: "One serenade will be excused as heat of emotion, but after that unless he pay, the serenader must spend time in the *calabozo*." To acknowledge this relatively expensive attention, the *senoritas* discreetly lit a candle that would be visible from the street.

Stevenson's health began to worsen, and he was depressed by Fanny's indecision about a divorce. Hoping the dry inland air would relieve his bronchial ailment and improve his spirits, he departed for a camping trip in the mountains above Carmel Valley. He almost died there. Two backwoods ranchers took him into their home and cared for him until he was able to return to Monterey. He rented a room in Madame Girardin's French Hotel, an adobe on Houston Street, which is now preserved by the state of California as the Stevenson House. The rooming house was frequented by both artists and sailors and tended to be a bit on the rough side. But it was cheap and near Simoneau's restaurant. As Stevenson's illness persisted, Jules Simoneau and his wife Martina often came across the back garden carrying nourishing broths.

Still pushing himself to write, Louis collapsed with pneumonia. Madame Girardin wanted no sick boarders in her house, so he was taken to the home of her son-in-law, Doctor Heintz, where the pregnant Mrs. Heintz was even less hospitable. Briefly, Stevenson was bedded down on the floor!

In the meantime, Fanny finally decided to sue for divorce and returned to Oakland to make arrangements. She had raised a storm of gossip, with her short-cropped hair, cigarettes, and ailing lover. Now Stevenson was left alone to live with the scandal. There was even a rumor that Lloyd Osbourne was his illegitimate son. Toward the end of December, he was thankful to leave "the tattling town" for San Francisco. He had been in Monterey only a short time, but in his writings on "The Old and New Pacific Capitals," he captured the essence of the place. He knew the cause of the native Californians was lost. Trusting and childlike, they were "curiously unfitted to combat Yankee craft." He predicted that the "native gentlemen of Monterey must perish, like a lower race, before the millionaire vulgarians of the Big Bonanza."

Six months after Stevenson's departure from Monterey, the Hotel Del Monte opened its doors, foreshadowing a new way of life for the old Mexican town. An advance guard of the future tourist invasion had come to the peninsula with the founding of a Methodist Retreat at Pacific Grove, but the Del Monte development was destined to center world-wide attention on the area.

In January 1880, the branch line of the Southern Pacific Railroad between Castroville and Monterey was completed. Since luxury hotels situated at beautiful spots adjacent to railroad routes were then in vogue, the rail tycoon Charles Crocker chose a site near Monterey for construction of the "most elegant seaside establishment in the world." More than 7,000 acres of land, at five dollars per acre, were purchased from David Jacks by the Pacific Improvement Company, a holding company organized in 1878 to control the financial interests of Crocker and his partners, Collis P. Huntington, Mark Hopkins, and Leland Stanford—the Big Four. The purchase included the site of the hotel as well as the

Ranchos Punta de Pinos and Pescadero, comprising today's Del Monte Forest and Pebble Beach.

The huge hotel, which could accommodate 500 guests, was erected in 100 days at a cost of one million dollars. Turreted and elaborately adorned, the pearl-gray two-story building was Swiss-Gothic in design, had great wings extending from either side of the main structure, and was topped by a tower. Situated in the midst of a 126-acre natural forest of pine and oak, the hotel grounds were landscaped with exotic shrubs and trees from all over the world. Flower beds, arranged in formal designs, flaunted a myriad of brilliantly colored blossoms. A seven-foot, topiary-trimmed cypress hedge formed a giant maze that covered several acres. Beside the bay, a glass-roofed bathing pavilion, decorated with hanging baskets of ferns and trailing tropical plants, offered a choice of four salt-water swimming pools heated to different temperatures. There was also a large lake and, at the boat landing, a clubhouse equipped with billiard tables, bowling alley, and bar. Furnishings were luxurious, the cuisine was superb, and rates started at three dollars per day. According to a contemporary newspaper report, "Even the most sanguine of the visitors were amazed and delighted at the magnificent scale of everything about them."

The first Saturday of June in 1880, the Del Monte held its opening celebration. A special train of six carriages, crowded to capacity, brought prominent guests from San Francisco. It was evening when they arrived. Illuminated by a thousand gas-jets reflecting in a multitude of mirrors, the spacious hotel stood waiting. A lavish banquet was followed by an inspection tour and a grand ball.

Overnight, the hotel became a success. Two trains ran to and from San Francisco daily, making the trip in three hours to Del Monte station a quarter of a mile from the hotel. Tallyhos and a large carry-all met the guests at the station. Soon the establishment was internationally famous, publicized as the "Queen of American Watering Places." Then, seven years after it opened, the hotel was in ashes. At the stroke of midnight, on April 1, 1887, fire broke out and raced through the wooden building, demolishing it in one hour. Fortunately, no one was injured, but for days, the charred ruins were sifted for lost jewelry and gold pieces.

By 1888, the hotel had been rebuilt on an even more lavish scale. The architecture was essentially the same, except that a third story was added to the main building. With its twin annexes, the new plant covered 16 acres. All the public rooms were now enormous. The dining room could serve 750 people at one sitting. A ton of meat, poultry, and vegetables arrived every evening on the Del Monte Express, and wagon loads of fruit and dairy products were brought from Carmel Valley, as was the company-owned water supply. So large was the enterprise that it published its own newspaper, the Del Monte *Wave*.

In the 1890s, several innovations were added for the entertainment of the guests. A golf course was constructed and the first California tournament held, a forerunner of the annual State Amateur Championship. Both a race track and a polo field were also built. These amusements were over and above the celebrated Seventeen Mile Drive, on which as many as 50 tallyhos made three trips a day.

The drive began by meandering through Monterey, which, at the turn of the century, was still a ramshackle village. The elegant tourists gazed in wonderment at the tumbledown adobes and the crooked neglected streets, while they listened to the story of the Spanish capital's historic past. The fortunes of the old city had been little improved by the Del Monte development.

Then, in 1906, a city engineer took office and instituted a quiet campaign to rehabilitate the slumbering community. Hampered by indifference and even hostility, Howard Severance shouldered this difficult assignment for three decades. Through his efforts, Monterey's tangled property lines were clarified and its haphazard thoroughfares straightened. A new civic consciousness was aroused. Businessmen and builders became interested in the area and an artists colony sprang into being. The flourishing Hotel Del Monte brought thousands of tourists who patronized newly established shops in the city. The presidio was reactivated and an army payroll swelled the city's coffers. But the biggest impetus to the economy came from the advent of a new industry—sardines.

The multimillion-dollar sardine business began modestly. In 1900, Frank Booth, who had a cannery on the Sacramento River, set up a tiny plant to pack salmon near present-day Fisherman's Wharf. Impressed with the large schools of sardines around the wharf, he experimented with canning the small silver-sided fish. Then his plant burned down, and for a time he operated a combination smokehouse and saloon on the waterfront. From this his sardines came to be called "soused mackerel."

After re-establishing his packing plant, at the foot of Alvarado Street, Booth felt the need of expert technical advice in processing the enormous quantities of sardines that glutted the bay. He found the man he needed in San Francisco—Knute Hovden, a young Norwegian graduated from the National Fisheries College in his native country. A throat ailment had forced Hovden to leave the cold climate of his home, and now he was at loose ends and looking for just such an opportunity.

Hovden was appalled at the primitive fishing and canning methods being used in Monterey. The fish were caught in gill nets, strung in the path of a school of fish and then hauled aboard the few sailboats that made up the fishing fleet. Only a small proportion of the fish became entangled in the nets, and of these many slipped away while being extracted and passed up to the cannery in wicker baskets. The fishing was erratic and the hauls varied from day to day, causing the cannery to be either overloaded or idle.

Canning techniques were even more inefficient. The fish were cut by hand and cooked in wire baskets that were pushed through troughs of boiling oil. Then they were hand-packed in hand-soldered cans. The clumsy procedure resulted in an output of about 400 cans per day.

Hovden's first improvement was a machine solderer. Then he turned his attention to the fishing problem and introduced purse-bottomed brails and impounding pens for more efficient catching and storing techniques. However, his most clever innovation was hiring Pietro Ferrante.

Ferrante had been a fisherman all his life. At the age of nineteen, he emigrated from Sicily on a cattle boat with only a few cents in his pocket. Taking a railroad job that paid a dollar a day, he worked his way to California, where he invested in a boat on the Sacramento River near Pittsburg and resumed the occupation he knew and loved. Ten years later, fire wiped out all he had earned, and he decided to make a fresh start in Monterey, whose rocky coast reminded him of his homeland.

There, Ferrante devised a version of the lampara net, which revolutionized the sardine industry. The net, which derived its name from the word *lampo*, meaning lightning, was similar to that used by Italian fishermen in the Mediterranean for a very fast cast and haul.

By 1913, there were four canneries in operation, and motorized fishing boats were bringing in as much as 25 tons of sardines in a single night. Cooking was done on chain conveyors moving through vats of boiling oil regulated to the proper temperature. The industry was out of its infancy.

Merchandising the product now became a problem. The California sardine was larger than the variety known to food buyers, and they were reluctant to try the unfamiliar species. Not until World War I cut off the supply of fish from European waters did sales soar. In 1918, for example, 27 plants lined Cannery Row, with an output of four million cases. And with regular improvements in the fishing and canning techniques, the industry grew steadily until Monterey rose to the position of third largest fish tonnage port in the world, with an industry payroll in 1939 of more than four million dollars. Cannery Row was Monterey's Comstock Lode. When the fishing boats returned and docked at the canneries, the whistles blew and the workers began streaming down the hill like ants converging on a lump of honey. Each whistle had a different tone and every worker knew which one belonged to his cannery.

Those were the days immortalized by John Steinbeck. Yee Won held forth at his general store named Wing Chong, which meant "Glorious-Prosperous." In the next block was the Lone Star, a cafe and whorehouse operated by Flora Woods. Despite the business she was in, everybody had only the best to say about Flora, for she was a contributor to every charitable cause and had fed a number of families during the depression of the 1930s. Across the street from the Lone Star was Edward Ricketts' Pacific Biological Laboratory. An eccentric and learned man, Doc Ricketts was a confidant and drinking companion of the lowly and Steinbeck's close friend.

Cannery Row had its share of ne'er-do-wells, bums, and winos, but most of its employees came from the industrious Italian–American colony, which originated when Pietro Ferrante began bringing his countrymen from Pittsburg and Sicily. He gave them room and board in his large house on Van Buren Street and helped them buy their own boats and homes. They idolized him as their leader, and he was instrumental in establishing both the Fishermen's Union and the Boat-Owners Association.

During the 1940s, the catch leveled off to an average of a quarter of a million tons a year. Repeated warnings that overfishing would result in a depletion of supply went unheeded, until, in 1945 the sardines began to disappear. Three years later, the season was the worst in the history of the industry. The big bonanza was over, and the community suffered a severe economic loss. Fortunately, in the interim, events had taken place that would lead to alternate sources of support.

These events began in 1915, when the Pacific Improvement Company sold its stock in the Southern Pacific Railroad and Charles Crocker lost interest in the development of the Monterey Peninsula. Samuel F. B. Morse, an energetic and imaginative young man who had been a classmate of Crocker's grandson at Yale, was hired to liquidate the company's holdings. The package on sale consisted of the 7,000 acres originally purchased from David Jacks, the Del Monte Hotel, the Monterey County Water Works, and scattered properties in the Carmel Valley. The price was $1,300,000.

At the time, the Del Monte Forest was practically an uninhabited woodland and only a log cabin stood at Pebble Beach. The once-famed Del Monte Hotel had slipped in status and its satellite attractions were in disrepair. But Morse had faith in the enterprise. He organized Del Monte Properties Company in 1919, with Herbert Fleishhacker and other San Francisco associates, and the new company acquired the holdings of the Pacific Improvement Company. Then Morse instituted a program of rehabilitation and expansion that ultimately brought new life to the city of Monterey as a resort.

Samuel Morse's program wisely preserved the scenic beauty of the Monterey Peninsula. Ninety-six percent of Del Monte Properties' waterfront acreage has been devoted to golf courses and green belt areas, and residential development in Del Monte Forest is rigorously restricted and controlled. The only commercial establishment in the area, except for a small sand-mining operation, is at exclusive Pebble Beach Lodge. The Del Monte Hotel, which was again destroyed by fire in 1924 and rebuilt on an even larger scale, is now the United States Naval Postgraduate School.

From the policies of Del Monte Properties, Monterey has reaped substantial benefits. With seven internationally known golf courses on the adjacent peninsula, it has become the "Golf Capital of the World." In addition, the Naval School has provided business incentives and job opportunities to the city's residents. But Monterey has done much on its own to change its image. Restoration of its adobes, spearheaded by the Monterey History and Art Association, and well-conceived urban-renewal projects have earned for it the reputation of a community uniquely concerned about the preservation of its historic past. This restoration and the city's superb natural setting have transformed it into a world-renowned mecca for tourists interested in the cultural heritage of California.

12

The Salinas Valley

Between the bright bare hills of the Gabilan Range to the east and the dark brooding wall of the Santa Lucias to the west lies the narrow swale of the Salinas Valley. Stretching southward from Monterey Bay for more than one hundred miles, the valley contains 640,000 acres of the richest soil in the state. Through it flows the Salinas River, fed by five tributaries originating in the surrounding mountains.

It was through the Salinas Valley that the Portolá expedition first came to the shores of what was to be the capital of California. And it was in the wilderness of the valley's waving grasses that the prominent families of Monterey held the great land grants that provided support for their adobe townhouses and carefree life style in Monterey. As late as 1850, the Salinas Valley was still a stock-raising district for the few families whose forebears had come with the first Spanish settlers. They owned most of the land, and the huge herds of black cattle, descendants of those brought by Rivera and Anza, roamed the virgin fields unhindered by fence or corral.

The days for such pastoral peace and security were numbered. In the aftermath of the gold rush and the American occupation, a flood of immigrants swept into California. Many headed for the mines, only to find that prospecting was hard and often unrewarding. They demanded that the vast tracts of fertile farm land in California be made available for settlement. In Monterey County, as in the rest of California, rancho land took in most of the finest agricultural areas, including the Salinas and Carmel Valleys. A harried Congress, thousands of miles away acted without complete or accurate information about the situation. In 1851, legislation was passed creating the United States Land Commission. It was set up to review the validity of land claims based on Spanish and Mexican grants.

Despite the provisions of the Treaty of Guadalupe Hidalgo, ending the Mexican-American War, in which the American government specifically promised to safeguard private property rights, the Land Act in effect challenged every title in California. Persons who claimed land were required to appear before the Land Commission and provide documentary evidence, along with the testimony of witnesses, to prove their claim. This proof had to be provided within two years of the date of the 1851 act. The legislation included a provision for interminable appeal, by the claimant or the government, to the United States District and Supreme Courts. All lands for which claims were finally rejected would be considered to be part of the public domain; for those approved, a patent would be issued.

The Commission carried out its assignment carefully and conscientiously, but once he had filed a petition with the commission, the native California landowner had to wait an average of seventeen years for his patent. In the interim, he struggled with a legal system and language he did not understand and used up any capital he had or could obtain. Unable even to sell his land until clear title was obtained, the ranchero had to mortgage his property to pay attorney's fees and then watch helplessly as squatters and speculators took over the land that was his only means of livelihood. The Americans were a practical people. They did not waste time on fiestas and games, give a horse or a steer for only the asking, or loan money with no security other than a handshake and a promise. But they were adept with mortgage foreclosures and sheriff's sales.

It was a time of trouble for all California rancheros, and those in the Salinas Valley had more than their share. Feliciano Soberanes lost the 21,884-acre San Lorenzo to a San Francisco land lawyer, and former Governor Alvarado's El Alisal was auctioned off in a sheriff's sale for $6,000. Mariano Malarín was struggling to keep the ranchos that had been left in his care after the death of his father. His education as an attorney, for which old Juan Malarín had sent him to Peru, was of little help. Finally, Malarín had to borrow $3,000 on his Rancho Chualar at 24 percent a year. The money came from David Jacks.

Among the earliest of the great ranchos to pass out of the possession of an old Spanish family was the Rancho Sauzal. The 10,242-acre tract, which had been granted to José Tiburcio Castro, was purchased by Jacob Leese in 1852 for $600. In that same year, James Bryant Hill bought the adjoining 6,633-acre Rancho Nacional. The present-day city of Salinas stands on portions of both ranchos.

The city had its start when Leese sold 80 acres of the Sauzal lands to Elias Howe, a Bostonian who was said to be the son of the sewing machine inventor. Howe built a tavern called the Halfway House at the intersection of the stage routes between Monterey and San Juan Bautista and between Los Angeles and San Francisco. Located in the midst of fields of mustard fifteen feet tall, the establishment seemed unlikely to succeed, especially since a well-established stage stop already existed at Natividad.

But clever Deacon Howe, so named because he had once presided at a funeral in the absence of a clergyman, devised a scheme for attracting customers. He began placing bets on which stage would arrive first at the tavern. Drivers on the two routes were soon whipping their horses into a white lather in their attempts to reach the Halfway House. Everybody gathered to drink Howe's good whiskey and to gamble money and even parcels of land on the stage arrivals. Business boomed and the rival establishment at Natividad eventually folded.

On the Rancho Nacional, James Bryant had another kind of success experience. Transforming the brush-covered acreage into fields of grain, he produced up to 85 bushels of wheat and 149 bushels of barley per acre, proving the potential of cattle-grazing land for agriculture. It was a significant development that foreshadowed the beginning of a new era for the Salinas Valley.

Meanwhile, the embryonic city of Salinas was growing. Deacon Howe's Halfway House now belonged to Alberto Trescony, who was also founder of the Washington Hotel in Monterey. Trescony was an enterprising man in his forties, who had landed at Monterey in 1842 after an incredibly varied career. Born and orphaned in Italy, he ran away from an unkind stepmother at the age of twelve and arrived in Paris alone and destitute. There, he learned to be a tinsmith; then worked his way to the United States as a cabin boy. He found employment in America on construction jobs and saved his pennies until he was able to buy a small herd of sheep, which he drove to Mexico. He then sold his sheep for a good price and walked from Mexico City to Mazatlan to preserve his capital. From Mazatlan, the tall, soft-spoken Italian took a steamer bound for San Francisco and landed at Monterey in 1842. The red-roofed adobes and rugged shoreline reminded him of his native Italy, and he stayed.

Living in a shack, the serious and reserved Trescony resumed his trade as a tinsmith, and the gold rush caused his business to flourish. At that time, tin pans were selling to prospectors at $35 each. Within a few years, Trescony accumulated a modest fortune and some properties.

His tavern in Salinas prospered, developing first into a hotel and then into stores and a stable, but he was not a happy man. He was not predisposed to be a hotelkeeper. Deep down in his heart he longed to work under the wide blue skies, and the memory of his experience as a shepherd was strongest within him. He was also very lonely, a problem that was soon resolved when a wonderful woman came into his life. There was but one difficulty—the woman was married.

Catherine Cotton Rainey had arrived in Monterey from New Zealand in 1850, with her husband and their infant son. Her husband Alexander Rainey, a shipwright by trade, was a rough and disorderly person who spent a good part of his time in court and grossly mistreated his gentle wife. Unable to bear the abuse showered upon the woman he adored, Trescony made a financial arrangement with Rainey to release her. Then he provided a home for her and her son, Alexander Jr. By 1862, Trescony had three children of his own. That same year, he got an opportunity to achieve his most cherished desire.

The Rancho San Lucas in the southern part of the Salinas Valley was for sale. The 8,875 acres of rolling hills and meadows, carpeted with deep natural grasses, had once belonged to Rafael Papías Estrada, stepbrother of Juan Bautista Alvarado. The easy-going Estradas had quickly lost their lands. James McKinley, the Monterey merchant, had picked up the San Lucas but the dry year of 1861 discouraged him, and he was willing to sell for $3,000. Though the isolated area showed little promise for development, it was ideal for raising sheep. On the day after Christmas in 1862, Trescony acquired the property.

During the Civil War years 1861 to 1865, great changes were taking place in the Salinas Valley. At what was then the mouth of the Salinas River, a small settlement was developing. It began around 1860, when Paul Lezer bought 300 acres at the river mouth from the State of California for one dollar an acre. Lezer installed a ferry across Elkhorn Slough and planned to establish a town called City of St. Paul. But another man's name was to be given to the locality. Charles Moss, a New England sea captain, saw the potential for a port that could handle the large quantities of wheat and barley being grown in the Salinas Valley. With Cato Vierra, an early settler from the Azore Islands, he built a wharf. Then, the Pacific Steamship Company organized steamer service to San Francisco, and warehouses sprang up near the landing, which came to be called Moss Landing. Charlie Moss ran barges down the Salinas River, carrying loads of grain, and wagons piled high with produce backed up five miles from the wharf waiting to unload.

Inland, a cycle of alternating droughts and floods brought an end to the pastoral economy of the rancheros. Their herds of small sturdy cattle, able to forage for themselves in normal seasons, could not survive the series of natural disasters. In 1860, there were 100,000 cattle in

Monterey County. Five years later, after the dreadful parched days of 1863–64, the number had dropped to 13,000! Helplessly, the rancheros listened to the pitiful bawling of starving cattle and smelled the stench of carcasses decaying under a blazing sun. Some mortgaged all they owned to buy feed, but the situation was beyond their control.

Francisco Soberanes lost 2,000 head of cattle, and most of the lands of the Mission Soledad, over which his father Feliciano had once proudly held sway, were in the hands of receivers. David Jacks foreclosed on Malarín's Rancho Chualar and was also eyeing Rancho Los Coches, the home of Joséfa Soberanes de Richardson and her husband.

Los Coches had long been a favorite stagecoach stop, and for a time the Richardsons had fared better than Joséfa's brothers. The Bixby Overland Stage, en route from San Francisco to Los Angeles, brought a lively trade, and the old adobe, with the cool shade of its long line of locust trees, was a popular inn. But by September 1862, Joséfa and her husband were heavily in debt to a merchant in Monterey and she was forced to mortgage the property her father had obtained for her. The $1,800 she borrowed came at two percent per month, with interest to be compounded four times a year.

At the Rancho San Lucas, Trescony suffered desperate hardships but held on. During the floods of 1862, he drove his sheep into the hills to keep them safe. But when the drought came and the sun turned his rich pasture land into burnt clay, he saw his flocks shrivel before his eyes. He sheared his animals and killed them, as many as a hundred a day, until 3,000 were put out of their misery. The tragedy of this loss for Trescony was made nearly unbearable by the recent death of his beloved Catherine, shortly after the birth of their third child. Sorrowfully, he closed up the little house he had built for her in Salinas and then placed the children with the kindly Señora Bonifacio in Monterey. "One thing he knew; he would never marry again."

While Trescony stayed on alone at San Lucas and slowly built up new herds of sheep, other rancheros were giving up the struggle. Even David Spence, who had been so proud to be a landowner, sold 7,500 acres of his Rancho Encinal y Buena Esperanza to Giles Kellogg and leased the Llano de Buena Vista to Carlisle Abbott. Men with new ideas and a different philosophy of life were taking over the Salinas Valley. They fenced off their property and built square, box-like houses. They planted acres of barley and wheat to replace the wild waving grasses. They introduced improved breeds of cattle which, for the protection of crops, fed in enclosed pastures.

Carlisle Abbott was typical of this new breed of men. Born into a farming family in Quebec, he came to the United States at the age of eighteen, crossing the plains for California. After a stint in the gold mines and a couple of years of farming in Sacramento and then Nevada, he migrated to Point Reyes in Marin County, where he built a prosperous dairy and stock-raising enterprise. In 1865, he moved to Monterey County bringing 600 head of cattle, and, before long, he purchased half of David Spence's property as well as 12,000 acres of the Rancho San Lorenzo. Bankrupted by the financial debacle of the Monterey and Salinas Valley narrow-gauge Railroad, Abbott subsequently lost his property in Monterey County and moved to Arizona.

Eugene Sherwood, who had acquired Rancho San Lorenzo before Abbott, was another representative of the new class of entrepreneurs moving into the Salinas Valley. He came from England to set up a chain of sheep ranches that stretched from Monterey County to San Francisco. He began in 1859, by buying San Lorenzo, the rancho that had once belonged to Feliciano Soberanes, for $1.50 an acre. At about the same time, he purchased the Castro grant, Rancho Sauzal, from Jacob Leese. His sheep business was successful, but the difficult years of flood and drought, which Trescony had patiently weathered, made Sherwood lose interest. There were other ways to make money in this burgeoning land of opportunity.

The Southern Pacific Railroad was creeping southward. In 1864, it reached San Jose, and there were rumors that it planned to cut across the Pacheco Pass and build its line to Southern California through the San Joaquin Valley. If it could be persuaded to lay the track through the Salinas Valley instead, the small settlement surrounding Trescony's Halfway House could become a rail stop and develop into a thriving town. Sherwood unloaded Rancho San Lorenzo to Abbott and concentrated on the Sauzal land, which emcompassed the site of the profitable little town he foresaw.

Sherwood got down to business in 1867, when Alberto Trescony sold his Salinas property, comprising the Halfway House and 160 acres, to a couple of developers named Riker and Jackson. Sherwood formed a partnership with them and, pooling their land, the three men laid out a city half a mile square. Then Sherwood offered the Southern Pacific free acreage for a right-of-way and a depot. A building boom promptly exploded in Salinas City. In 1868 alone, 50 buildings were erected in four months. Progress had come to the rancho that once belonged to José Tiburcio Castro.

At the same time, a rival town was developing on the 30,000-acre Rancho Bolsa Nueva y Moro Cojo, which had been granted to José Tiburcio's brother, Simeon Castro. Juan Bautista Castro, with his sister, had inherited the rancho when he was only six years old. As soon as he came of age, he assumed management of the property and decided to subdivide. He realized that subdivision was the only way to save the land from *gringos* like those who had grabbed the Sauzal, and he knew that they had plans for Salinas City. But the Castros would have their own city.

Castroville was laid out in 1863, over a portion of the rancho that was divided into small lots. Castro worked fast to beat the developers in Salinas City. When his lots did not sell, he leased them. At one point, he even gave them away, transporting squatters from neighboring settlements to his land and helping them build housing facilities. His strategy brought results. More of his property was subdivided and Castroville boomed. In 1868, the town boasted more than twenty business establishments, four hotels, and a flour mill.

The railroad crept ever closer and it looked as if Castroville might gain the coveted depot. Then Juan Bautista made a mistake. Instead of offering the Southern Pacific Railroad land for the roundhouse they wanted to put in his town, he asked a high price. It was a tactical error that in the end caused Castroville to be eclipsed by Salinas City.

Soon, Salinas City also pushed Monterey aside. As early as the 1860s, agitation had begun for moving the county seat from Monterey. The competitors for its new location were Castroville, Salinas City, and Hollister. Hollister, which stood on the 54,000-acre Rancho San Justo that had belonged to Francisco Pacheco, had been recently established by the three men, Hollister, Flint, and Bixby, who had bought the property. The residents of Hollister were opposed to the inconvenience of coming to Colton Hall to transact official business, since they were separated from the rest of the county by the Gabilan Mountains. The Salinas City group led by William Vanderhurst, an influential merchant and agricultural entrepreneur, insisted that their town was the logical site for the county seat since it was centrally located and the railroad was about to reach it. Juan Bautista Castro had high hopes that the honor would go to the city that bore his name.

In 1870, an election was held. Surprisingly, the majority went to Monterey. Hollister claimed a small share, and the remaining votes were almost evenly split between Salinas and Castroville. The Salinas contingent then made a deal with the residents of Hollister and the San Benito Valley. The latter agreed to vote for Salinas in the next election, if the Salinans would support Hollister in a petition for a separate county. Thus, in the election of November 6, 1872, Salinas won the county seat by an overwhelming majority—1,436 votes against Monterey's 448 and Castroville's 265.

In other ways as well, 1872 was a big year for Sherwood's city, set amidst the fields of tall yellow mustard. In September, the town had been incorporated and, that same month, cheering crowds had greeted the first train to roll into its fine new depot. Although Castroville was also on the railroad's main route, it was only a twenty-minute stop. Hollister eventually received its due when the county of San Benito was created in 1874 and Hollister became the county seat. The Southern Pacific constructed a branch line through its boundaries.

Sherwood's shining success with Salinas Valley prompted other men to follow his example. One was David Jacks, who persuaded the Southern Pacific's Big Four to push their railroad southward to his Rancho Chualar. He gave land for a right-of-way, laid out a town, and guaranteed a large freight business. He was now owner of the Rancho Los Coches, having picked up Joséfa Richardson's land in a sheriff's sale, and the Rancho Zanjones as well. He rented the farming land on shares and took a third of the profits. The Scotsman who had acquired the city lands of Monterey in 1859 had now increased his holdings to 60,000 acres in Monterey County, with portions of as many as ten land grants in his possession.

Two more men who quickly took advantage of the advancing railroad were the sons of Teodoro Gonzales, Alfred and Mariano. The rancheros had been smart enough to outwit the land speculators, and now the path of the railroad was directed toward their 15,219-acre Rancho Rincon de la Punta del Monte. They acted immediately, laying out the town of Gonzales and deeding a 100-foot right-of-way to the Southern Pacific.

Another shrewd *Californio* was the very capable Doña Catalina Munrás, the widow of the Spanish trader Estéban, who had come to Monterey 50 years before. The 19,979-acre Rancho San Vicente still belonged to the Munrás family, and Doña Catalina remembered well what her husband had told her: "Hold oñ 'to the land and when the time is right subdivide for a township. Give one lot for a church, one for a school, and one for a cemetery." As the steel ribbons of the railroad began to approach the venerable lady followed her instructions but wisely added a fourth gift of land—for the railroad right-of-way. On December 20, 1872, the railroad reached the site Doña Catalina had selected for a town, which she named Soledad in honor of the brave padres who had founded the now-abandoned mission across the river. For the next thirteen years, Soledad remained the terminus of the Southern Pacific, and as the shipping point for grain from the southern portion of the country, the town attained prestige and great prosperity.

By 1874, the Salinas Valley was a rich grain-growing community with 80,000 acres under cultivation. That year it exported 32,000 tons of wheat and 12,000 tons of barley in addition to growing large quantities of potatoes, beans, and other crops. Day after day, trainloads of immigrant farmers arrived to stake out their share of this bonanza. Farm land was selling for as much as $150 an acre, but huge tracts of unsurveyed government land were open for settlement. Some of the newcomers chose the Jolon country in the mountains west of the valley, making the long hazardous trip from Soledad by stagecoach.

From the gold rush days of 1849, travelers on the Santa Fe Trail bound for the gold mines passed through the San Antonio Valley of the Santa Lucias, coming into the Salinas Valley by way of Reliz Canyon and proceeding to Natividad and the Pacheco Pass. To meet their need for a place to stop and rest, Antonio Ramirez built a small adobe inn on the site of what would become Jolon. Later, the hostelry was an important stage stop on the route between Los Angeles and San Francisco. Then the settlement was given additional impetus, in the 1870s, when placer mining began nearby and some 70 families settled on adjoining farm land.

The settlers acted in good faith in taking the Jolon land, believing the acreage to be part of the public domain and open to pre-emption under the laws of the United States government. However, Faxon Dean Atherton, a San Francisco financier, insisted that the settlers were squatting on his land and ordered them to vacate the property. Atherton had acquired the old Rancho Milpitas, which stretched for many vaguely defined miles along the San Antonio River, and he claimed that the rancho comprised thousands of acres more than those recorded in the careless Mexican records. The adobe inn, by then a two-story hotel owned by George Dutton, and the rest of the little town of Jolon were included in Atherton's claim. The so-called squatters brought suit in the United States Circuit Court against Atherton, asking that he be restrained from evicting them. They lost.

Eviction notices were sent, but the settlers refused to leave. Then, when Faxon Atherton died, in 1877, his son George took over management of the Milpitas. Accompanied by his young wife Gertrude and their small baby, George Atherton set forth to oust the intruders. Mrs. Atherton provides a pungent account of the experience in her autobiography, *Adventures of a Novelist:*

"Such a trip! When we were not rattling over narrow mountain roads along the edge of precipices, sometimes slipping over but rescued by the terrified plunging horse, we were fording rivers whose waters roared above the hubs of the wheels . . . We arrived before night at

Salinas Valley

Home of Feliciano Soberanes' son, Mariano Guadalupe Soberanes, in the center portion of the Soledad Mission lands. The house is believed to have been built in the 1850s.

Mariano married Francisca Stevenson, daughter of an English trader, and they had eleven children. Photograph courtesy of the Monterey City Library.

The Soledad Mission about 1880.
Feliciano Soberanes was appointed
administrator of the mission in 1841.
On January 4, 1846, he was granted
the 8900 acre mission tract in
payment for a claim of $800
against the Mexican government.
Photograph courtesy of the
Monterey County Library.

The William Hartnell house and
school on Rancho El Alisal or
Patrocíno. Early in the 1830s,
Hartnell began ranching on the
property and later opened a boarding
school for boys. The family home
is on the right, with the large
doorway on the extreme right leading
into the chapel. Students were housed
in the building to the left. The
small, adjacent adobe was the blacksmith shop, and at an earlier date
may have been the kitchen.
Amelie Elkinton Collection.

Governor Alvarado's ranch house on El Alisal. The
governor purchased the rancho, exclusive of the portion
which belonged to Hartnell, from Feliciano Soberanes
in 1841. Alvarado spent much time there until 1849,
when he retired to his wife's Rancho San Pablo in
Contra Costa County. In 1852, he lost El Alisal
to Bruno Bernal in a sheriff's sale.
Mayo Hayes O'Donnell Library Collection.

(*top and bottom right*)

The home of María Soberanes de Richardson, daughter of
Feliciano Soberanes, on the Rancho Los Coches (the pigs),
east of Mission Soledad. William Brenner Richardson
began construction of this adobe in the early 1840s.
It became a favorite stagecoach stop on the route from
San Francisco to Los Angeles. Later it was also used
as a hotel and a post office. It is now a
State Historical Monument. Photograph taken in 1918
by S. L. Slevin, courtesy of the Bancroft Library.

Natividad was a rival stage stop to the Halfway House in budding
Salinas City. It was located on the route between San Juan Bautista
and Monterey. Near the Natividad Hotel was the site of Isaac Graham's
distillery and saloon, notorious hangout for deserters from foreign
ships and seedbed of insurrections. Photograph taken in 1917
by S. L. Slevin, courtesy of the Bancroft Library.

150

Old stage at
the Salinas Rodeo
in 1918.
Photograph by S. L. Slevin,
courtesy of the
Bancroft Library.

The Sherwood ranch
on the Rancho Sauzal
in about 1914.
Eugene Sherwood, who
purchased El Sauzal
from Jacob Leese,
was one of the new
class of entrepreneurs
who descended on
the Salinas Valley
in the 1850s.
Amelie Elkinton Collection.

The Salinas Valley

Claus Spreckles, emigrant
from Germany, brought industry
and prosperity to the Salinas
Valley when he built his
$2,700,000 sugar refinery on
the Rancho Llano de Buena Vista
in 1897. Photograph taken
in 1939, courtesy of
the Monterey City Library.

The town of Soledad, founded
by Doña Catalina Manzanelli de
Munrás in 1873, on the Ranchó
San Vicente. For 13 years, it
was the terminus of the Southern
Pacific Railroad and shipping
point for grain from the
southern portion of the Salinas
Valley. Photograph taken
in 1915, courtesy of the
Monterey County Library.

Bradley was the southernmost of
the towns in the Salinas Valley
resulting from extension of the
Southern Pacific Railroad. Named
after Bradley Sargent, one of the
largest landowners in central
California, it was located on his
La Pestilencia ranch. Photograph
probably taken about 1915, courtesy
of the Monterey County Library.

The town of Pleyto, on the
San Antonio River in the Santa
Lucia Mountains, was one of the
settlements resulting from an
influx of homesteaders in the 1870s.
Photograph taken in 1915, courtesy
of the Monterey County Library.

The Dutton Hotel, located at Jolon on the Rancho Milpitas, began as a small adobe inn built by Antonio Ramirez. Later it became an important stage stop on the route between Los Angeles and San Francisco. Part of property claimed by the Athertons, it was repossessed by its owner, George Dutton, for $1000. Mayo Hayes O'Donnell Library Collection.

Jolon, a straggling village on the edge of the ranch, where we were
to remain until one of the squatter's houses could be put in order for
our occupation. The 'hotel' was a long narrow building, and our room
had neither fireplace nor window . . .

"The business of evicting began on the following morning. . . . At
the first farm where George and the sheriffs stopped, six men were
drawn up in a row with rifles at their shoulders. Our heroes sprang
to the ground, brushed the fire-eaters aside, marched into the house
and flung the furniture out of the windows. Not a shot was fired. Then
the sheriffs collected the guns and retired. At other farms there was
not even a show of resistance. The men cursed but submitted."

Actually, the settlers raised money to send a representative to Washington, D. C., to plead their case, but they received no satisfaction.
George Dutton bought back his hotel for $1,000. Others also managed
to repossess their property, but some homesteaders simply moved away.
Eventually, the Milpitas was sold to William Randolph Hearst for over
a million dollars. Today, it is part of the Hunter Liggett Military Reservation, and the old hotel has fallen into ruin.

As early as the 1860s, a few hardy homesteaders had chosen to
settle at the southern end of the Salinas Valley, in the rolling foothills
of the Gabilan Range. The acreage was mostly unsurveyed government
land and suitable for sheep raising and the cultivation of fruit orchards.
The settlers made their homes in the beautiful little valleys that traversed
the rugged mountainous terrain, and gave the valleys beguiling names
like Priest and Peach Tree. Isolated except for narrow wagon trails,
the settlers could make trips to town for supplies only twice a year.
From Priest Valley, for example, it took over a week to drive a herd
of hogs to Soledad.

Life became easier for homesteaders in the southern portion of the
Salinas Valley when the railroad was extended through the Rancho San
Lorenzo in the 1880s. What prompted the Southern Pacific to push
its line southward was the agricultural successes of the new owner of
San Lorenzo, Charles King. In 1884, King, who had become a millionaire
in the redwood lumber business, purchased the San Lorenzo acreage
for $105,000. At the time, the land was believed to be too dry for farming.
But King stubbornly ordered that 6,000 acres be sowed in wheat, and
the venture was a great success.

Soon agriculture was under way on a grand scale in a part of
the county that had been previously limited to stock raising. As a result,
in July 1886, the railroad reached the newly constructed station on the
site of Charles King's proposed townsite, King City. A year later, sub-

division began and the town was laid out. It became the important freight station for ranchers from the surrounding valleys of the Santa Lucia and Gabilan Mountains.

King built a race track, rivaling the one Sherwood had laid out in Salinas City, and constructed a flour mill that offered competition to the Salinas Milling Company. Manager of the mill was Ernest Steinbeck, father of the famous writer whose novel *East of Eden* is in part based on the experiences of his grandparents in the Salinas Valley. The innovative Mr. King next brought a man named Winterhalter from Germany to experiment with growing sugar beets. The crop failed because of wind and rust, but it foreshadowed the next farming development for the valley.

Meanwhile, the railroad moved on southward through the property of Alberto Trescony, which included in addition to the San Lucas, the adjoining Rancho San Benito and a portion of the Rancho San Bernardo, which once had belonged to the Soberanes family. Trescony even had huge acreage across the mountains in the Carmel Valley. Although sheep raising had made him a very rich man, he continued to live in a quiet and unassuming manner.

He was especially loved by the large number of Basque shepherds he had helped to come to the Salinas Valley. Some he brought from Europe, but he met many others at a Basque hotel which he frequented in San Francisco. The hotel provided another kind of matchmaking when Trescony's son Julius fell in love with Kate Aguirre, the daughter of the hotel's owners. They were married and lived on the San Lucas, managing the ranchos and 20,000 sheep while the elder Trescony retired to the Abbott Hotel in Salinas.

In 1892, death came to Alberto Trescony. He was eighty years old. October sunshine warmed the golden hills of the Salinas Valley as a special train, its engine draped in black, took his body to be buried on land at a point that overlooked his three ranchos. The shepherds he had befriended filed sorrowfully past the coffin of the Italian tinsmith, lying in state at the Pleasant View Hotel in San Lucas. In the funeral party, Indians and *paisanos* in faded blue jeans mingled with finely attired folk from San Francisco. All were anxious to pay tribute to the generous and kindly man.

By renting land that had been used for grazing to tenant farmers, Julius Trescony transformed his father's vast acreage into fields of wheat and barley. Then he built the largest grain warehouse south of Salinas City, which helped to establish another new town in the valley, San Lucas. As the shining rails of the railroad advanced, San Lucas, situated

in the midst of Trescony's three ranchos, became the supply station
and shipping point for the southern portion of the Salinas Valley, eventually eclipsing King City. By 1890, lots 50 by 120 feet in the developing
business district of San Lucas were selling for $175.

Before the railroad moved beyond the boundaries of Monterey
County, it resulted in two more towns. San Ardo stood on the Rancho
San Bernardo, of which a part was owned by Brandenstein and Godchaux,
a San Francisco firm of wholesale butchers. Nearer the county line was
Bradley, located on Bradley Sargent's 12,000-acre La Pestilencia ranch.
Sargent had been a resident of Monterey for over 30 years and had
large holdings in the central coast counties and San Joaquin Valley.

Industry came to Salinas Valley in 1897. For five years, prominent
businessmen of the Salinas City board of trade had tried to interest
Claus Spreckels in building a sugar refinery near Salinas. The emigrant
from Hanover, Germany, who already had sugar beet factories in San
Francisco and Watsonville, had been working to develop sugar beet
seed that would resist rust and wind, and he had bought thousands of
acres of the Rancho San Lorenzo from Charles King, presumably for
growing the beets. But he was a shrewd man; before he consented to
build a plant in the Salinas Valley, farmers had to contract to grow
beets on at least 25,000 acres for five years. When this had been accomplished, a five-story factory rose on the Rancho Llano de Buena
Vista.

The Spreckels factory provided a tremendous impetus to the valley's
economy. Erected at a cost of $2,700,000, it was the largest beet-sugar
refinery in the world, providing employment for 500 people and consum-
ing over 3,500 tons of beets per day. Some beet farmers made as much
as $40,000 a year on 7,000 acres.

In 1898, another innovation came to Salinas Valley, when an agricultural commune was formed by the Salvation Army. The commune
was on property situated near the Soledad Mission that had once belonged
to Francisco Soberanes. His son Benito had lost the 600-acre tract in
a mortgage foreclosure, and it had been picked up by the brother-in-law
of David Jacks, Charles Romie, who then sold it to the Salvation Army.
The Army divided it into ten-acre pieces and recruited impoverished
city dwellers to colonize Fort Romie. Everything was furnished the
settlers free of charge, from seeds to two-room shacks. In return, they
contracted to make yearly payments of $100 for ten years, after which
they would own the land.

Unfortunately, most of the people who came knew nothing about
farming. To add to their misery, it was the year of a terrible drought.

The sun blazed, the wind howled, and crops would not grow. Some of the hardier souls managed to hang on and eventually bought the land on which they toiled. The majority moved away, and the land was sold to Swiss farmers who fed their dairy cattle on beet tops and sugar pulp from the Spreckels factory. The barracks that had been built for prayer meetings was made into a general store, and an evaporated milk processing plant went up just a few miles from the ruins of the mission.

Soon after the turn of the century, a second development was started by a firm of Los Angeles real estate promoters. It was on 4,000 acres of the Rancho Arroyo Seco, part of the 16,523-acre tract that had been granted to Joaquín de la Torre. The developers organized the California Homeseekers Association and advertised for buyers of twenty-acre sections, at $20 an acre. Named Clark Colony after one of the promoters, the subdivision was located at the mouth of the Arroyo Seco Canyon in an arid, wind-swept area referred to as "Three Mile Flat."

Settlers arrived to draw lots for the site of their twenty acres. A tent village sprang up, then small houses were erected. Using scrapers pulled by two horses, the men began clearing off the sand which buried the soil. But after they spent a year at the task, the drifting sand was carried back by strong summer winds. They also dug wells and planted rows of eucalyptus trees—hard unrelenting work which was seemingly hopeless.

Then the developers took action to save the community. They obtained the water rights to 218 square miles of watershed and built a canal from the Arroyo Seco River. The irrigation experiment was a great success. Water became available at one dollar a year per acre, and soon thriving farms developed. The town of Greenfield came into being, and other irrigation projects were instituted in the Salinas Valley. The Spreckels Sugar Company constructed steam-powered plants to pump water from the Salinas River to ranchos near King City and Soledad. Huge tracts of land were planted in hardy, blight-resistant sugar beets. With the advent of irrigation, the threat of disastrous droughts was over.

In 1909, the man who had played a pioneer role in the development of the Salinas Valley was dead. A special train carried mourners from Salinas to Monterey for the funeral of David Jacks. There were many on that train who had feared and even hated the man. There were also many who remembered him with deep affection. Among them were the people he had helped in time of trouble, dispensing baskets laden with food, and the children who recalled him as a kindly bearded man who told stories of the "old days" and distributed fruit and candy. Life had disappointed David Jacks in many ways; he had no grandchildren and the career accomplishments of his sons did not meet his expectations. But the most difficult cross he had borne was the animosity which had been heaped upon him and which he never really understood. His driving ambition and huge fortune had brought him little happiness.

The next great agricultural development to come to the Salinas Valley began in 1921 near the mouth of the Salinas River. Lettuce was introduced on a few plots of ground. The heads were huge and the crop yielded 400 crates to the acre. Before long the crop was expanded and began to take over land previously planted in beets, and within ten years, the first lettuce shipment of 68 freight cars had swelled to 20,000 cars a year. Vast stretches of the long valley were devoted to the new bonanza.

Today, the Salinas Valley is one of the most productive agricultural valleys in the world. Crops are diversified and organized into three climatic zones. The coastal zone yields year-round crops of vegetables, such as artichokes, which flourish in relatively high humidity and a narrow temperature span. The next adjoining area produces lettuce, carrots, celery, and other truck vegetables on a year-round basis. Farther up in the valley, tomatoes and other crops that thrive in hot weather are grown during the summer.

Many serious problems haunt the agricultural industry of the Salinas Valley today. The hard-pressed growers, plagued by problems of inflation, mechanization, urban sprawl, and labor unrest, have recently been offered tax incentives by the government in order to help them continue in production. It can only be hoped that this measure and others will allow the long valley, where once roamed the cattle herds of the first families of Monterey, to remain a multi-patterned tapestry of lush green harvests.

13

Pacific Grove

"I walked through street after street, parallel and at right angles, paved with sward and dotted with trees, but still undeniable streets, and each with its name posted at the corner, as in a real town. Facing down the main thoroughfare . . . I saw an open-air temple, with benches and sounding-board, as though for an orchestra. The houses were all tightly shuttered; there was no smoke, no sound but of the waves, no moving thing. I have never seen a place so dream-like. . . . Indeed it was not so much like a deserted town as like a scene upon the stage by daylight, with no one on the boards."

The place was three miles west of Monterey, the description by Robert Louis Stevenson. Walking in the woods, on an unfamiliar trail, he had suddenly come upon the encampment grounds of the Methodist Episcopal Church, abandoned during the winter months except for one clergyman and his wife.

Four years earlier, in 1875, this "Christian Seaside Resort" had come into being. Sequestered in a dense pine forest, on 100 acres of what once was the Rancho Punto de Pinos, the Pacific Grove Retreat began as a summer camp and setting for church meetings. Advertised as "a haven for the gentle, the refined, the cultured, where carousing and dissipation are unknown," the community was to become a town unique in all of California. Its laws would exclude "all disreputable, unruly, and boisterous characters, and all unwholesome and demoralizing sports and pastimes." For its origins, Pacific Grove Retreat, and Pacific Grove, were indebted to the interest and support of the ubiquitous and incredible David Jacks.

The Scotch land baron, who owned the 7,000 acres comprising the Monterey Peninsula, was a pious man. Aware that the elders of the Methodist Church were planning a religious resort on the California coast, he took steps to bring the stretch of shoreline east of Point Pinos to their attention. First, he induced a Methodist minister named Ross, who suffered from an acute respiratory ailment, to try the salubrious effects of an outdoor life among the pines on his property. Fortunately for Jacks' plans, after the minister had spent a few months in a shack, which he built himself in the vicinity of present-day Lighthouse Avenue and Sixteenth Street, he was miraculously cured.

The following year, he returned with his brother and both their wives, all of whom were ill of the same complaint. Sleeping in hammocks under the trees and subsisting on fish and game, they too were restored to health. With high enthusiasm, the Reverend Ross then invited Bishop Peck, a prominent member of the Methodist Retreat Association, to sample the climate and scenic beauty of the site he had discovered. Properly impressed, the bishop recommended that a tract be purchased from David Jacks, and at a meeting of church elders, held in San Francisco on June 1, 1875, the Pacific Grove Retreat Association was born.

Jacks knew how to be generous when it suited his purposes. Eschewing the acceptance of payment in connection with such a worthy cause, he donated 100 acres of land between the waterfront and Lighthouse Avenue, adjacent to the present location of the museum. He also loaned the Retreat Association $30,000 to meet the expense of laying out streets, erecting buildings, and making other initial improvements. To solve the water problem, he agreed to provide a supply from a spring located on his land about a mile from the grounds.

The resident managers of the new enterprise, the Reverend J. O. Ash of Salinas and the Reverend J. W. Ross of Alameda, plunged into elaborate plans for the resort, which was to be modeled after the encampment at Ocean Grove, New Jersey. The acreage was plotted into residential lots, a park, a grand avenue, minor streets and avenues, and the embryo of a town. The principal building planned was the preacher's platform, facing an amphitheater large enough to seat an audience of 5,000. Other projected construction included a restaurant, dormitories, a central laundry, several stores, and a commodious bathhouse situated on the bay.

Lots were divided into sections, with sizes ranging from 30 by 50 feet for tents to 30 by 125 feet for larger dwellings. The minimum price per lot was $50. In the first year, fifteen cottages were built and a sufficient number of tents set up to accommodate 450 people. Then on August 8, 1875, the inaugural church meeting took place. Held in a huge tent, in the vicinity of today's Jewell Park, it lasted three weeks, with services morning, afternoon, and evening. Some of the prayer sessions were held outdoors, causing the adjacent rocky prominence to be called "Lovers of Jesus Point." The conclave became an annual event and was the forerunner of a variety of convocations, best known of which was the Chautauqua Assembly.

The campground was also open to guests. Tents could be bought at wholesale prices or rented at low rates. Campers not attending meetings were charged 50 cents a head, which included wood, water, and cleaning up. The Pacific Grove Retreat was in business. A temporary set-back was encountered when the association was unable to meet its mortgage payment to Jacks, and the unsold portion of the tract reverted to their benefactor. But he continued to sell lots and the popularity of the "little Paradise in the Grove" increased.

Then, early in the 1880s, the officers of the Retreat Association had cause for real concern. Their landlord had sold the old Ranchos Pescadero and Punta de Pinos, including the Pacific Grove acreage, to the Pacific Improvement Company. The association was worried that under the new management the high moral tone of the retreat might be threatened. But David Jacks soon allayed their fears. The provisions of the sale stated that the Pacific Grove Association would continue to have moral and prudential control over the grounds, and this control would be extended to a distance of one mile from the geographical center of the original survey. All the safeguards which the officers of the association had so carefully written into their bylaws were retained.

They also made haste to establish some new ones. Deeds to all property contained restrictive covenants forbidding the use of intoxicating beverages and gambling, with automatic cancellation of title to land if violations occurred. The gambling edict covered cards, dice, and billiards. All dancing was forbidden as well, and the Sabbath was strictly enforced, with no bathing or swimming allowed and stores permitted to sell only medicine.

The design of bathing costumes was severely circumscribed. It was unlawful to appear on the beach unless attired in clothing of opaque material "worn in such a manner as to preclude form, from above the nipples of the breast to below the crotch." The law further specified that bathing suits must have "double crotches or a skirt of ample size to cover the buttocks."

A curfew law prohibited any person under eighteen from being on the streets after eight P.M. in the winter or nine P.M. in the summer. It also stipulated that the shades in all houses must be kept up until ten P.M., at which hour they were to be lowered and the lights extinguished. Finally, to insure that no untoward influences would contaminate the community, a fence was erected which encircled the entire retreat except for the side facing the bay. The vehicular gate was padlocked, so that if residents wanted to unload their luggage at their front doors, they had to enter through a turnstile and hike a mile to the retreat office for a key. Tradesmen from Monterey, peddling their wares from pushcarts and wagons, were kept outside.

Besides being incredibly insular, the budding town of Pacific Grove was also isolated. At its back was a somber thickly wooded forest of pine and oak. Westward lay a wilderness of sand, with the grey stone lighthouse a lonely sentinel on Point Pinos. And to the east, about half a mile along the road to Monterey, an exotic hamlet hugged the rocks at Point Cabrillo. This was Chinatown, a community with which the retreaters were unlikely to be neighborly.

Situated in the vicinity of the present-day Hopkins Marine Station, the Chinese settlement consisted of a single narrow street that wound between a double row of ramshackle wooden shacks. On the shore side, the huts hung out over the water and were supported by stilts. In the 1870s, about a hundred people dwelt in this short stretch, most of whom were men. They had drifted to the coast when completion of the Central Pacific Railroad threw thousands of Chinese laborers out of work. A few subsequently brought their wives from China, and children began to appear in the crowded quarters of the village.

The mainstay of their economy was fish, most of which they salted and dried in the sun for export to San Francisco. Abalone shells were also collected in great quantites and found a ready market at $20 a ton. But the richest harvest was obtained from squid. Frequently, this fish was caught at night, and the fleet of one-oared sampans, fashioned after the ancient designs and each illuminated by a fire of pitch logs at its bow, reflected in flaming pools on the black water of the bay.

Once a year in autumn, junks with giant lateen sails anchored off the village and loaded the squid for transport to China. They also brought strange and wondrous wares to the village store. Among these was opium, which was sold quite openly. A vial of the substance could be obtained for ten cents. In one shanty along the crooked street, there was a back room with bunks three-deep where habitues gathered.

For a decade, Pacific Grove remained primarily a setting for camp meetings. Then, gradually the religious orientation of the Grove was supplanted by real estate development. It began when the Del Monte Hotel in Monterey opened its doors in 1880, bringing a great influx of tourists to the general area. Then, seven years later, when the Del Monte was destroyed by fire and was being rebuilt, the El Carmelo Hotel in Pacific Grove came into being.

A property of the Pacific Improvement Company, the three-story hostelry was strategically located on Lighthouse between Grand and Fountain Avenues, with beautiful gardens at its front and a view of the bay at its rear. It also boasted 114 rooms and, for safety against fire, three broad staircases as well as an elevator run by hydraulics. After the re-opening of the Del Monte, the El Carmelo became a mecca for vacationers of moderate means. It stressed its homelike qualities and reduced its rates to two dollars per day for room and board.

Many who came to visit began to buy land and build permanent dwellings. Lots were selling from $135 to $250, with small down payments and interest rates at seven and eight percent. A three-room house, completely furnished, could be purchased for $650. In May of 1888, the first issue of a weekly "real estate journal" was distributed free of charge. Named the *Pacific Grove Review*, its purpose was to serve the interests of buyers and sellers of property and to disseminate information about the advantages of the Grove as "a summer resort and sanitarium." The publication quickly assumed the function of a smalltown newspaper, giving full reports of conventions and assemblies, but its main message was that the price of choice lots was rapidly increasing and small fortunes could be made by prudent investors.

Large two-story residences began to appear, some of which are still standing and are fine examples of Victorian architecture. A business section sprang up in the center of the community. Stores provided a wide selection of merchandise and took "orders for anything not in stock," except, of course, wines and liquor. In 1891, Rensalaer Luther Holman opened a small dry goods establishment, which came to be called "The Popular" and later grew into a big department store.

The program of summer meetings also expanded, filling the calendar from June to September and featuring, in addition to the Methodist Encampment, conferences of the Y.M.C.A., the W.C.T.U., a Farmers' Institute, a School of Music, and the renowned Chautauqua movement. Pacific Grove became the west coast headquarters of this home-study program as well as the site of its popular ten-day seminar series. Subjects of its seminars included natural history, botany, Bible study, physical culture, cookery, and art. Student tuition for the entire course of instruction was $1, and the public could obtain a season ticket providing admission to all lectures and musical entertainments for $2.

The Chautauqua meeting place, Chautauqua Hall, was a squarish edifice of raw-boned simplicity which still stands at Sixteenth and Central Avenue. The hall was also used for other community meetings in Pacific Grove until the elegant new Methodist Episcopal Church was completed in 1888. A year later, the Chautauqua also moved to the larger facilities of the new church, which was situated three blocks west of the El Carmelo Hotel. With its cool, dimly lighted interior, stained glass windows, and stately twin towers, the church had the lovely look of a small Gothic cathedral. It was torn down in 1964 and only its massive golden pipe organ remains, housed in a stunning modern church on the outskirts of town.

By 1890, the permanent population of Pacific Grove had grown to about 1,500, but every summer it exploded into five or six times that number. A tent city, centered between Eighteenth Street and Grand Avenue, rose overnight with the summer season's arrival. Beneficent influences of the Pacific Improvement Company and the Southern Pacific Railroad were very much in evidence everywhere in the town. The Pacific Improvement Company had contributed $10,000 of the $25,000 construction cost of the new church. In addition, the community no longer had to depend upon wells for its water supply; it shared the 25 miles of iron pipe and two reservoirs which brought the headwaters of the Carmel River to the Del Monte Hotel. The railroad extended the Southern Pacific Line through the tiny town in 1889, hauling thousands of campers and vacationers in and out of town and offering reduced rates to those attending the Chautauqua or other specified conferences.

Always at the train station were smartly equipped buses and buggies from the Mammoth Livery Stables. This was a magnificent establishment, rated as the largest, handsomest, and most complete livery on the coast. Two blocks in length, it was situated on Laurel Avenue between Forest and Fountain. An 80-foot-high tower topped its three floors, which contained rooms for hostlers and grooms, dining and kitchen facilities, storerooms, and ice house, and space for the storage of feed. It provided 150 square feet for rolling gear and enough stalls to house almost 100 horses. The Mammoth Stables were built in 1884 by a man named Johnson to take care of horses and carriages that belonged to guests of the Del Monte Hotel and to provide conveyances for hire. Four years later, the stables, equipment, and livestock were acquired by Henry Kent in exchange for his ranch in Hollister. The new owner maintained the same high tradition of perfection, adding a colorful note with a train bus painted carmine and cream and adorned with gilded scroll work.

The Grove lost its physical boundaries early in the 1880s, when State Senator Benjamin Langford, who owned a summer home in the Retreat, grew weary of the rigamarole attendant upon getting inside its gate. Late one evening, he arrived with his family and, wielding an axe, reduced the offending barrier to kindling wood. Within a few years, the fence was completely gone and the community was no longer separated from its neighbors. Still, it wanted no connection with Monterey, feeling a strong sense of superiority to the old Spanish town. Instead, a movement for incorporation was begun, and in July 1889, Pacific Grove became a city of the sixth class.

A board of trustees, pledged to protect the unique qualities of the original Christian resort, was duly elected, and restrictions were made even more stringent. Some property owners dissented and even rebelled, arguing that the "blue laws" could cause a financial depression by driving people away and discouraging the investment of capital. But most residents gloried in the high moral tone of their town and considered themselves fortunate to live there.

When the summer visitors departed, townspeople drew a deep sigh of relief and reverted to normal patterns of daily existence. Once again the beach and bathhouse belonged to them. The latter had deteriorated into little more than a dilapidated shed, but oldtimers still speak of it with misty-eyed nostalgia. Throughout the central part of town, streets were lined with the stark bare frames of tents dismantled for the winter, their canvas stored in Chautauqua Hall. The businesses were battened down for a long stretch of reduced revenues, and the life style of the community became one of incredible simplicity.

The individual contributions of public-spirited citizens shone with unusual clarity in this environment, and two such people, Oliver Smith Trimmer and Charles K. Tuttle, are warmly remembered by early residents. Oliver Trimmer, a Salinas physician, and his nephew, Charles Tuttle, a pharmacist, settled in Pacific Grove in the latter part of the 1880s. Both served on the city's first board of trustees, of which Dr. Trimmer was president. Before long, Tuttle's drugstore, across the street from the grounds of the El Carmelo Hotel, became a beacon of security for the little town. In a time when telephones were a rarity, a wire was installed between the Tuttle establishment and Dr. Trimmer's home at Sixth and Laurel Avenue. Then if people became ill at night, they sent someone to the drugstore to arouse the pharmacist who summoned his uncle, rode with him to the patient's house, and then put up the required medicine which the doctor in turn delivered. This kind of consideration deserved the deep affection it earned.

Another person whose memory is enshrined in the recollections of Pacific Grove residents is Julia Platt. The mention of her name never fails to elicit an emotional response—"She was a grand old gal," "She was hell on wheels," "She was our most outstanding citizen." Certainly no more colorful personality ever participated in the community's affairs.

Born in San Francisco and educated in Vermont, Julia Platt first came to live in Pacific Grove at the age of 33. As a scientist, with a doctorate in zoology and a specialty in embryology, she attracted much attention in the staid community. When the marine biological station opened near Lovers Point and Miss Platt, an unchaperoned maiden lady, became a close associate of the staff, there were some who even questioned her morals. To the church people of fundamentalist persuasion, it did not seem quite proper for her to discuss the processes of reproduction with members of the opposite sex.

A tall woman, who walked vigorously and wore peculiar clothes, she soon became a familiar figure about town. Often, she would be seen in a long purple dress, with blue sunbonnet and yellow gauntlets, trundling a wheelbarrow and scattering nasturtium seeds to beautify the streets. In the 1890s she left for Europe to engage in advanced study at Freiburg University in Germany and to serve as director of the renowned Naples Zoological Station in Italy. But Pacific Grove had not seen the last or the best of her. Her most sensational performances were to take place after her return.

Meanwhile, the monotony of the residents' lives during the uneventful winter months was occasionally broken by attendance at exotic festivities in the Chinese village. Among these was the celebration of Chinese New Year in February, but an even more exciting event was the Ring Day festival. For this occasion, members of the tong organization gathered from far and near. Dressed in their best blue garments, they displayed bright red buttons atop their round caps signifying their rank. In a field adjacent to the village, a huge pole was erected and completely covered with red and green firecrackers. At the top of the pole was a giant yellow firecracker a foot high, on which was perched a gold-colored ring encased in straw. Everybody watched wide-eyed as a fuse was ignited and exploding firecrackers filled the air. At last, with a great thunderclap, the massive one on top went off, flinging the ring sky high. Then the young Chinese men surged forward, fighting and clawing to get hold of the ring. Blood ran and the battle was not something to forget. He who obtained possession of the ring became top man in the tong organization and gained good luck for the year.

The people in Pacific Grove were gradually learning to accept and even to like their strange neighbors in Chinatown. The community came to depend on the Chinese for most of its menial work, and housewives looked forward to the daily visits from Sam, the fish vendor, who came each morning with two baskets suspended from a pole across his shoulders. Still, there were those who resented the unsightly appearance and offensive odors of the village, and real estate developers had begun to eye the stretch of waterfront with increasing avarice. Matters came to a head in May of 1902, when a great quantity of smelly drying squid, spoiled by a sudden shower, was dumped into the bay and washed back up on shore. The stench was overpowering. The Pacific Improvement Company, owners of the land on which the village stood, issued an edict. Henceforth, the squid-drying operation would be prohibited. Everyone assumed that the Chinese, deprived of their main source of support, would now have to leave. But they lingered on, and more drastic measures had to be taken.

In November 1905, the Pacific Improvement Company gave an outright order to the Chinese to vacate the land. Plans were announced to convert the 30 acres into villa sites and to extend Ocean View Avenue into a scenic drive to Monterey. Preliminary arrangements were made to move the Chinese to a location near Seaside, but when the owner of the property discovered the acreage was to be used for the erection of Chinese shanties, he terminated negotiations.

The Pacific Improvement Company next threatened eviction with the aid of the county sheriff, but, in February of 1906, the Chinese were still there. Then, shortly before eight o'clock on the evening of May 16th, fire broke out in a barn at the west end of Chinatown. Many felt sure arson was its cause. Strong headwinds fanned the blaze, and the Pacific Grove volunteer fire department, for some reason, had difficulty obtaining sufficient water. The flames swept through the village and, by ten o'clock, only the Joss house was still standing in the midst of heaps of burning debris.

No one knows how many Chinese were killed. They seemed to vanish, while their possessions were pillaged by looters from neighboring towns. On the front page of the *Pacific Grove Review*, a letter from an outraged resident of that city appeared: "It seems incredible that American citizens could become so lost to all sense of moral obligation as to behave as I saw them behaving at the Chinatown fire. Conscience, honor, delicacy, decency seemed thrown to the winds." The protest was signed by Edward Berwick, chairman of the board of trustees of Pacific Grove and famed orchardist of Carmel Valley.

The Chinese community of humble, happy, hardworking people was gone, virtually overnight. Ironically, no imposing real estate development replaced it. Instead, economics dictated that the land immediately to the south of it would be the site of Cannery Row. Perhaps the smell of sardine reduction plants was less offensive than that of drying squid.

Another fire in the early 1900s destroyed the Mammoth Livery Stables and almost wiped out the city of Pacific Grove. Cause of the conflagration was uncertain, but it started shortly after the delivery of 80 tons of hay to the stable. With this enormous quantity of dry material to feed the flames, the fire spread too quickly for all the horses to be evacuated, and some of the injured animals had to be killed with axes. The meagre equipment of the fire department was inadequate to cope with the blaze, and when a wind came up in the afternoon, townspeople expected the flaming tower to fall and spread the fire. Fortunately, the wind changed, and finally the fire was subdued. But for days the smell of burned horseflesh lingered in the air.

In a happier vein, the beginning of the twentieth century brought a spurt of civic improvements to Pacific Grove. William Smith, sometimes referred to as "Bathhouse Smith," acquired the property at Lovers Point and made some startling changes. By dynamiting the bluff back of the beach, he made room for construction of a spacious new bathhouse, with a heated salt-water swimming pool and a restaurant, auditorium, and pier. Then, in an elegant grace note, a Japanese Tea Garden was built on the point, replete with rock garden and arching bridge, as well as authentic architecture and decor. Tea and rice cakes were served by attractive girls in oriental costume.

The new century also brought the flamboyant Julia Platt back to town. Embittered because her scientific discoveries were too advanced to be acknowledged, she had abandoned research and was now focusing her formidable energies on community problems. Once again, she was seen pushing a wheelbarrow full of plants and garden implements through the city streets on missions of improvement. One of her projects was the parkway between upper and lower Lighthouse Avenue, where she not only superintended the workmen but personally wielded rake and hoe. Though her clothes had become a bit more conservative, she now usually combined a mannish hat with a long full-skirted dress and a grandmotherly shawl about her shoulders.

Participating in every council meeting, Miss Platt pounced on any "irregularity, evasion, or sentimentality," causing council members considerable irritation and the public unfailing entertainment. It was she who, in 1927, drafted the city charter and circulated the petition for its adoption, thus providing Pacific Grove with a city manager form of government. And when new owners acquired Lovers Point and blocked public access to the beach with a padlocked gate, she was the one who chopped it down. By this time, the tea house was gone, the other buildings in disrepair, and the garden choked with weeds. She devoted much of her time to restoring a modicum of beauty to the grounds.

In 1931, at the age of 74, Julia Platt was elected mayor, and one of her first official acts was to bring to fruition a long-cherished dream. About ten years earlier, the city had acquired the shoreline between Point Pinos and the Monterey city limit. Now Mayor Platt obtained state legislative action establishing a marine refuge along the waterfront.

Energetic to the end of her life, Julia Platt died of a heart attack in 1935. She was shrouded in canvas and buried at sea in accord with the provisions of her will. Since tradition required that the "city fathers" accompany the body in an official funeral, the leaders of the community found themselves in a small launch twelve miles out on an exceedingly rough ocean. Even in death, Miss Platt was capable of causing them discomfort.

Sheldon Gilmer succeeded Miss Platt in office, and during his administration, major steps in community development were achieved. The city floated a bond issue and acquired the bathhouse property. The old buildings were torn down and a huge new swimming pool constructed.

For many people Pacific Grove remained a favorite seaside resort, but the face and flavor of the place had changed considerably. The tent city had given way to rows of tiny wood and stucco houses. Much of the pine forest had been cut, resulting in a colder climate. The handsome El Carmelo Hotel had been razed. Colorful Chinatown had been replaced by the new plant of the Hopkins Marine Station, a department of Stanford University.

Still, there remained a section of Pacific Grove in which something of the spirit of the old "Christian Seaside Resort" had been preserved. This was Asilomar, begun in 1913 under the sponsorship of Phoebe Apperson Hearst as a campground for the Young Women's Christian Association. Its name originated as a contraction of the Spanish words *asilo del mar*, or refuge by the sea. Today, Asilomar is a 60-acre conference site of serene beauty and impeccable standards. Property of the state of California, the wild dunes, virgin pine forest, and rock-bound shores of this beautiful sea-haven are an appropriate reminder of the old Pacific Grove.

Pacific Grove

The Point Pinos Lighthouse was a lonely sentinel westward of the budding town of Pacific Grove. Erected in 1855, it is the oldest operating light station on the West Coast. Photograph taken in 1890, courtesy of the Monterey City Library.

For about thirty years, an exotic
Chinese fishing village hugged the
rocks at Point Cabrillo, in the
vicinity of the present-day
Hopkins Marine Station. In 1906,
the community was wiped out by fire.
Photograph taken about 1900,
courtesy of the Monterey City Library.

The Joss House, or Chinese
temple, was a picturesque part
of Chinatown. Offerings of
roast pig often adorned its altar.
Winnifred Beaumont Collection.

In the center background is
the Mammoth Livery Stable,
which spanned two blocks on
Laurel Avenue between Forest
and Fountain. It was rated
as the largest and most
complete livery on the coast.
To the left, on Grand Avenue,
is a part of El Carmelo
Hotel, and on the right are
some of the small bungalows
converted from what were
originally tents. Photograph
courtesy of Betty Shields.

Built in 1887 by the Pacific Improvement Company, El Carmelo Hotel was located on Lighthouse between Grand and Fountair Avenues. Surrounded by trees and flowers, the 114-room hostelry overlooking the bay was a mecca for vacationers for many years. In 1918 it was torn down and its site is now occupied by the Holman department store. Winnifred Beaumont Collection.

In the foreground are the grounds of
El Carmelo Hotel. Across Lighthouse
Avenue is Charles K. Tuttle's
drugstore, a beacon of security for
early residents of Pacific Grove.
In the background on the right is the
tower of the Mammoth Livery Stable.
Winnifred Beaumont Collection.

Pacific Grove about 1890, when much
of the beautiful pine forest was
still intact. Forest Avenue is the
thoroughfare in the center of the
picture. The small building at the
foot of 16th Street is the "lookout"
from which a path led down to the
original bathhouse. Photograph taken
from Lovers Point, courtesy of
the Monterey City Library.

The Pacific Grove Beach after the
turn of the century. Across the bay
is Lovers Point. The small building
to the left of it is the "lookout"
erected by the Civic Club. Next is the
Japanese Tea Garden, built by
Mr. Sugano and the Nakamuras. In the
lefthand corner is the windmill that
pumped water to the marine biological
station. At the extreme left is the
home of William Smith, sometimes
referred to as "Bathhouse Smith."
Winnifred Beaumont Collection.

Carmel Valley

The Boronda adobe on the Rancho Los Laureles
in Carmel Valley. The three-room adobe was
once the home of José Manuel and Juana Cota de
Boronda. In the 1880s it was a center for the
Pacific Improvement Company's dairy operation.
Mayo Hayes O'Donnell Library Collection.

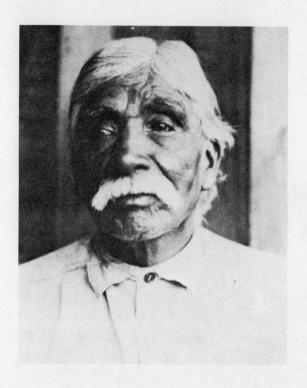

(*top left*)

Manuel (Panocha) Onesimo,
descendant of Juan Onesimo.
Marion A. Crush Collection.

(*bottom left*)

María Juana Cota
de Boronda, born in 1806
at the Presidio of
Santa Barbara. Married
José Manuel Boronda on
May 2, 1821 at the
San Carlos Church in
Monterey. Photograph
courtesy of the
Monterey City Library.

Original
Carmelo School
built by
James Meadows.
Marion A. Crush
Collection.

Jonathan Wright's cabin in Robinson
Canyon, where Robert Louis Stevenson
recuperated from a serious illness.
Seated in front of the cabin
are Anson Smith and two of
Wright's children. Mayo Hayes
O'Donnell Library Collection.

Joe Stewart threshing beans
on the Martin ranch, also
called the Mission Ranch.
Joe was one of the sons of
the widowed Elizabeth Stewart
who married John Martin.
Photograph taken in 1910 by
S. L. Slevin, courtesy of
the Bancroft Library.

The W. E. Martin Ranch
in Carmel Valley, 1917.
William Martin was
and grandson of William
and Agnes Martin, and the
son of John Martin.
His wife was Anna Hatton.
Photograph by
S. L. Slevin, courtesy of
the Bancroft Library.

The Hatton ranch
at the mouth of
the Carmel Valley.
Photograph by
S. L. Slevin, courtesy of
the Bancroft Library.

The home of William and
Kate Harney Hatton, which was located
on land that is now Carmel Knolls.
It was completed in 1894.
Marion A. Crush Collection.

14

The Carmel Valley

It was the year 1840. Don José Manuel Boronda rode at the head of the pack train that carried the family's possessions. Beside him was his eldest son, the eighteen-year-old Juan de Mata, and at the rear, in the bulging *carretas* that lumbered up the steep trail out of Monterey, were Doña Juana and the younger children. Emerging from the deep shade, they saw the Carmel River, glistening between willow-bordered banks below them. Beyond were the tawny flanks of the towering Santa Lucias, tapering to a dark green sea-girt point.

They descended the hill to the desolate Mission San Carlos, then continued along the dusty trail that wound through golden oak-studded hills into the beautiful Carmel Valley. It was a great day in the lives of the Borondas. They were on their way to occupy their land grant from Governor Alvarado, the 6,625-acre Los Laureles.

The only dwellings along their route were occasional shacks in the Indian *rancherías*. Dispersed by the secularization of the mission, many of the Indians had suffered great hardship and few had been able to keep their allotments of mission property. Men like José Antonio Romero, the first of the Carmel mission's civil administrators, were ambitious and more than ready to exploit the Indians. Romero had also tried to get Los Laureles for himself a few years earlier, but Governor Alvarado had given the land to Boronda, son of the retired corporal.

There had been other land grants bestowed in the Carmel Valley. In 1839 the 4,367-acre Rancho Cañada de la Segunda, through which the Borondas were passing, had been granted to Lazaro Soto. And mounting the wild reaches of the Santa Lucias to the southeast was the 4,307-acre Rancho Potrero de San Carlos, granted to Fructuoso del Real in 1837, as well as the 8,814-acre San Francisquito, given in 1835 to Doña Catalina Manzanelli de Munrás. But none of the grantees had chosen to occupy their land.

At the eastern end of the valley, beyond Los Laureles, Rafael Gomez had built a two-story adobe on the Rancho Los Tularcitos, granted him by Governor Figueroa in 1834. But the poor man was killed when he became entangled in the reata of a horse he was trying to drive away from newly planted grain. Of course, his lovely widow, the former Joséfa Antonia Estrada, could not live alone on the 26,581 acres of untamed wilderness. So, Don José Manuel Boronda would be the first ranchero to take up permanent residence on the Rio Carmelo.

As the red ball of the sun sank behind the somber wall of mountains, the Boronda family came to their adobe, which was nestled in laurel trees near the river. The house consisted of three rooms, with dirt floors, a crudely raftered ceiling, and a thatched roof of tules tied on with rawhide thongs. The original building had once housed an Indian family charged with care of the mission's cattle, but Don José Manuel and his eldest son, with the help of mission Indians, had altered the building so that it was not unlike the Boronda adobe in Monterey.

The Borondas worked hard at Los Laureles, and gradually they were able to enlarge their small herd of stock. In the spring they planted grain, and Doña Juana made great, round mounds of yellow cheese from the rich milk that became plentiful. There were gay times, too. Friends and relatives made the long trek to Los Laureles from Monterey and the Salinas Valley for fiestas and a delicacy like bull's head wrapped in wet sacking and slowly steamed in a pit of glowing coals.

For the first years, the Borondas' only neighbor was a gentle, friendly Indian family headed by Juan Onesimo, who as a boy worked to build the mission and whose most treasured possession was a violin which the padres had given him and taught him to play. Onesimo lived with his daughter Loretta, her husband Domingo Peralta, and their two children Jacinta and Madalena.

The devout and industrious Loretta had been a great favorite of the padres and, when the mission lands were divided, she and Domingo had been given a large tract. They cultivated the land, planting corn, tomatoes and onions to sell in the markets of Monterey. Soon they hoped to have enough money to buy cattle, but almost every week, men like civil administrator Antonio Romero came to threaten the Peraltas with ouster or worse.

Doña Juana sent gifts of her golden Spanish cheese to the Peraltas and old Onesimo, and she urged her husband to talk to the governor about the harassment of these innocent people. But Don José Manuel considered the problem hopeless, especially since his patron Alvarado had declared himself too ill to govern.

Still, the kindly Doña Juana continued to protest until, one day, the dead body of Domingo Peralta was found in a gulch. Then, even she had to agree that the situation seemed hopeless and that the widowed Loretta should abandon her land and seek work as a servant in Monterey. Both of the Borondas failed to reckon, however, with the role to be played by a British sailor who had just returned from fourteen months in the prisons of Mexico.

James Meadows had first set foot on the shores on Monterey in 1837, a seaman on a merchant ship out of London. Hot-tempered and independent, he resented the kind of treatment he had received enroute. Monterey looked good to the twenty-year-old youth, so he decided to desert. The Peraltas helped him hide until his ship had sailed, and a friendship quickly developed.

For a couple of years, Meadows worked contentedly as a *vaquero* on the Rancho El Sur, the property of a fellow Englishman, Juan Bautista Roger Cooper. But he was unable to stay away from the Isaac Graham tavern, a notorious hangout for deserters from foreign ships, and on an April morning in 1840, the government, alarmed by reports that Graham's cohorts planned insurrection, arrested all foreigners who had no passport. Meadows was among the 46 foreigners shipped to Tepic for imprisonment.

Lengthy negotiations between the British consul and the Mexican authorities ensued. Finally, clemency was obtained for some of the prisoners and, in July of 1841, Meadows returned with a tattered group of twenty. The following year, he married Loretta Onesimo de Peralta and assumed responsibility for her land. After that, no one was inclined to challenge her claim to the 4,592 acres, between the Rancho Cañada de la Segunda and Los Laureles.

The adobe house that Meadows built near the river became a favorite gathering place for the area. Despite a testy disposition, Meadows was well-known for his generosity; anyone could get a loan, borrow a farm implement, or receive sound advice on a business problem. He donated land for the first school in the valley and constructed the building and furniture. Many prominent men began their careers with his support and encouragement. William Brainard Post, for example, who was later to become a pioneer rancher in the Big Sur area, worked on the Meadows land. He also married Anselma Onesimo, Loretta's sister.

James and Loretta Meadows had four sons and one daughter, Isabella, who was born on July 7, 1846, the day the American flag was raised over the Custom House in Monterey. Miss Isabella's reminiscences of intimate details of mission life in the days of Juan Onesimo, as told to her by her mother, served as the basis for much of Anne Fisher's novel *Cathedral in the Sun*. Miss Isabella ended her days in a blaze of glory, when it was discovered by the staff of the Smithsonian Institution that she was the last living person to know the speech of the Costanoan Indians. At the age of 89, she was taken to Washington, D.C., where for five years she worked to record the language before it was completely lost. Then, quite suddenly, this remarkable woman simply died in her sleep.

In the American military contingent that landed in Monterey on the day of Isabella's birth was Isaac Hitchcock. After receiving his military discharge, he acquired a piece of land in the area and soon became acquainted with the Meadows family. Isabella's half-sister, Madalena, captured his heart and they were married. Three decades later their son Joseph, one of the best loved characters in the Carmel Valley, came to work on the Rancho Los Laureles, which, by then, no longer belonged to the Borondas.

Late in the 1860s, Don José Manuel's son Juan de Mata, who had inherited the rancho, sold it to Nathan W. Spaulding of San Francisco. When Spaulding looked upon his property, he saw a place of incredible beauty, with deep-pile emerald green grasses, flower-frosted chamise, and great spreading oaks. Much of the Carmel Valley was still an untamed wilderness, with wildcat and coyote roaming the countryside. Only on the isolated Meadows ranch were there signposts of civilization.

He placed the rancho under the management of his brother-in-law Kinzea Klinkenbeard, who initiated innovations in its operation. Flumes were installed to irrigate the land, lumber for fences was brought from San Francisco, and new cattle breeds were introduced. Klinkenbeard and his family resided briefly in the Boronda adobe, until they could build the more modern dwelling which eventually became the nucleus of Los Laureles Lodge. Then, the Boronda adobe fell into disrepair and was used to house cattle. A different way of living had come to the Rancho Los Laureles. It was a harbinger of the future.

By 1875, none of the five land grants in Carmel Valley were held by their original owners. Lazaro Soto had sold the Rancho Cañada de la Segunda for $500. It had then passed through several hands until it became the property of Faxon Dean Atherton, father-in-law of the well-known writer Gertrude Atherton. Both the Rancho Potrero de San Carlos and the San Francisquito had been purchased by Bradley Sargent, who, with his three brothers, had acquired about 80,000 acres in central California. Los Tularcitos, at the upper end of the valley, now belonged to Andrew Ogletree, for Joséfa Antonia Estrada de Gomez had married a dashing German sea captain, Charles Wolter, and preferred to live elsewhere.

While the old Monterey families were disposing of their Carmel

Valley property, other men were finding new ways of cultivating the rugged area. One of these was Edward Berwick. Born in London, he spent his early years as a clerk in a banking house. Then in 1865, at the age of 22, he sailed for California and courageously embarked upon a new career by investing in a cattle ranch in southern Monterey County. He lost money but maintained himself and learned a great deal about the dairy and stock-raising business.

In 1867, he sent to England for his fiancee, Isabella Richardson, and the newlyweds made their home in a sparsely settled area near King City where Mrs. Berwick did not see another woman for eight months. The Carmel Valley seemed civilized by contrast, and Isabella suggested wistfully that they might live there someday. When Berwick discovered 120 acres of the old Meadows tract for sale in the valley, he bought it for $500 in gold. He planned to supplement his income by teaching at the Carmelo School and use his dwindling capital for some experimental agricultural projects he had in mind.

Loretta Onesimo Meadows had told Berwick about the wonderful pear orchards that had been part of the mission gardens, where a few gnarled old trees still filled the air with fragrance every February. They had been grown from cuttings brought by Father Lasuén in 1795. Berwick determined to try planting some of his own, and his success as a farmer was phenomenal. The Berwick orchards became world famous. Carloads of Winter Nelis pears were shipped each year to London and Paris. High praise was also accorded the apples, walnuts, and strawberries raised on his acreage.

The tall, blue-eyed Mr. Berwick also developed quite a local reputation as a scholar. He was seldom seen without a book of philosophy or poetry, and he was often observed stopping at the end of a long furrow to sit down and read. He was an ardent pacifist and published voluminous writings in his endeavor "to rid the world of that idiocy called war." In 1881, Berwick built a house in Pacific Grove and from then on commuted to his work in the Carmel Valley. Everybody liked the genial outgoing man, who was always ready to engage in spirited conversation.

Edward Berwick's agricultural achievements attracted other enterprising farmers to the valley. South of the Berwick tract, near the entrance to a lush canyon that led into the Rancho San Francisquito, Richard Snively had a thriving dairy and fruit farm on land that once had belonged to Mariano Soberanes, a cousin of the Borondas. Snively branched out to include apricot, nectarine, and cherry trees and was experimenting with growing almonds.

About nine miles up the canyon, two retired sea captains, Anson Smith and Jonathan Wright, were trying their luck at bee-keeping and the growing of grapes and peaches on land rented from Bradley Sargent. They also kept a herd of goats, which Wright tended, and Smith spent his spare time hunting grizzlies, still abundant in the Santa Lucias.

Robert Louis Stevenson credited Jonathan Wright with saving his life in 1879, when he had set out, despondent and desperately ill, on a solitary camping trip in the warm sun and dry air of the mountains. After spending a night at the Berwick ranch, he made his camp, and for a few days all went well. Then one night, it suddenly turned cold, and by morning he was too miserable and pain-racked to move. Dimly in the distance he heard the tinkle of goat bells as he fell into a stupor. Wright found him two days later and took him to his cabin, where he and Smith nursed the emaciated writer back to a modicum of health.

In his later essays on "The Old Pacific Capital," Stevenson wrote of the Carmel Valley with a brooding nostalgia, suggesting his premonition that this land would soon be changed. His forecast came to be only two years after his visit, when Rancho Los Laureles was sold for a second time. The buyer on this occasion was not another rancher but the Pacific Improvement Company, the holding company that represented Crocker, Stanford, Huntington and Hopkins, their Central Pacific Railroad, and Crocker's elegant Del Monte Hotel. The newly opened spa needed a large water supply, as did the rest of the 7,000 acres the Big Four had purchased from David Jacks. The Carmel River would be that source.

Los Laureles ranch house became the company headquarters for the purchase, which included besides Los Laureles a portion of the Rancho Los Tularcitos and several thousand acres of back country. Soon 700 Chinese laborers were put to work building the original San Clemente Dam and laying twelve-inch pipe to bring water out of the valley. It proved to be a very difficult undertaking. The pipe-line crossed the river in five places, and, at the entrance to Robinson Canyon, it had to be elevated on a five-foot trestle. The job was accomplished and the Pacific Improvement Company hired William Hatton to manage the dairy and ranching operations of Los Laureles.

Hatton was a man of long experience and established reputation as a farmer and rancher. Born in Ireland, he had left home at the age of thirteen to become a merchant seaman. After seven years of seafaring, he settled in Charleston, South Carolina, where he worked for a year as an agent of the United States Revenue Service and met and married the charming Kate Harney. In 1870, they came to California, and Hatton took his first job as an apprentice on the St. John dairy ranch near

Salinas. The thrifty and industrious Hattons eventually saved sufficient money to buy this 640-acre piece of property, in addition to land south of the mouth of the Carmel River. Then in 1888, Hatton became manager of both the widowed Dominga Doñi de Atherton's Rancho Cañada de la Segunda and the vast acreage that belonged to the Pacific Improvement Company. It was a formidable challenge, but the energetic Will Hatton responded easily.

On the Rancho Los Laureles, he increased the stock and modernized the dairy operation, still located at the old Boronda adobe. Huge vats and presses were installed to manufacture great quantities of the golden cheese, which once had been made by Doña Juana. The process was the same, except she had used a simple keg with a heavy board pressed down across its top by a jack—which, some say, is how the cheese came to be called Monterey Jack.

Soon, Del Monte Dairy was sole supplier of milk products for the Del Monte Hotel. Then, in 1890, Hatton built an auxiliary dairy a few miles up the valley. The unique construction of the tower at the newer farm was designed to ventilate the milk house. Forty years later, the building was converted into an inn, then to an art gallery. It is still standing in Carmel Valley Village.

The Hattons lived in the house built by Kinzea Klinkenbeard. There they raised their seven children and spent congenial times with their neighbors: the Meadows, the Snivelys, and the Berwicks. Another name came into the friendly valley roster when Joseph Hitchcock, son of Isaac and Madalena, came to work for Hatton. Joe Hitchcock lived in a small house in the canyon which still bears his name, and his son, Joe Jr., wrote many colorful memories of the early days in the valley.

It was a good life, despite long hours and hard work. Family activity centered around the black, cast-iron stove in the kitchen. The day began before five in the morning, with the sound and smell of coffee being ground in the mill attached to the wall. After breakfast each member of the household went to his task: milkers to their stools, *vaqueros* to their bronchos, field hands to their plows, and teamsters to their wagons. A round trip to Monterey or Salinas, with a four-horse wagonload of butter or cheese took at least eight hours. And in the rainy season, when the twisting dirt road became a ribbon of mud, it took even longer.

The women had the job of feeding the hired help as well as their kinfolk, churning homemade dairy products, and sewing clothes for their large broods. Their only piece of mechanical equipment was a primitive sewing machine. Often, twenty loaves of bread were baked in each family's wood stove. Many of the women were equally at home riding in their side-saddles, or driving a team of horses, and almost all helped out in the fields during the harvest season.

A wonderful camaraderie existed among these first families. Neighbors worked together in periods of peak workload and turned them into festive occasions. One such time was the annual *matanza*, or butchering of cattle, when the meat had to be quickly converted into salami, corned beef, and jerky. Another was when a new building, such as a school, was being constructed. As soon as the floor was down and the roof-beam raised, a dance would be held. Then the men went to work putting up the partitions.

Frequently, surprise parties were given to celebrate a birthday or anniversary. For these popular festivities, settlers, like the Steffanis, the Bertas, and the Jameses, would come from as far up the valley as the Cachagua to join residents of Los Laureles. After dark and when they were sure the household was asleep, they would gather near the unsuspecting host's house, surround the place, and then the musicians in the group would start to play. Gleefully, they would watch the kerosene lamps being lit in the rooms, and then as the door swung wide, the women would troop in with huge quantities of sandwiches, pie, cake, and freshly ground coffee. To the strains of the accordion, banjo, and harmonica, the dancing went on until four o'clock in the morning, when the revelers had to get home in time to milk their cows.

Until 1890, all of the celebrations were held in the residents' homes. Then, in the kind of joint endeavor for which it was famous, the community built a clubhouse. Land and materials were donated, and every able-bodied man who possessed a hammer and saw took part in constructing what came to be called the Farm Center Building. Delos Goldsmith, then developing real estate in Carmel City, was hired to design the structure, and the Martins, prominent ranchers at the mouth of the Carmel River, helped to supervise the project.

Located at the midway point in the valley, near the entrance to Robinson Canyon, the building became the setting for many a joyous occasion. A *quadrille* at midnight became the traditional highpoint of the evening, after which supper was served by the ladies and the dancing continued until dawn. A few formalities were established. Gentlemen were expected to have been introduced to the ladies whom they asked to dance, there was no liquor served, and musicians were to be paid for their services with a donation from each couple.

By 1892, Will Hatton had purchased the Rancho Cañada de la Segunda, which he had been managing. He and Kate built an elegant, eighteen-room Victorian house at the entrance to the valley, on the land which is now Carmel Knolls. Set in the midst of spacious gardens, it was the showplace of the area. Tragically, the year that the house was completed, 1894, William Hatton died. He was only 45.

Mrs. Hatton managed the property, with the help of her brother John Harney, until at the turn of the century, her sons took over. About the same time, James Meadows, then in his eighties, relinquished control of his ranch to his son Edward, from whom it passed in turn to his son Roy Meadows. On Los Laureles, the Pacific Improvement Company enlarged the original ranch house and added a number of small cottages, since the ranch had become a popular destination for guests of the Del Monte Hotel. They usually came for lunch in tallyhos and, if they were interested in hunting or fishing, stayed overnight.

In the early 1900s, the Pacific Improvement Company liquidated its holdings on the Monterey Peninsula, and Del Monte Properties, a group of financiers spearheaded by Samuel Morse, acquired the lands. The new company decided to subdivide its Carmel Valley acreage and tried unsucessfully to find a developer who would take the entire 10,000 acres for $150,000. In 1923, then, they offered the land in eleven parcels, termed "gentlemen's estates," at $60 an acre. Easterners staying at the Pebble Beach Lodge became interested. International golf champion Marian Hollins bought the 2,000 acres which later became the valley village and the C. E. Holman ranch. Sam Fertig, a Pennsylvanian, purchased the part of Los Laureles that included the old Boronda adobe and the embryonic Laureles Lodge. But the pioneer real estate developers of the valley were the Frank Porters of Salinas.

In 1926, the Porters acquired 600 acres on a deeply wooded hillside in the southeast corner of old Rancho Los Laureles. They named the tract "Robles del Rio" and began carving roads into the steep terrain in preparation for subdividing the land into small plots. It was still relatively wild country. Mrs. Porter recalls "bobcats almost as plentiful as deer" and the "winding pretzel of a road" that was their tenuous link with Salinas.

After many obstacles, forested hills were divided into lots, many measuring 75 by 150 feet, and these were offered at $90 apiece. Robles del Rio Lodge was built to promote the sales. Slowly, where once there had been only sycamores and oaks, weekend cabins appeared, followed by houses. Jet Porter now had neighbors, although even into the 1930s, she remembers the sound of cowbells floating up from the valley floor and the rolling acres of land carpeted with wildflowers and silver grain. For at that time, subdivision had still not extended beyond the Porters' portion of Los Laureles.

A different kind of activity came to the gigantic Rancho San Francisquito y San Carlos. In 1923, the heirs of Bradley Sargent sold the
22,000-acre property to the eastern millionaire sportsman George Gordon
Moore. Moore built ten miles of private road into the mountains and,
on a great swale of land, cupped in the Santa Lucias, erected a 35-room
mansion. The main room was 75 feet long, overlooking a sweeping polo
field. Paddocks for 80 ponies were provided, and famous polo teams
came from all over the country. No expense was spared for lavish entertainment. For the pleasure of his guests, Mr. Moore built a golf course
and introduced Russian boar hunting, importing the animals from his
North Carolina estate.

It was fabulous while it lasted, but in 1929, the market crash wiped
away Moore's fortune. Hard-pressed to satisfy his creditors, he sold the
ranch to Arthur C. Oppenheimer. It is rumored that the price was less
than a quarter of a million dollars, about a fourth of what Moore had
been offered in his heyday. The Oppenheimers have preserved the house
and maintained the property as a working cattle ranch.

Los Tularcitos, largest land grant in the valley, was lost by Ogletree
to Alberto Trescony in a mortgage foreclosure. The former Italian tinsmith, who had become a wealthy landowner in the Salinas Valley, later
leased a portion of the property to Carlisle Abbott. Chinese were employed to operate a dairy in part of the old adobe built by Rafael Gomez.
In 1924, the major portion of the rancho was sold to John and Robert
Marble. It is still one of the most beautiful pieces of land in the valley,
almost entirely in its natural state.

Progress continued in the remainder of Carmel Valley at an ever
more accelerated pace. The Porters acquired a portion of the Hollins
ranch and sold it to Byington Ford, a prominent Monterey Peninsula
real estate developer who was imaginative as well as enterprising. He
built the first commercial development in the valley, comprising an
airport and business district. The shops were designed to look like a
Mexican village, with murals painted in glowing colors on the fronts
of the buildings. They lent a romantic aura to the area and attracted
the attention of tourists.

For a time, Muriel Vanderbilt Phelps Adams owned what had been
the Fertig property, and on it she raised race horses. Then, the Porters
bought that acreage too and subdivided. The Los Laureles ranch house
was purchased by Sanborn Griffin, who converted it into the present-day
Los Laureles resort. Only the old Boronda adobe, with its crumbling
walls and fallen roof-beam, stood as a reminder of the days of the dons.

At last, in the 1940s, it came into the possession of someone who appreciated its unique value. With loving care, George Sims restored the neglected building that was more than a hundred years old. A protective coating of plaster was applied outside of the three-foot thick walls, plank flooring was laid down with hand-made pegs, modern conveniences were unobtrusively installed, and the roof was repaired with antique tiles. Once again the home of the Borondas became a private residence filled with life and laughter.

Today, great stretches of the Carmel Valley are occupied by clusters of houses, and the fragrant pear orchards have given way to shopping centers and a variety of building complexes. Still, in the springtime, buttercups and shooting stars sprinkle the meadows, and poppies flaunt their gold over fields of deep blue lupine. Cattle can be seen browsing on a hundred hills, while venerable oaks, like hunched-over sentinels, spread their dark green shade. And the wonderful sense of camaraderie, of everyone being wanted and needed, continues to characterize life-style in the valley.

CHAPTER

15

The South Coast

South of the Carmel River, for 70 miles on the seaward side of Monterey
County, the Santa Lucia Mountains rise abruptly to heights of over 3,000
feet within a span of three miles from the sea. Beyond the first ridge
of these multi-layered mountains, peaks soar to almost 6,000 feet, with
steep valleys in between. The face of this range, gashed by deep ravines
and plunging perpendicularly to the sea, forms the boldest and most
compact shoreline in California. A narrow marine terrace threads the
escarpment at elevations of several hundred to a thousand feet above
the surf.

Under the Mexican government, two land grants were bestowed
in this spectacular country. In July 1834, Governor Figueroa gave Juan
Bautista Alvarado title to the 8,949-acre Rancho El Sur, between the
Little Sur River and what is now named Cooper Point. A year later,
Teodoro Gonzales received the long slender tract of land called Rancho
San José y Sur Chiquito—8,876 acres bounded on the north by the Carmel
River and on the south by the Palo Colorado Canyon. Neither grantee
took up residence on his land. A different breed of men were to make
this wild and beautiful coast their home.

A few years after the American occupation, unappropriated public
lands in California became available to settlers in parcels of 160 acres.
The process was termed pre-emption and could be initiated by anyone
who filed a declaration of intent, settled on and improved the land,
and paid the purchase price of $1.25 an acre within twelve months.
In 1853, all acreage on the south coast, exclusive of the two land grants,
was open to such pre-emption. George Davis, a resident of Monterey,
was the first to take advantage of the opportunity. He chose a tract
deep in the redwood groves of the Big Sur River and built a cabin
along the river bank, not far from where the Mount Manuel trail begins
in what today is Pfeiffer Big Sur State Park.

Meanwhile, Juan Bautista Roger Cooper had acquired the Rancho

El Sur from his nephew, the improvident Alvarado. And although Cooper continued to live in Monterey, he ran cattle on the south coast rancho and erected a house, surrounded by a charming garden. Located in the sheltered Little Sur Valley, it made a delightful vacation spot for Doña Encarnacion and her two children.

Among the *vaqueros* who worked on the Rancho El Sur was the Indian, Manuel Innocenti. Born and educated at the Santa Barbara Mission, he had come north on a cattle drive to Watsonville and was employed by Captain Cooper, who eventually made him head *vaquero*. One day, early in the 1860s, Innocenti rode past George Davis' cabin and learned that Davis was willing to sell his claim for $50. Eagerly, Manuel closed the deal and brought his wife, Francisca, and their small family to the idyllically situated new home. The Innocentis cleared the land and planted fruit trees, melons, and vegetables, and started a flower garden. Trout, deer, and quail were plentiful, and for a number of years, the Innocentis lived well and happily in the wilderness with their five sons and a daughter.

In the late 1860s, they were delighted to discover they were about to have neighbors. William Brainard Post, owner of the nearby acreage, had laid claim to his land under the provisions of the Homestead Act, signed by President Abraham Lincoln in 1862. By its terms, settlers could acquire 160 acres free of all charges except for a nominal filing fee. Final patent was issued after five years residence and cultivation of the land.

Bill Post had arrived in Monterey in 1848, an affable and energetic youth of eighteen, who had sailed from Connecticut for San Francisco. Sturdily built, he obtained work at the whaling station on Point Lobos. After two years, including a six-month stint at sea, he was ready for a change. Riding up the Carmel Valley, he met James Meadows and Meadows' sister-in-law Anselma Onesimo. He remained in Carmel Valley and, that same year, married Loretta Meadows' pretty sister.

Intrigued by stories Meadows told of his days as the *vaquero* on the Cooper Ranch, Bill Post began exploring the south coast and fell under the spell of the country. He resolved that someday a part of it would be his and that, meanwhile, he would make the most of whatever opportunities lay at hand, the most lucrative of which was bear and deer hunting in the Santa Lucia Mountains.

As a hunter and buckskin trader, he traveled into the northern part of the county. There, he saw the need for a warehouse to store grain from the Salinas Valley while it awaited shipping. He built one at Moss Landing and at the same time took a position as agent for a steamship firm. By the time he was in his early thirties, he had started a couple of businesses and had become foreman of that portion of the Rancho San José y Sur Chiquito, south of Malpaso Creek, which then belonged to the Soberanes family.

With his customary enthusiasm, he staked out his claim to four 160-acre parcels in the country below the Big Sur River. At the time he was constructing his house, the rough wagon road from Monterey extended only as far as Wildcat Creek, below the present-day Highlands Inn. From there, a trail followed the contour of the coast to Granite Creek, then wound inland over the mountains to the Big Sur River. Stoves and other equipment that could not be made on the premises had to be packed in on mules. Beyond his place, even the tortuous trail disappeared in the wild brush of the Big Sur country.

In the fall of 1869, the man whose name was to become synonymous with the Big Sur country came ashore at Monterey. No stranger to the vicissitudes of pioneering, Michael Pfeiffer had crossed the plains and mountains from Illinois in a wagon train. He and his sixteen-year-old bride, Barbara, settled first at what is now Vacaville, northeast of San Francisco.

When their rented farm began to prosper, a sharp increase in rent drove them to look for better conditions. They moved to Tomales Bay but experienced the same treatment. Then they heard of good grazing land, open to homesteading, in Monterey County, and on a gray windy day in October, the Pfeiffers embarked on the old sidewheeler, *Sierra Nevada,* from San Francisco. On board for the two-day voyage were their four children as well as their small stock of cattle and horses. The sea was rough and the trip was miserable, but the most difficult part of the journey still lay ahead.

Bravely they began the long slow trek along the great sea-wall toward Pacific Valley, 70 miles through unknown country to the southern tip of the county's coastland. Far, far below, the ocean, like crinkled blue satin, seemed to stretch into infinity. After a brief respite at the Soberanes Ranch, they climbed into the bronze folds of the mountains. In the distance they glimpsed the off-shore giant of Point Sur, then descended into the Little Sur Valley. After a night's stay at the Cooper ranch house in Little Sur, they came to the mouth of the Big Sur River the following day.

Soon they were immersed in tall, cathedral-like spires of wine-colored redwood, and looking for a place to rest, they discovered a canyon, golden in the light of sun-struck sycamores. Nearby was a spring and some flats which, when cleared of brush, could be plowed. Michael

Pfeiffer saw the pleading in Barbara's eyes; they would stay here at least through the winter.

Using split redwood, Pfeiffer hastily erected a crude shack on the south slope just above the beach. Fortunately, the weather was not harsh that winter. Early rains brought grass for the cattle, and there was an abundance of game, trout, and abalone for the Pfeiffer family. Soon they learned about their neighbors, the Innocentis, but not until the spring did they meet. Francisca, who spoke little English, was shy about visiting the light-skinned lady but understood it to be a proper courtesy. She paid her call, presenting a little bunch of flowers and saying, haltingly, "I have come to see my white sister." Later in the day, one of the Pfeiffer boys noticed the barefoot tracks along the trail on the mountain between the river and Sycamore Canyon. The tracks ended just short of a view from the Pfeiffer cabin and became shoe-prints, mute testimony to the discomfort Francisca was willing to endure for the sake of her pride and responsibility. Throughout the ensuing years, she continued the same pattern, coming once a year and always bringing a gift of flowers or some treasured seed.

The Pfeiffers were happy in their new home despite the grueling work. They labored from before dawn until after dark, with nine-year-old Charles and his younger brother John helping all they could. The most back-breaking toil was grubbing out the brush and getting the ground ready for the planting of crops. Michael had cattle, sheep and pigs to care for in addition to planting and harvesting. Hunting and fishing were also a necessity to augment the family's food supply, and when cash was needed to buy provisions, such as flour, sugar and coffee, Pfeiffer earned money by working as a farmhand in the Salinas Valley.

Barbara had a full workload of her own—milking and churning butter, planting the vegetable garden, sewing all the family clothes, curing meat and making sausage, as well as the usual household chores. And when Michael was away, she assumed also all of his tasks. Above all, it required real courage on her part to stay alone in the wilderness with young children. Both grizzly bears and mountain lions were prevalent in the area. Of the two, the lions were the lesser threat, as they fed mostly on deer. But twice a colt was killed and eaten, and frequently sheep were carried away. The grizzlies were a great menace to the cattle, knocking them down with a hard blow that crushed the animal's ribs.

Finally someone told Pfeiffer how best to kill bear. The method was to wrap some strychnine in a ball of fat, taken from a freshly killed animal, and hang it in the branches of an oak tree high enough so it was beyond the reach of the family's dogs. As added insurance in attracting the bear, a bit of fat was smeared on the tree trunk. The bait was infallible.

Trips to Monterey were infrequent for the Pfeiffers, since the travel consumed three to four precious work days. Occasionally, butter was packed in small barrels and taken on horses, along with chickens, eggs, venison and quail, to be traded for staples in the stores. Always, winter supplies had to be packed in before the rains began, as there were no bridges over rivers and canyons and the trail was quickly submerged in a mass of mud and rubble.

Settlers of the south coast pleaded with the county government to widen the precarious path into a wagon road. The government responded that the settlers must first demonstrate that such a road was feasible by building it across Malpaso Creek, notorious as a bad crossing, and as far south as the Garrapata. Sweating and swearing, the settlers tried. With pick and shovel they hacked at the granite and dug out the shale. Primitive plank bridges were built across creeks and ravines.

It was a big help when Charlie Bixby became one of the road bosses. Bixby was a hard-driving ambitious rancher who had filed for a homestead at Mill Creek, the stream which now bears his name. Hiring men at $1.25 per day, with food and a place to sleep, he used them as a combination road gang and ranch crew. It was an advantageous arrangement for everybody concerned, for, in the 1870s, even the jingle of a few coins in a man's pocket meant security. The road-building requirement was finally met, with Bixby's help, and Bill Post went to the county for the aid it had promised. The road they had built was just adequate to get a wagon through as far as the Bixby Ranch.

Meanwhile, determined men continued to push the threadlike trail farther down the coast. In 1872, David Castro, who was employed as a *vaquero* on the Cooper Ranch, staked his claim to acreage just below the Post place. Two years later, John Partington came to seek his fortune in timber and tanbark oak, 35 miles south of the Carmel River. With him he brought a wife and five children.

Laura and John Partington had been married nine years. She was "a fiery little woman, about as big as a minute," who had known searing tragedy in her youth. Married at nineteen to a soldier in the Union Army, she was widowed and bereft of their baby before the Civil War had ended. Alone, she sailed to San Francisco, where she had a brother, and there she married Partington, an engineer, ten years her senior, who had come from the eastern seaboard in 1850.

Initiation into the rigors of coastland travel came on the second day of the Partingtons' journey out of Monterey. Their pack train of fifteen mules, laden with pots and pans, groceries, crockery, and such sundry items as a sewing machine, was picking its way along the mountainside when it happened. One of the animals lost its footing, plunged over a sheer bank, and dragged three other mules with it.

Laura led the children to a place of safety, while John retrieved what he could from the wreckage. He hardly dared tell his wife that the prized machine, needed to sew all the family's clothes, was smashed beyond repair. But there were more serious problems. One of the mules had been killed, and Tom Slate, one of the three men who had volunteered to help the Partingtons move from Monterey, was seriously injured.

Slate, along with Phil Dolan and Jim Anderson, were bachelors who had acquired land far down the coast. Place names on modern maps still show the locations of their homesteads. Dolan's was just north of Big Creek, Anderson's was just below a concrete bridge that now bears his name, and Slate lived at the Hot Springs, which today is known as Esalen. Slate had come to California as a boy from Missouri and worked as a woodchopper in the Santa Cruz Mountains. When he became crippled with arthritis, an old Indian told him of miraculous healing waters that poured out of a mountainside to the south. Two friends transported the young man over the hard trail to the hot mineral baths, and he was cured. He bought the springs and surrounding acres from the squatter occupant and made the place his home. Now he lay bruised and bleeding, under the blue bowl of the sky. Dolan and Anderson carried him to the nearby Palo Colorado Ranch, which belonged to a Captain Cushing, and the pack train moved on. Three days later, the Partingtons arrived at their destination.

High above a canyon thickly forested in redwood, fir, and the tanbark oak that had brought them, the Partingtons climbed over the great golden shoulder of the ridge. Then they saw the sheltered valley, its long, blond summer grasses swaying in a gentle breeze. The family camped nearby while John Partington, with the help of his affable neighbors Anderson and Dolan, began the building of what someday would be a seven-room house. Before the rains came, Laura had started a vegetable garden. Within a short time, it was expanded to an acre, including fruit trees, a grape arbor, and every variety of flower.

A government survey was the first step in the business part of the Partington enterprise. As soon as this was completed, Partington and his business partner Sam Trotter commenced the construction of trails and a sea landing at the foot of the cliff; for before the completion of Highway 1, the most practical way to send and receive large quantities of heavy goods was by sea. Muleback and wooden sleds were used to bring tanbark and timber out of the forest. The mechanics of a landing consisted of a cable attached to a supporting framework at the top of a bluff and fastened, at its other end, to a heavy anchor or offshore rock. The ships anchored at a safe distance from the rocky coastland and transferred their cargo to small boats, which drew in under the lower end of the cable. Goods were then hauled up and lowered in slings or cages via a horse-powered windlass.

The tanbark industry was just beginning to develop. In the next decade, several other landings were built to load the bark, used in the manufacture of tannic acid, and to ship the lumber cut from prime redwood. Among them was Godfrey Notley's landing, near the mouth of the Palo Colorado Canyon, around which a thriving village sprang up. Jim Anderson also had a landing near the bridge that is named for him and there was another at the mouth of the Big Sur River. Perhaps the most spectacular was Partington Landing, at which goods had to be transported through a thousand-foot tunnel to the base of the cliff. At its heyday, the Partington and Trotter operation included a 40-man crew and the cutting of about 10,000 cords of bark. Lumbering was a good source of income for a number of settlers. Some of them, like Partington and Post, combined it with raising cattle and hogs.

For several years, the Pfeiffers, Posts, Castros, and Innocentis constituted the entire population of the Big Sur area. To the north lay the Cooper and Soberanes Ranchos and a few homesteads near the mouths of creeks and canyons. To the south were the Partingtons, Tom Slate, who was courting the lovely Bersabe Soberanes, and the bachelors Anderson and Dolan. Before the turn of the century, two families—the McWays, and Waters—had homesteaded between the Partington Ranch and Slate's Hot Springs. The Waters property was called Saddle Rock Ranch for the saddle-shaped rock at the mouth of McWay Canyon. The rock and adjacent waterfall is still a beautiful landmark below the cliff-side trail of today's Julia Pfeiffer Burns State Park.

Below the great divide, where the precipitous seaward face of the Santa Lucias made travel impractical, a couple of old Spanish families from Monterey had put down roots. Vicente Avila, who hated the *gringos* with all his heart, was one who shortly after the American occupation took his family and a pack train carrying all their possessions to an isolated valley to the north of the Mission San Antonio. Surrounded by steep mountains, his rancho was named Salsipuedes, which meant "Get out if you can." By the 1870s, Avila's sons had accepted the challenge and crossed over the range to homestead on the coast, near the site of present-day Lucia. Descendants of the old Spanish soldier Manuel Boronda, also had staked their claim to acreage close by.

In 1876, the first American family came to live in this untamed insular land. They were of stalwart stock, brave and fiercely independent. Gabriel Dani had been a scout on the pioneer wagon trains that broke a path of empire across the continental United States. His wife Elizabeth had come from England to St. Louis, in 1860, with plans to travel westward. It was during the long trek by covered wagon to Salt Lake City that the two bold spirits met.

In the 1870s, they moved on to California, settling first in Wilmington. From there they sailed for San Francisco and, from the deck of their steamer, they looked in awe at the plunging hills of the great, seamed, and tip-tilted country. Its savage beauty; unblemished by signposts of civilization, reached out to them with a magnetism they would not forget. Two years later, the Danis, and their five children, made the hazardous trip from Soledad, the terminus of the Southern Pacific Railroad, across the tangled web of mountains.

The first leg of the three-day journey was by stagecoach. They crowded with difficulty into the shabby, two-seated vehicle, which a couple of small horses reluctantly dragged over the dusty rutted trail. After a night's stay at the Dutton Hotel in Jolon, the adventure was continued on horseback as they began the dangerous ascent of the higher ridges of the Santa Lucia. Two cinches were used to hold their saddles in place, and, along some of the steeper stretches, the children clung frantically to the manes of their horses to keep from falling backward. On equally sheer descents, the nine-year-old Ada Dani's feet were often on a level with her horse's ears.

At the top of the first summit, a magnificent view met their startled gaze. To the right, a gigantic system of cleavage, extending for many miles and interrupted by intervening canyons, had a raw unfinished look. Peaks were thrown in rough and fantastic outlines, some formed of huge, bare boulders piled loosely on top of one another. To the front and left, the skyline of the great ridge was etched in spear-like pines, many of which were bare of foliage and seemed to pierce the sky with gaunt silvery arms.

Occasionally, their trail led into the cool dimness of a canyon, filled with stately redwoods and rose-stemmed madrone. There on a fragrant groundcover of flowering herbs, they rested their animals and drank from a spring surrounded by fern and alder. They were emerging from such a canyon when the ocean first burst upon them, sparkling under sunbeams yet partially veiled in a soft moving mist.

The trail continued to rise and fall with the spurs of the ridge, until it came to the final descent, a rugged, gorge-broken series of declivities. Standing on a bluff, high above the many-splendored sunset sea, the Danis saw the long creaming shoreline curving to the south and heard the muted roar of the surf as it stroked the jagged rocks in exuberant explosions of spray. They knew that they had come to the end of their search.

For their homestead, they chose the site of the present-day Camaldoli Hermitage. Out of a couple of young redwood trees, beams and joists were hewn for a house and split-shakes were formed into walls. The rest of the lumber was fashioned into a few pieces of crude furniture.

The good-natured carefree Borondas and Avilas were ideal neighbors. They soon taught "Riel," the Yankee newcomer, the tricks of survival in a land with the contours of a gabled roof. They showed him how to sow a field of barley on horseback, riding the furrows full tilt while tossing handfuls of seed with both hands and controlling the colt with his knees. They pointed out the light soil of the little hollows, nestled between steep slopes, where potatoes and corn could be grown. And at harvest time, they demonstrated their ancient yet effective method of threshing, termed "tramping out the beans." The bean crop was strewn on the hard dirt floor of a corral, then family and neighbors rode in on horseback, whipping up their ponies to a good pace and trotting around till the job was accomplished.

Cattle and hogs were the chief products of the region. Elizabeth Dani learned that milking and caring for the pigs were considered to be exclusively feminine occupations, along with the routine of cleaning, washing, and sewing clothes, and raising great broods of babies. She became very popular with the Spanish and Indian women of the area because of her skill as a midwife, and when she gave birth to a child of her own, they clustered around her and suggested that she name the girl Lucia, "after the mountain."

Almost ten years went by before another American came to live in the little settlement. Wilbur Harlan had come to California from Texas. His mother died when he was a small boy and his father sent him to live with an aunt in Santa Cruz. An urge to strike out on his own brought him to the south coast. Carrying what clothing he had in a sack over his shoulder, he hiked from Soledad along the same trails traversed by the Dani family. His traveling companion was an old German man, Philip Schmidt, who also wanted to homestead in the area.

Harlan staked his claim to acreage near the Danis, and, before long, he and their daughter Ada were married. He worked hard to clear his land of thick underbrush, tilled its steep slopes with a two-handled plow, and raised livestock. To care for his rapidly increasing family, which eventually totaled ten, he also got a job with the nearby Rockland Cement Company at Limekiln Canyon.

The Limekiln operation, which began in the 1880s, came as a great boon to the community. About three miles to the south of the Harlan homestead, the mountain held a rich deposit of calcareous rock. Below the site, three canyons united, their waters breaking through the rocky shore to form a smooth beach and tiny harbor. Here the Rockland company constructed a landing, installed three large kilns, and built houses for the workmen. Schooners began to call regularly at Rockland Landing to pick up limestone bricks and deliver supplies.

Wilbur Harlan made a yearly trip to San Francisco on one of the ships, taking orders for provisions from the entire neighborhood. Settlers gathered from miles around on the day the two-masted *Bonito* anchored off Lucia Cove, enroute to Rockland Landing. Sacks of flour, macaroni, rice, sugar and salt, even bolts of yardage, were unloaded in huge piles. It was the long awaited opportunity to stock up on everything that could not be raised or made at home.

When the cement company terminated its operation, isolation closed in on the little community again. Once more, everything had to be packed in from King City, and there was no mail service beyond Jolon, a distance of 70 miles round trip. In winter, when the San Antonio and Nacimiento Rivers rose or snow lay on the upper ridge, it could be two months before contact was made with the outside world.

The settlers had to be self-sufficient and they were. Turkeys and chickens were plentiful and venison was usually available. Everything from carpentry to shoemaking was done by members of the group. As one old-timer put it, "We were independent of depressions." Even if their children had never seen a wagon, much less a train, they had a school. Teachers were boarded with the local families and constituted an excellent source of wives. Ten such brides were wooed and won by the sons of just two homesteaders.

In the late 1880s, the rugged mountain fastness, fifteen miles south of Lucia, was suddenly invaded by a roaring burst of activity. Gold was discovered near the head of Alder Creek! The first report of gold in Monterey County had been made in 1849, when a deposit was found not far from the San Antonio Mission, on the Rancho Milpitas. It marked the beginning of a settlement that in 1870 became the town of Jolon. But serious placer mining did not commence until 1876, after the mother lode country had been thoroughly ransacked. Two years later, the Athertons evicted prospectors from their property on the Milpitas.

Then, in 1887, came the great day when William Cruikshank, who for years had been combing adjacent public lands, discovered his vein of gold. He called his claim the "Last Chance" and proceeded to develop it. Soon hordes of propectors swarmed into the area, making additional discoveries and opening more mines. The Los Burros Mining District sprang into being with three stamp mills, and a boom town, named Manchester, mushroomed on Alder Creek. In its heyday, Manchester boasted four stores, a restaurant, five saloons, a dance hall, and a hotel.

The mining operation was doomed by its inaccessibility. Gold ore had to be sent out on the rough trail to Jolon; and, though once a year a ship brought machinery and equipment to a landing at the mouth of Willow Creek, most supplies came via the inland route. By 1895, when the best ore had been exhausted, the boom began to fade. Sporadic mining activities have continued in the area to the present day, but no vestige of the once-thriving town of Manchester remains.

As the nineteenth century drew to a close, more settlers came to live on the south coast. Those who stayed at its upper end had the limited convenience of an undulating wagon road which, by 1889, had been constructed almost entirely by homesteaders as far as the Castro property. It was so steep and narrow that, in some spots, small wagons had to be unhitched and held over the side of the cliff to let larger vehicles pass. And it was still a three day round trip with a wagon from the Pfeiffer or the Post Ranch to Monterey.

Constellations of families, at both ends of the seventy-mile coastland, sought comfort in each others company on rare but exceedingly joyful occasions. The whole family went visiting on horseback, often with babies transported in panniers on a trusty pack-mule. With them, they took a plethora of food—big loaves of fresh bread, cream cakes, preserves, and their finest honey and home-cured hams. Visiting days were spent helping with the ranch work; men split timber, built fencing, and mended equipment, while the women pared and sliced apples, pickled vegetables, and stuffed pillows with fluffy goose feathers. Best of all, they all talked, blessed release from weeks of loneliness.

The festivities culminated in a picnic or a barbecue for which two beeves might be slaughtered. Then came the dancing, to the music of accordion, banjo, violin, and guitar, and it lasted until dawn. One of the favorite songs heard at these gatherings was the "South Coast Waltz."

Open-handed hospitality was a byword with all the Big Sur settlers in the early 1900s, but the Pfeiffer and Post ranches were most frequently the center of social activities. The Posts had increased their holdings by almost a thousand acres. Bill Post's sons, Frank and Joseph, had each homesteaded 160 acres, and various relatives had acquired tracts totaling another 640. Their land stretched as far south as the site of the present-day Nepenthe restaurant. The ranchhouse, which still stands on Highway 1 at the top of what is now called "Post grade," was much enlarged. In the canyon back of it, Joe built a home for his wife, the former Mary Elizabeth Gilkey, and their son, Bill II. Frank's homestead was on land where many years later his daughter Alice established the Loma Vista Inn.

Big Sur's early post office and its second schoolhouse were on the Post ranch. The ranch was also headquarters for pack trips, on which Joe and his father led hunting and fishing parties into the back country. In 1889, when the Point Sur Lighthouse was installed, Joe and his brother got the contract for construction of the road into the station. Joe was also employed as foreman of the Molera Ranch, the southern portion of Rancho El Sur, which had been inherited by Juan Bautista Roger Cooper's son-in-law, Eusebio Molera, after the death of the 80-year-old captain. In 1898, ill health forced Bill Post to retire to Monterey, and Joe moved to the family homestead.

The Post daughters both married men who had acquired land a mile or so south of the Castro property. Ellen became the wife of Edward Grimes, an Englishman who was the nephew of James Meadows. Mary became Señora de la Torre when she married José, the grandson of the old presidio soldier Joaquín de la Torre. The Grimes and de la Torre acreages eventually were purchased by the Castros and Alejandrino Boronda, a handsome young *caballero* who had found the isolation around Lucia too tame for his high spirits.

Michael and Barbara Pfeiffer's family grew to eight children. The Pfeiffer boys homesteaded additional land adjoining that of their father. John Pfeiffer's first claim was on a mountainside between Sycamore Canyon and the Big Sur River. The cabin he built is still standing in the Pfeiffer-Big Sur State Park, near the foot of Oak Grove and Mount Manuel trails. Close by, a rough circle marks the burial ground of the Innocenti children, all of whom died before they reached maturity. Their mother, Francisca, who lived to almost a hundred years was buried beside them.

Shortly after the "proving up" on this land, John Pfeiffer bought additional acreage from the Wurld brothers, whose house stood on the site of the present-day Big Sur Lodge. Then, in 1898, he took off for Alaska to seek his fortune in the gold rush. The trip was not successful financially, and he returned to resume the occupation of farmer and apiarist. In 1902, the 40-year-old bachelor married the eldest daughter of the Swetnam family, who in 1896 had purchased the Palo Colorado Ranch.

Florence Swetnam Brown was an attractive young widow with two children. Possessed of a tremendous amount of energy and managerial ability, she soon put the Pfeiffer ranch on a paying basis. John was something of a dreamer and had paid little heed to the costs of the numerous guests who continually dropped in uninvited and unannounced at the ranch. As a result, the Pfeiffers were slipping ever deeper into debt. One day, Florence's patience was tried a bit too much. She was contemplating the stacks of dirty dishes and piles of linen that had to be washed in water carried up from the creek, when she saw one of their free-loading boarders beating his mule with a heavy picket. Outraged, she rushed out, gave him a sound dressing down, and informed him that henceforth he and his friends would pay for their bed and board. It was the start of the resort business, with rates set at three dollars per day.

The dynamic Mrs. Pfeiffer also reactivated a lumber mill, situated one-half mile up the river in the present-day Pfeiffer Park, to obtain material for the construction of additional accommodations at the ranch. The mill had been established by the Ventana Power Company as one of the many commercial projects involving the tanbark industry; but when the timber was depleted, the company closed down.

Another transitory attempt at industry in the area was at Bixby Creek, which had been Charlie Bixby's holding. In 1906, the Monterey Lime Company bought out Bixby for the limestone they found on Long Ridge. An aerial tramway was built and the lime was transported by cable to the mouth of the creek, where it was hoisted aboard steamers. For four years, the region hummed with activity, until the best of the calcareous deposits had been mined and the operation became too expensive to maintain. Then, the heavy rains of a long wet winter washed out the trails and swept away 22 bridges installed by the company.

With the end of the liming operation, the days of industrial enterprise on the south coast were about over. Commercial development on the coast would henceforth be devoted entirely to the recreation business. The Big Sur country had already been attracting hunters and fishermen for decades. Now the Pfeiffer resort had a rival for the business of these sportsmen. The Hotel Idlewild, located on the banks of the Little Sur River, advertised rates of $1.50 a day and guaranteed a limit of trout "even to those who used a bent pin and had never fished before." A stagecoach left Monterey three times a week and made the trip to the resort in ten hours.

In 1906, a physician from San Jose, Dr. Charles Wayland, established a private campground on land across the river from the present-day Big Sur Lodge. At first, Dr. Wayland and the 40 families that joined him in the venture set up tents on the grounds for their summer homes or vacation spots. Later cabins were built on land Wayland leased from Pfeiffer and for over twenty years, the 40 families came every summer and contributed substantially to Mrs. Pfeiffer's thriving business. Both the Post and Castro Ranches also opened to paying guests.

The only deterrent to the south coast becoming a mecca for tourists, as well as sportsmen, was the hazardous road that could not be kept open all year. The idea for a year-round scenic highway originated with Dr. John Roberts, the founder of Seaside, who for many years had ridden the treacherous trails and serpentine roads of the south coast in order to care for his patients. As a member of the county board of supervisors, he aroused public interest in the project, believing it could be accomplished for $50,000. When the county could provide only half that sum, State Senator Elmer Rigdon spearheaded pressure for a state appropriation.

It was 1917, and the legislature's defense committee ruled that priority must be given to roads of urgent military importance. Instantly, the lobbying group in Sacramento dropped the word "scenic," and when the Military Highway bill was passed, the Carmel-San Simeon highway was included as one of six roads necessary for defense. In 1919, through a bond election, $1,500,000 was appropriated for its construction.

Three years later, the allotment of money had been consumed and work had not progressed beyond the northern section of the road. The highway commission cancelled its contract with the builder, but he continued construction, sued the state, and won. Still, there were no funds until another bond issue was passed, and work was resumed with prison labor. By this time, it was 1931 and the road extended to Anderson Creek from the north, and to Salmon Creek from the south. Thirty of the most difficult miles were still to be built.

Many of the original settlers were enraged by the devastation the construction had caused. Machinery blasted through the great cliffs, scarring granite promontories and defiling canyons and waterfalls with debris. Some old-timers, who felt they had an inalienable right to their mountains, looked upon the highway crew as an invasion of vandals. Others, more concerned about the commercial value of their property, fought proposed zoning restrictions.

At last, on June 27, 1937, the highway was completed, at a cost of approximately $8,000,000. Dedication ceremonies began at San Simeon, and from there the procession of dignitaries moved up the coast to Big Sur for the culmination of festivities. A way of life had ended, and a new era began for the beautiful country.

Since the 1920s, eager entrepreneurs from San Francisco and Los Angeles had been badgering the Pfeiffers to sell their land for real estate developments. One had offered $240,000 for the entire 1,200 acres. But John Pfeiffer's love for his homeland was too deep to allow its development. Instead, in 1934, he sold 706 acres to the state for the nucleus of the 822-acre Pfeiffer Big Sur State Park. He also donated half of the purchase price. The rest of his acreage was divided between his children, and a few moments spent in the soft-spoken company of Esther Pfeiffer Ewoldsen and her husband, Hans, give certain evidence of their far-sighted determination to preserve the beloved country.

Others have heeded the call to keep the unique coastline in sacred trust for generations yet unborn. The Lathrop Browns, who purchased Saddle Rock Ranch, gave the 1,700 acres which constitutes Julia Pfeiffer Burns State Park. Twenty-one acre John Little State Park, which was originally part of the Slate property sold to Milton Little, was donated by Elizabeth Livermore. Frances Molera, granddaughter of Juan Bautista Roger Cooper, placed 2,000 acres in trust for the Andrew Molera State Park in the Big Sur area. These are but islands in the land, however; the threat to the radiant green and golden shoreline, brought by the highway, requires constant vigilance.

Of the original homesteaders, who knew how to live in harmony with its natural splendor, few remain. But artists and writers have become the new settlers, and they also value the grandeur and isolation of this magnificent landscape. Robinson Jeffers immortalized its gut-gripping quality in his narrative poems. Their stories are inextricably interwoven with the phenomena of the "multi-form coast-range hills."

Recently, the mass-recreation seekers and real estate promoters began pressuring for conversion of Highway 1 to a freeway, with the concomitant proliferation of roadside businesses and housing developments. But, fortunately, through the efforts of concerned residents, a master plan, providing for strict zoning regulations and building restrictions, was adopted in 1963. At about the same time, the California legislature was persuaded to remove Highway 1 from the projected state freeway system. On the interpretation, as well as the enforcement, of these controls rests the future of one of the most breath-stoppingly beautiful stretches of coastline in the world.

16

Carmel-by-the-Sea

Year after year, the ancient amber-colored walls of the San Carlos Mission came alive again with the sound of singing on only one day—the feast of Saint Charles. November sunlight streamed through the roofless church, ruthlessly exposing rubbish three feet deep on the floor. Squirrels scampered across the debris. Yet a crowd of boisterous merrymakers from Monterey thronged the mission door. And in the small sacristy, the Indians in their bright dresses, faces alight with joy, knelt and chanted the old familiar Latin words.

Father Casanova listened to his mixed flock with deep affection and sadness. Theirs was the voice of the high-hearted past in which Carmel had begun. It was also all that remained. Fervently he resolved to restore dignity to the sacred ruins, where the dreams that became California had been nurtured.

The year was 1870. Outside the crumbling stone walls were the scant seven acres which the Church had been given by the United States government patent. To the west and north, beyond the straggling willow hedge, stood the 200-acre Mission Ranch, property of the Martin family.

William Martin, an industrious Scotsman, had emigrated to Canada in 1840, with his wife Agnes and their six children. Then, lured by the call of gold, he moved his family to California, taking the arduous route through the Isthmus of Panama. Perhaps because the rugged beauty of the Monterey coast reminded the Martin family of their native Scotland, they chose to settle near the mouth of the Carmel River, where the thunderous roar of the sea echoed up to the eaves of their simple dwelling.

The Martins had no neighbors on the bay, except for a few Portuguese whalers at Point Lobos and a small colony of Chinese fishermen near Pescadero Point. To the north lay a large unoccupied acreage of wooded hills belonging to Honore Escolle, a Monterey businessman. Escolle had come from France to the United States at the age of fifteen.

After five years in New Orleans, he moved in 1852 to Monterey, where he opened a bakery and general store. Soon, the enterprising youth was a prosperous merchant and had picked up several thousand choice acres in Monterey and San Luis Obispo counties. But as his interest lay in ranching, he lightly valued the steep slopes above Carmel Bay, called Las Manzanitas for the masses of manzanita that grew among the pines. Suited neither to fruit orchards nor cattle grazing, the property was worthless in his opinion.

Others were to take a different view of this unique piece of coastline. David Starr Jordan, later to become president of the newly created Stanford University, encountered the deep blue bay while engaged in an ichthyological survey for the 1880 census. His description was ecstatic. "Of all the indentations of the coast of California, the most picturesque and most charming is the little bay of Carmelo." His accolade appeared in several published accounts.

As the decade of the 1880s got under way, California became involved in its first gigantic real estate boom. One contributing factor was the arrival of the Southern Pacific Railroad. Promoters, aware of the potential of increased immigration, bought huge tracts of land for next to nothing, had them surveyed into "paper towns," and launched flamboyant campaigns to snare investors. In Monterey, the Southern Pacific Railroad's luxurious Hotel Del Monte was attracting distinguished visitors from all over the world. It was even possible that the Southern Pacific would extend its line to Carmel.

S. J. Duckworth, of Monterey, was among those who foresaw the gleam of opportunity, particularly in the Escolle property. Inspired by the flourishing Methodist community at Pacific Grove, Duckworth saw Carmel as an ideal spot for a Catholic summer colony, with a refurbished mission as the main attraction. Due to the efforts of Father Casanova, restoration of the Carmel Mission was already under way. By 1882, the debris had been cleared out of the sanctuary, revealing the tombs of the padres Serra, Crespí, Lopez, and Lasuén. Much publicity for Casanova's project was obtained through announcement of a public viewing of the remains of the four missionaries. Some 400 people gathered at the mission for the event, and a fund-raising drive resulted, led by Mrs. Leland Stanford and involving more than 50 prominent citizens of California. In 1884, work was begun on repair of the church.

Early in 1888, Duckworth approached Escolle about the purchase of part of Las Manzanitas. The Frenchman was delighted to sell. A survey was made of the townsite and, in May, Carmel City's first official map was filed with the county recorder. Ignoring such natural impediments as gullies and ravines, the town plot showed an orderly layout of imaginary streets, bounded to the west and east by present-day Monte Verde and Monterey and, to the north and south, by First and Eleventh Avenues.

Next, a brochure was floated, describing the development in rhapsodic terms: "A golden opportunity is here presented for men of enterprise to reap a golden harvest by directing their attention toward the advantages possessed by Carmel City for commercial purposes." Discussion about subordinating business to the artistic aspects of the community was to come much later. Within two months, 200 lots were sold. Then, following the pattern set by land developers throughout the state, Duckworth built a hotel to house prospective clients. It was on the northeast corner of Ocean Avenue and Broadway, later to be called Junipero Street. A traveler, stopping in Carmel in the summer of 1889, described the hostelry as "a comfortable eighteen room structure." As an added attraction, a bath house was built at the foot of Ocean Avenue. It provided a glassed-in observation platform and outdoor showers, the water for which was supposedly warmed by the sun and came from a tank on the roof. Bathing suit, towel, and dressing room could all be rented for 25 cents.

But after the first flush of enthusiasm, sales tapered off. By the early 1890s, Duckworth was running into financial problems. Total collapse of his venture was temporarily averted only through the support of several wealthy San Franciscans. Notable among them was Abbie Jane Hunter, who organized the Women's Real Estate and Investment Company and sent a personal representative to promote the project. Her brother Delos Goldsmith built the Hotel Carmel at the corner of Ocean Avenue and San Carlos Street. It was a two-story frame building with a homey atmosphere, in keeping with Mrs. Hunter's campaign to present Carmel as an ideal family resort.

Despite these efforts, Carmel City remained a "paper town." A Chautauqua-type organization did not exist to interest the Catholics, and the mission was far short of restoration. In addition, widespread depression had dealt the tourist boom a severe blow, and Carmel had no hotel comparable to the Del Monte to attract the affluent. An example of the going rate for real estate, in 1893, was Escolle's sale of 27 lots on the block where Magnin's store now stands for ten dollars!

Not until about 1900 did another promoter attempt to build a city on Carmel Bay. This time it was a developer with extensive experience, James Franklin Devendorf, who already owned subdivisions in San Jose, Morgan Hill, Gilroy, and Stockton. Trading his Stockton holdings for

the Carmel property, he acquired additional land from Escolle and
formed the Carmel Development Company in November 1902. As his
partner, he chose the tall affable Frank Powers, a San Francisco attorney.

A map was filed for the new subdivision, now named Carmel-by-
the-Sea. The new plan differed little from that of the first Carmel City,
still representing a grid pattern of non-existent right-angle streets. Even
Ocean Avenue was little more than a wide path through the pines, known
as "the devil's staircase" because of the huge, chuck holes that pocked
its sandy surface.

The dignified and portly Devendorf was perfect for the job of colo-
nizing Carmel. Early settlers describe him as being "wonderfully kind."
He spared no effort to help prospective buyers feel at home, from finding
them temporary housing facilities to having a fire ready on the hearth
when they arrived. Clients referred by Powers came down from San
Francisco on the Del Monte Express. From the depot at Monterey, an
open two-horse carriage brought them up the old dirt road over Carmel
Hill. It was a long hard pull, taking well over an hour and often requiring
the male passengers to get out and walk to the top in order to save
the steaming horses. Rounding a hairpin turn, the narrow road entered
Carpenter Street and zigzagged into what there was of a town.

A handful of stores, with square "false fronts," huddled in the two-
block stretch of Ocean between San Carlos and Lincoln. One of these
doubled as the post office, with two short tiers of mail boxes under
the wooden canopy adorning its front. This became a favorite gathering
place for the villagers, rivaling the old covered-over watering trough
that stood in the center of San Carlos Street.

Lots were offered for as little as five dollars down and five dollars
a month. Often, Devendorf allowed payments to accumulate for years,
with a refund of the principal that had been paid if foreclosure became
inevitable. Nor did his altruism end with the terms of the sale. He gave
advice on construction plans and landscaping, donated trees, and even
supplied building materials garnered from older shacks being demolished.
Once he ordered some cottages in San Francisco dismantled and sent
down. When the shipment arrived, it comprised mostly doors. Undaunted,
people used them to build what later came to be called "door houses."

In 1903, the hotel that Duckworth built was moved on rollers five
blocks down Ocean, to form the nucleus of the present Pine Inn. Tents
were erected on an adjoining lot, now the site of Lobos Lodge, to take
care of the overflow. The new inn opened with much fanfare on the
Fourth of July, and crowds came from the San Joaquin Valley, jamming
Ocean Avenue with wagons, surreys, and two-seaters. On the same day,

an enterprising couple from Pacific Grove opened a restaurant in a hastily put together tent building two doors from the post office. Meals were twenty cents.

Soon Carmel could claim 75 residences and a permanent population of 32 families. For the most part the houses were small and unpretentious, little more than tiny flat boxes clustered in the pines on the upper slopes. The stretch above the beach, west of the street called Camino Real, was an open grassy plain. There were few conveniences in the town; a couple of telephones, no electricity, and wooden sidewalks only in the sparse business section. Ocean Avenue was a muddy stream bed in the rainy season, despite the pines planted along its center and sides to stem the water. But beauty in a great and overflowing abundance was free for "the mere labor of looking."

Villagers woke to the fragrance of pine, sun-warmed or drenched in mist from the sea and mingling with woodsmoke and whiffs of bacon frying on the outdoor grills. Trails led from the cottages through sprays of sky-blue ceanothus or bright-berried manzanita to the corner grocery, where a blackboard outside gave news of the nation along with the price of canned goods and potatoes. Spring brought the village solid sheets of shooting stars and the pale pink globes of fairy lanterns nestled among the manzanita. Simple amusements wiled away the hours; foraging for driftwood and bouquets of wild iris, gathering mussels from the rocks at Lobos or the river mouth, visiting among neighbors. And always there was the sound of the singing surf, a creamy, billowing, high-flown fringe to the peacock blue of the bay. An early resident reminisces, "It was the absolute simplicity and openness of everything that made it such a wonderful experience."

This was the life style that lured the poet George Sterling to settle in Carmel. The central figure in San Francisco's celebrated Bohemian Club, he soon gathered about him the group of writers and artists who gave the sleepy hamlet its bohemian mystique. Sterling was 36 years old at the time. The maverick son of a solid Sag Harbor, Long Island, family, he had come to California in 1890, trailing the tatters of a three-year education toward the priesthood. Harnessing himself to employment in his uncle's San Francisco insurance firm, he had married the blond, statuesque Carrie Rand and become a seemingly conscientious, somewhat stodgy suburbanite in Piedmont, across the bay. Then, as escape from unbearable boredom, he took to spending the twice-daily, half-hour ferry trip to San Francisco scribbling verse.

At first, Sterling wrote only for his own pleasure, but friendship with the influential critic Ambrose Bierce brought impetus to his endeavor. Under the tutelage of this exacting mentor, he began to take his work seriously. Added encouragement came from close association with a group of established writers, many of them neighbors in the Berkeley Hills. Most stimulating were Joaquin Miller, "Poet of the Sierras," the short-story writer James Hopper, and Harry Lafler, editor of a small literary magazine. But none of them could meet the exhilaration that Sterling found in the advice and friendship of the zestful Jack London.

With their meeting in 1901, a new life began for Sterling—open houses on Sunday afternoon with the colorful Mexican artist Xavier Martinez, frequent festive gatherings at the London home, and long nights with London on San Francisco's Barbary Coast. Sterling was living up to his name of "Greek," given him by London. But he also was making progress with his poetry.

In 1903, his first collection of verse, *Testimony of the Suns,* was published to considerable critical acclaim. When several short pieces sold and his next long poem received high praise, Sterling was convinced that the time had come to cut loose his chains. Fifteen years of toil at a job he loathed, albeit spiced by other activities, had become abrasive. Now, he could dare to devote full time to his art. It was at this point that he met the woman who precipitated his move to Carmel.

Mary Hunter Austin had recently published her successful *Land of Little Rain,* a book of sketches about life in the Owens Valley. Sterling read the book with admiration and, hearing that Mrs. Austin was in San Francisco, asked her to have dinner with him at Coppa's, a favorite rendezvous of the bohemian crowd. She accepted eagerly, taking it as an invitation to join the "inner circle."

A year older than Sterling, Mary Austin was patently plain, with a short stocky figure and tragic brooding face, to which only the lovely eyes and abundant golden-brown hair lent grace. Product of a lonely childhood and loveless marriage, she was avid for appreciation and affection. Of these, the magnetic Sterling seemed to provide ample promise. Over a meal of succulent shrimp, almond tarts, and wine, she told him about the novel she was writing, for which she wanted to gather background material at the Mission San Carlos. He offered to take her there and act as her guide, having himself been interested in the area by Frank Powers, Devendorf's partner in the development of Carmel.

It was the early summer of 1905. An idyllic interlude ensued in Carmel, about which Mary Austin later wrote in her autobiography. They spent much time alone together, wandering in the old mission orchards, striding over the hills "looking for pitch pine and bee trees,"

The South Coast

The Post ranch house, which still stands on Highway 1 at the top of what is called "Post grade." Mayo Hayes O'Donnell Library Collection.

In 1885 Wilbur Harlan staked his claim to acreage near the Danis, and before long he married their daughter, Ada. His homestead cabin was built of split logs, with brick for the fireplace brought in by pack train. Amelie Elkinton Collection.

The John Pfeiffer House in Big Sur, originally the Wurld cabin. Florence Pfeiffer came to live there as a bride in 1902. Photograph taken in 1913 by S. L. Slevin, courtesy of the Bancroft Library.

(*top right*)
In 1876 Gabriel and Elizabeth Dani settled in the area that came to be called Lucia. For their homestead they chose the site of the present-day Camaldoli Hermitage. In the 1890s, this substantial house replaced their first roughhewn cabin. Hester Harlan Collection.

(*bottom right*)
In 1902, Wilbur Harlan built a fine house for his growing family. It was destroyed by fire on December 12, 1926. Both Hester Harlan Collection.

William Brainard Post came to
Monterey in 1848, married Loretta
Meadows' sister, Anselma Onesimo,
and homesteaded large acreage below
the Big Sur River. Photograph
courtesy of the Monterey City Library.

Mrs. Wilbur Harlan
(Ada Dani) in 1893, with Aaron,
Lulu, and George Harlan.
Hester Harlan Collection.

Schoolteachers of the south
coast had to be a hardy lot,
traveling many miles on
treacherous trails. Mayo Hayes
O'Donnell Library Collection.

Notley's Landing near the mouth of the Palo Colorado Canyon.
Tanbark was an important industry on the south coast.
Landings were built to ship the bark, used in the manufacture
of tannic acid. A thriving village developed around
Godfrey Notley's landing. Photograph taken in 1919
by S. L. Slevin, courtesy of the Bancroft Library.

Slate's Hot Springs (*Below left and right*)

Today's Esalen was once called Slate's Springs, because
it had been the property of Thomas Benton Slate. About the
turn of the century, it was acquired by John Little,
who sold a portion of the land, including the springs, to
a Doctor Murphy. He hoped to build a sanitarium on the site.
In the 1930s there was a lodge, cabins, and open air
baths on a platform wedged into the cliff above the ocean.

A flag was raised at the top of the path leading to the springs
to alert bathers when the tubs were in use. It was a courtesy
to clean and partially refill the tub so that the water
would not be too hot for the next user. The water turned green
after standing a short time, and those "not in the know,"
thinking it was dirty, emptied it. They suffered a long wait
while their boiling bath cooled.
Photographs taken in 1934
by S. L. Slevin, courtesy of the Bancroft Library.

The Monterey-Big Sur stage in 1904.
A stagecoach left Monterey three
times a week and made the trip
to the Hotel Idlewild, on the
Little Sur River, in ten hours.
Shortly after this picture was taken,
a front wheel collapsed. Mayo Hayes
O'Donnell Library Collection.

The limekiln on Long Ridge above
Bixby Creek. In 1906, the Monterey
Lime Company bought out Charlie
Bixby's holdings for the rich
deposits of limestone. The region
became a beehive of activity.
An aerial tramway transported
the lime by cable to the mouth of
the creek, where it was hoisted
aboard steamers. Depletion of the
calcareous material and the heavy
rains of a wet winter, which swept away
22 bridges, brought the operation
to an end. Robinson Jeffers
used Bixby Landing as the
setting for his narrative poem
Thurso's Landing. Photographs
taken in 1919 by S. L. Slevin,
courtesy of the Bancroft Library.

Boat landing supplies for construction of the San Simeon Highway.
Dr. John Roberts initiated the
movement for construction of
an all year, scenic highway along
the south coast. Funds were first
appropriated for the road in 1919.
It was completed in June, 1937.
Photograph courtesy of
James Knapp. Mayo Hayes
O'Donnell Library Collection.

Carmel

San Carlos Mission, 1853, copy of
a painting by J. N. Alden. Original
is at the Mission Santa Barbara.
Photograph was the gift of Father
Maynard Geiger to Harry Downie,
renowned restorer of California

missions. Under Mr. Downie's meticulous
supervision, restoration of the
Mission San Carlos to its present
state was begun in the 1930s. His
research and craftsmanship has given
the restoration its rare authenticity.

San Carlos Day procession.
Every year in November, in
celebration of Saint
Charles Day, the Mission
San Carlos was the scene
of a joyous and solemn
celebration. Photograph
taken in 1910 by S. L. Slevin,
courtesy of
the Bancroft Library.

The Pine Inn in 1904.
The prior year, the hotel
had been moved from its
original location on the
northeast corner of Ocean
Avenue and Junipero Street.
Tents were erected to
accommodate the overflow
of guests. Photograph was the
gift of Lillian Devendorf
Hohfeld, courtesy of
the Carmel Library.

Chris Jorgenson,
noted pioneer painter
of Yosemite, built
a studio on
Camino Real in Carmel.
Later it became
the nucleus of
the La Playa Hotel.
Photograph taken in 1912
by S. L. Slevin,
courtesy of the
Bancroft Library.

Ocean Avenue in 1909.
Pine trees were planted
along its center and sides
to stem the water that turned
it into a stream bed in the
rainy season. The sparse
business section had wooden
sidewalks. Photograph
taken by S. L. Slevin,
courtesy of the
Bancroft Library.

Mary Austin and Jimmy Hopper in her
"wick-i-up," a platform built high in
the branches of a great oak, where she
wrote each morning. Photograph
courtesy of the Carmel Library.

The water trough, in the center
of the street at the intersection of
San Carlos and Ocean, was a favorite
gathering place. Photograph
courtesy of the Carmel Library.

The future Nobel prize winner
Sinclair Lewis acting the part of a matron
at the annual Dutch Fair. With him
is Opal Peet. Photograph taken in 1909,
courtesy of the Monterey County Library.

"Milk shrines" were stationed
at two-block intervals in early Carmel.
Residents often picked up their milk
supply while still attired in their
dressing gowns. Photograph taken in
1924, courtesy of the Carmel Library.

taking their favorite walk to Lobos, "no poet's stroll, but a stout climb, dramatic, danger-tipped, in the face of bursting sprays." Both became enraptured by Carmel, and Mary, undoubtedly, was strongly attracted to Sterling. She described him as "handsome as a Greek faun, shy, restless, slim and stooping." They left to go their separate ways, both with resolutions to return. And on the last day of June, Sterling came back, bringing two friends recruited to help him build a house.

He chose a site on a wooded hillside, in the uninhabited 80-acre tract southeast of town. The location was on what is now Torres Street, between Tenth and Eleventh Avenues. Lupine-covered meadows sloped down to a cobalt sea, and the far-flung view swept over the mission, up the winding river valley, and across to the dramatic Santa Lucias. A tent was pitched on the property, and the men went to work.

Sterling leased three acres of adjacent land for farming. His ambition was to wrest a living from his "potato patch," while pursuing the practice of poetry. In August, his slightly skeptical wife Carrie joined him, but before long, she too fell under the spell of the simple life.

By October, the 30-foot long redwood living room was ready to entertain the old Piedmont crowd. Gathered in front of the tall, chalk-stone fireplace, they partook of "Thackeray stew," a fish chowder named for Thackeray's "Ballad of Bouillabaisse," and downed great quantities of muscatel and ale. A conversation piece was the sacred grove, back of the house, with its altar-like stone fire-pit and encircling trees, each decorated with the skull of a horse or a cow. Intended for votive offerings to the forest gods, it became the scene of many a mussel roast in those mellow autumn days.

Friends shuttled back and forth from San Francisco, enjoying abalone picnics on the beach and exclaiming over the wonders of Carmel. All declared that Sterling had made a fantastic discovery, and gradually they began migrating down. First to come was Arnold Genthe, famous photographer, bachelor, and *bon vivant*. His spacious redwood bungalow, on Camino Real and Eleventh, was distinguished by having the only cellar in Carmel.

In January, Mary Austin came back, settling in a picturesque log cabin on North Lincoln Avenue. For a studio, she had a platform built high in the branches of a great oak. She called it her "wick-i-up," and each morning ascended a rickety ladder to work on her latest book. Dressed in long Grecian robes, with her hair hanging to her waist, she soon became the talk of the town. The friendship with Sterling was resumed, apparently with somewhat less enthusiasm on his part.

Early on the morning of the 18th of April, Carmel shook to the earthquake that brought disaster to San Francisco, and many of Sterling's friends sought permanent refuge from the devastated city. The writer Jimmy Hopper came with his family, renting a house on Dolores and Ninth for six dollars a month. A stocky little man, with a cherubic face and a thatch of curly yellow hair, Hopper made a lively addition to the colony. It was reputed, however, that his wife was not such "a congenial Bohemian." Other colorful refugees were Nora May French, the incandescent and impoverished young poetess, Ina Coolbrith, one of the founders of *The Overland Monthly*, shaggy-haired editor Harry Lafler, and the Mexican artist Xavier Martinez, with his brilliant black eyes and flowing crimson tie.

Jack London and his new wife, Charmian, became habitual guests of the Sterlings. Often, their arrival was the signal for a party lasting several days. According to Mary Austin, there were mussel roasts by moonlight, tea beside driftwood fires, abalone feasting around Sterling's outdoor altar, and "ambrosial, unquotable talk." It was at this time that the celebrated "Abalone Song" originated. It comprised an unending round of rollicking verse, lusty and irreverent, composed as the gang rhythmically pounded away at the abalone pulp:

> The more we take the more they make
> In deep sea matrimony
> Race suicide cannot abide
> The fertile abalone.

> Oh! Some think the Lord is fat,
> And some think he is bony;
> But as for me I think that He
> Is like an abalone.

The Sterling group took frequent jaunts over the Seventeen Mile Drive to Monterey, where there had long been an art colony. A favorite gathering place there was the home of the gifted but improvident artist Charles Rollo Peters, who had a great flair for entertaining. A familiar figure at these festivities was a recent resident of Monterey, Charles Warren Stoddard, who was famed for his Tahitian stories.

Arnold Genthe tells of a time when he arrived at the Peters' hacienda to find his host in despair. The other guests were expected momentarily, and the sheriff had just put his seal on every piece of furniture in the place. Genthe asked if the sheriff happened to be a friend. "We're the best of friends," Peters replied. "Then, make it a party in his honor," Genthe suggested. "The Carmelites and other Bohemians will probably guess the truth. The others will think the seals just a stunt." Peters followed his advice, and the party was a huge success.

All was not frivolity in Sterling's forest Eden. London tried to maintain his regime of writing a thousand words a day, taking advantage of editorial help from Sterling, whose opinion he held in high regard. Mary Austin was collaborating with Hopper and Sterling on a number of projects. And Sterling's own poetry was developing a new quality and depth. It was a carefree but wonderfully creative and productive period upon which all participants were to look back with profound nostalgia.

Abruptly the halcyon days ended. The Londons left for their ill-starred voyage on the *Snark*. Jimmy Hopper became embroiled in bitter domestic problems. Mary Austin, convinced she had cancer, departed to die in Italy. Both Rollo Peters and Charles Stoddard were seriously ill. And Nora May French, in debt and despondent, ended her life with a dose of potassium cyanide. The Christmas of 1907 brought small cause for rejoicing to Carmel's bohemian group.

Meanwhile, the other villagers went their quiet ways, paying little attention to the antics of the inhabitants of what they called the Barbary Coast. The Carmel Development Company had expanded its holdings, purchasing a portion of the old Martin Ranch, so that lots were now available on what today is called Carmel Point. The first house to go up in the area—the driftwood cottage at its southernmost tip on Scenic Road—is still standing. Population increased at the rate of 80 percent a year and now included some retired capitalists and several Stanford professors who built summer houses on Camino Real.

On the same street, the noted pioneer painter of Yosemite, Chris Jorgenson, built a beautiful stone studio which later became the nucleus of the La Playa Hotel. Other artists like Jorgenson, with stable work habits and restrained life styles, lent a new air of propriety to the cultural life of Carmel. Townspeople organized an Arts and Crafts Club and erected a clubhouse in which to hold art shows, musical programs, and other community events of an artistic or intellectual nature. An old barn on Ocean and Mission Street, called Manzanita Hall, came to house the village socials.

Everyone, regardless of occupation or economic status, lived a carefree communal life. A typical notation on the bulletin board, outside the post office, read "Lost—two loaves of bread. Will finder please return to ____, at ____. If eaten, please bring 25 cents." Another excellent example of the mores of the time was the "Milk Shrine." Sets of open shelves were stationed at two-block intervals for the delivery of milk.

At night, the people of Carmel would leave money on the shelf marked with their name, and in the morning, often in their dressing gowns, they would pick up their milk.

Several important new arrivals came to town in 1908. Most sensational was Upton Sinclair, who at 30 had completed his tenth book. Broke and on the verge of a nervous breakdown, he came with the hope of establishing a replacement for Helicon Hall, a cooperative colony in Englewood, New Jersey, recently destroyed by fire. Sterling, a fellow socialist, greeted him with enthusiasm, and Genthe gave him the use of his house. But being an ardent teetotaler and proselytizing vegetarian, Sinclair soon wore out his welcome. When he departed within three months, the bohemians were not sorry to see him go.

Two other ex-inhabitants of Helicon Hall were Alice MacGowan and her sister Grace MacGowan Cooke. Serious professional writers, they also were too sober for Sterling's crowd. Buying a substantial two-story house on San Antonio and Thirteenth, above what became known as Cooke's Cove, they set up a schedule of working hours that left little room for parties.

It was the MacGowan sisters who brought Sinclair Lewis to Carmel. A gangling freckle-faced youth, with bright red hair and piercing blue eyes, the future Nobel Prize winner was just beginning to write. "Hal" Lewis had met the MacGowans at Helicon Hall, where he worked as a furnace stoker. Strongly attracted to Grace's pretty daughter Helen, he eagerly accepted the sisters' invitation to act as part-time secretary and to collaborate with them on a novel. Settling in a small cottage called the "Brownie," on Monte Verde near Ninth, he was soon joined by William Rose Benét, a former classmate at Yale. During their six-month stay, the young bachelors became popular men about town, Lewis even acting the part of a loquacious matron, in full costume, for the annual Dutch Fair.

Most important arrival of the year was Herbert Heron Peet. Descendant of a family abounding in writers and actors, he had high ambitions to be a poet and playwright. He came to Carmel to visit Sterling and Stoddard, both of whom he greatly admired. With him he brought his mother, a well-known writer and sculptress, and an exceedingly youthful wife and two-year-old child. Instantly aware of the possibilities Carmel offered for little theater, he moved from Los Angeles the following summer. Approaching Frank Devendorf with his idea for an outdoor thespian venture, he was given the use of an entire block of wooded property without charge.

By the spring of 1910, the Forest Theater Society had been formed and a play was in rehearsal, with villagers acting the parts. The site, located not far from Sterling's house on present-day Mountain View Avenue, was a natural amphitheater, with the bare ground for a stage and logs for seats. The first production was an original biblical play entitled "David." Heron, who had by this time dropped the name Peet, played the title role, with Alice MacGowan and Helen Cooke in supporting parts. A picturesque touch was provided at the premiere when the audience lit their way up the path through the pines with improvised lanterns fashioned of candles and tin cans. The San Francisco *Chronicle* carried a highly complimentary review of the play, and the Forest Theater, the first open-air community playhouse in California, was off to an excellent start.

The Sterling household remained the center of the artistic and social life of the community. Xavier Martinez visited often, accompanied now by his spirited 17-year-old bride Elsie, daughter of the writer-adventurer Herman Whitaker. Harry Lafler, another frequent guest, was now as interested in real estate as he was in editing and was trying to interest Whitaker and a newcomer, a journalist named Perry Newberry, in starting a colony at Big Sur. Lafler built a one-room dwelling there, made almost entirely from marble quarried from the government land he was homesteading high above the sea. But the others were unwilling to settle on the remote, forbidding coast, and Lafler himself eventually abandoned the house, returning to San Francisco to make his fortune on Telegraph Hill.

Newberry and his wife Bertha, nicknamed "Buttsky," became permanent members of the Carmel colony, building a house near the beach. The 40-year-old Newberry, with his tousled blond mane and engulfing smile, was destined to cut a broad swath in the politics of his adopted town.

In May 1910, two visitors from Los Angeles came to spend a week at the Sterling home. Out of their sojourn came one of the most flamboyant articles ever written about Carmel. Willard Huntington Wright, called "the boy iconoclast of Southern California," was a writer who someday would be famous as editor of *The Smart Set* and creator of the character Philo Vance. With him was the satirical cartoonist Gale. Their joint product, published in the Los Angeles *Times*, carried the title, "Hotbed of Soulful Culture, Vortex of Erotic Erudition: Carmel in California, where Author and Artist Folk are Establishing the Most Amazing Colony on Earth."

There was both truth and fiction in their report. Carmel was described as a one-street temperance town, where the drugstore sold liquor on the sly. Artists and writers were divided into two groups; the "Respectables," headed by Sterling, who ate underdone ducks and drank martinis and mint punch, and the "Eminently Respectables," led by the MacGowan sisters, who did not drink, went to bed early, and worked hard. The article alleged that there was "more hair per capita" in Carmel than in any town in the nation, and the predominant subjects of discussion were "scenery, soul, and art." Though Mary Austin was still abroad when Gale and Wright visited Carmel and they had never seen her, they gave her a merciless lampooning.

Despite this kind of publicity, Carmel actually was becoming a rather staid resort. Almost 400 houses had been built, many quite substantial. In addition to the three hotels in town, the Del Monte Lodge had been established, and the picturesque collection of shacks, making up the old Chinese Village at Pebble Beach, had been razed. There were a dozen stores, a school and a library, two livery stables and a garage, a Wells Fargo office and a lumber yard, and a clutch of souvenir shops.

In 1912, Mary Austin, having recovered from her "fatal illness," returned from Italy. She was just in time to witness and contribute to a painfully difficult year for her old friend George Sterling. Soon after her arrival, she acted with Sterling in a production of one of her plays at the Forest Theater and managed to conjure a romantic dalliance. But by the following season, they had quarreled bitterly over both personal and artistic affairs. At about the same time, Sterling's wife Carrie, unwilling to tolerate any longer George's philandering and drinking, filed for divorce. Lonely and disconsolate, Sterling spent days wandering down the Big Sur coast and into the Santa Lucias. His work was going badly, and a switch from poetry to short stories, for which he had no talent, brought added frustration. Many of his old friends no longer had time to spend with him. Some solace came from close friendship with Harry Leon Wilson, the playwright and novelist then living in the Carmel Highlands and married to Helen Cooke. But by 1914, Carmel had changed sufficiently so that Sterling was no longer "High Panjandrum" of the colony. Turning his house over to Jimmy Hopper, he left for New York's Greenwich Village.

That same year Mary Austin was again off and away, paying only an occasional visit to the house she maintained until 1924. The two people who had been most responsible for launching Carmel on its "gleaming years" were gone. In a sense, it was the end of an era. Robinson Jeffers, who shortly after arrived with his wife Una, stumbled upon Sterling's stone altar and saw it as the "last of the sacred groves."

From this point on, commercial success was to color the Carmel story. In 1916, concerned residents voted for incorporation, in order to exercise firmer controls on development of their town. They won the election, but for thirteen years the cultural and business factions continued to fight over their disparate interests. The art group even brought suit against the city's board of trustees to prevent the paving of Ocean Avenue. There was dancing in the streets when they won on a technicality.

Then, the "progressives," the commercial faction, planned a large Spanish-style hotel on the water-front, and outraged citizens retaliated with a gigantic "Art versus Dollars" campaign. As a result, the village was bonded for $30,000 to purchase the property along the shoreline, and the Carmel Development Company deeded the block that became Devendorf Park as a dividend. In 1922, a city planning commission was established to protect Carmel from undesirable commercial ventures, but the number of stores and specialty shops continued to increase. Ocean Avenue was paved, and a new highway ran from Monterey to the mission. And when a professional planner was hired to outline a traffic pattern that would keep automobiles out of town, the business community rose up in arms and voted the city council out of office.

In 1929, the battle reached a rousing climax with an election in which the slogan was "Keep Carmel Off the Map!" Perry Newberry ran for the office of city trustee on the following platform:

"Believing that what 9,999 towns out of 10,000 towns want is just what Carmel shouldn't have, I am a candidate for trustee on the platform, DON'T BOOST! I am making a spirited campaign to win by asking those who disagree to vote against me.

DON'T VOTE FOR PERRY NEWBERRY:
If you want to see Carmel become a city.
If you want its growth boosted.
If you desire its commercial success.
If concrete pavements represent your civic ambitions.
If you think a glass factory is of greater importance
    than a sand dune, or a millionaire than an artist,
    or a mansion than a little brown cottage.
If you truly want Carmel to become a boosting, hustling,
    wideawake, lively metropolis,
DON'T VOTE FOR PERRY NEWBERRY."

He was elected, and the same year, a zoning ordinance was passed which stated, in effect, that business development must forever be subordinated to the residential character of the community.

But the struggle was not over. It was inevitable that a place such as Carmel would in time become too popular to retain the wonderful simplicity with which it started. The Second World War, with a burgeoning Fort Ord, brought an enormous influx of tourists. Motels mushroomed and eventually took over much of the town. Still, the residents continued to fight for preservation of the unique character of their community and, in large measure, they succeeded. The stately pines stand tall, with no high rise buildings to diminish them. The great white beach stretches to the cerulean sea, unsullied by commercial activity. The night sky is undimmed by street lights or neon signs. The scented air, soft and clear, is filled with the sound of the singing surf. Beauty is still free for "the mere labor of looking."

Cry, the Beautiful Country

The Monterey area is not so much a place as a beckoning promise. Millions of tourists light up with nostalgia at the mere mention of its name. Some of the world's finest writers have laid the fruits of their imagination upon its superb natural beauty. Residents tend to be either extravagant in their praise or unbelievably casual, although they all seem to acknowledge that in Monterey County even a trip to the market can be a scenic drive.

Ironically, the very attributes that have created the cherished ambience of Monterey threaten the future of the beautiful country. Neither nostalgia nor adulation will be able to stem the tide of the ever-increasing population and development that is inundating the area. And only a highly sophisticated and concerted effort towards conservation will hold off sprawling urbanization, smog, and ruin; for the same topographical and meteorological conditions exist in the Salinas and Carmel Valleys as in the Los Angeles Basin and other coastal areas that have been urbanized. An inversion layer forms a ceiling, trapping heat and atmospheric pollutants. The daily sea breeze is a low-level wind which pushes pollution inland but does not dissipate it. Accelerated development along the coast will inevitably lead to the interior valleys being socked in with smog much of the year.

On the other hand, change and development of some kind seems inevitable, and present-day rancheros are embittered by what they consider to be lack of understanding for their problems. Owners of large tracts of land in the choicer areas of Monterey County will not be able to preserve them in their natural state for much longer. The tax burden alone is becoming prohibitive.

If change is inevitable, what enlightened solutions can be proposed? One is that industrial and major residential development be concentrated midway up the valleys and not on the coast. There a more efficient atmospheric waste disposal is possible because of the lay of the land.

Another great hope for which a number of conservation groups are striving is the public purchase of open space, especially adjacent to the shoreline. In addition, there is cause for optimism in the creation of such parks as the 4,800-acre Toro Regional Park and the 500-acre Jacks Peak Park.

It can only be hoped that the will and the way will be found to protect the many-splendored image of Monterey. It represents the best of what is left of California's splendid heritage. Future generations are entitled to have the opportunity to experience it.

Selected Bibliography

The brief bibliographical notes that follow are not intended to cover the complete range of sources related to the history of Monterey County. Nor do they include more than a small selection of the references used in the preparation of this book. Their purpose is to provide suggestions for additional reading to those who wish to deepen their understanding of the subject matter presented or simply to partake further of the glorious entertainment that history can be.

For solid background material on the history of California, the serious reader will want to consult Hubert Howe Bancroft, *History of California* (7 volumes, 1884–90). For those who prefer a comprehensive but not exhaustive account, several good one-volume histories are available. Especially concise and readable is Walton Bean, *California, An Interpretive History* (1968).

The most authoritative volume on California's first inhabitants is Alfred L. Kroeber, *Handbook of the Indians of California* (1925). Much interesting information about the life style of the Indians of the Monterey Peninsula can be found in James Culleton, *Indians and Pioneers of Old Monterey* (1950). But for an appreciation of the intrinsic nobility of the Indian character, Theodora Kroeber, *Ishi in Two Worlds, A Biography of the Last Wild Indian in North America* (1961) is strongly recommended, even though it is the story of a Yahi Indian.

The chronicle of Spain's early years in California is given thorough and interesting coverage in Charles E. Chapman, *A History of California: The Spanish Period* (1921). In addition, fascinating first-hand accounts are available in the journals of the explorers. Those of Cabrillo and Vizcaíno are in Herbert E. Bolton, *Spanish Exploration of the Southwest, 1542–1706* (1959). The original narratives of 1769–70 written by Portolá, Constansó, and Fages appear in the *Publications* of the Academy of Pacific Coast History (1910–11). The diary of Fray Juan Crespí is in the second volume of Herbert Bolton's translation of Francisco Palóu,

Historical Memoirs of New California (1926). A dramatic account of the Portolá expedition's long and arduous trek from Baja California to Monterey is presented in Richard F. Pourade, *The Call to California* (1968).

The best biography of Father Serra is Maynard J. Geiger, *Life and Times of Fray Junípero Serra* (2 volumes, 1959). For the complete story of the Anza expeditions, the basic reference is Herbert Bolton, *Anza's California Expeditions* (5 volumes, 1930). The first volume, reprinted as *Outpost of Empire*, is Bolton's summary of the two epic expeditions. The rest are documentary, with Fray Pedro Font's diary, an enthralling eye-witness account, in volume 4.

A realistic description of Monterey's early years is provided in Culleton's *Indians and Pioneers of Old Monterey*. An excellent pictorial presentation, with brief historical narrative, can be seen in Jeanne Van Nostrand, *Monterey: Adobe Capital of California, 1770–1847* (1968). Romantic accounts of the period include Bancroft's *California Pastoral* (1888) and *Spanish Arcadia* (1929), by Nellie Van de Grift Sánchez.

Three reports of distinguished visitors are Jean François Galaup, Comte de La Pérouse, *Voyage Round the World* (2 volumes, in translation, 1798–99); George Vancouver, *A Voyage of Discovery to the North Pacific Ocean* (3 volumes, 1798); and Donald C. Cutter, *Malaspina in California* (1960). The search for the sea otter, which played an important part in the early history of Monterey, is best described in Adele Ogden, *The California Sea Otter Trade, 1784–1848* (1941). For emphasis on the military aspects of Monterey, a comprehensive source is Kibbey M. Horne, *A History of the Presidio of Monterey, 1770–1970* (1970).

Life in Mexican California has been sketched by a number of observers who left interesting records. Among these are Richard Henry Dana, *Two Years Before the Mast* (1840); Alfred Robinson, *Life in California* (1846); William Heath Davis, *Seventy-five Years in California* (1929); and Doyce B. Nunis, Jr., editor, *The California Diary of Faxon Dean Atherton, 1836–1839* (1964).

Biographies afford an especially entertaining presentation of historical material. Those pertinent to the Monterey story include Susanna Bryant Dakin, *The Lives of William Hartnell* (1949); Rueben L. Underhill, *From Cowhides to Golden Fleece* (1939), a biography of Thomas Oliver Larkin; Myrtle Mason McKittrick, *Vallejo, Son of California* (1944); and Madie Brown Emparan, *The Vallejos of California* (1968). For the serious reader, a wealth of supplementary detail may be found in *The Larkin Papers*, edited by George P. Hammond (10 volumes, 1951–64).

The story of California's land grants is a fascinating aspect of Monterey history. The subject is covered in clear and cogent style in W. W. Robinson, *Land in California* (1948). Two beautiful books by Robert Becker may be used to complement this basic work. They are *Diseños of California Ranchos* (1964) and *Designs on the Land* (1969), both collections of early California rancho maps, including several in Monterey County.

In illuminating the years immediately preceding and following the American occupation, letters and memoirs make a most significant contribution. Three books in particular add much to an appreciation of the period: John A. Hawgood, editor, *First and Last Consul: Thomas Oliver Larkin and the Americanization of California* (1962); Walter Colton, *Three Years in California* (1854); and William Robert Garner, *Letters from California, 1846-47, Edited, with a Sketch of the Life and Times of their Author, by Donald Monro Craig* (1970). A classic fictional account of the period is Gertrude Atherton, *Splendid Idle Forties* (1902), a collection of short stories based on actual happenings.

John Charles Fremont's activities are chronicled in a highly informative and enjoyable biography by Allan Nevins, *Fremont: Pathmarker of the West* (1939). Contrast to Nevin's sympathetic treatment of his subject is provided in Cardinal Goodwin, *John Charles Fremont, An Explanation of His Career* (1930). Some readers might also find pleasure in the romanticized account given in Irving Stone's *Immortal Wife* (1944).

A lively picture of life in Monterey during the constitutional convention is provided in volume one of Bayard Taylor's *Eldorado, or Adventures in the Path of Empire* (1850). Among the many books on the proceedings of the convention, the most readable is Samuel H. Willey, *The Transition Period of California* (1901). Readers who wish to consult the official record can refer to J. Ross Browne, *Report of the Debates in the Convention of California, on the formation of the State Constitution* (1950).

Published historical material on Monterey County after 1850 is extremely sparse. Except for Anne B. Fisher's *The Salinas Upside-down River* (1945), no comprehensive narrative is available. Mrs. Fisher gives a zestful account of the Salinas Valley, replete with anecdotes, and utilizes her novelistic skills to entertain the reader. For a terse and factual presentation of some of the same material, enhanced by many pictures, a useful reference is Robert B. Johnston, *Old Monterey County, A Pictorial History* (1970).

Significant episodes in the story of the city of Monterey are concisely covered in Robert W. Reese, *A Brief History of Old Monterey* (1969). The feeling and flavor of Monterey in the 1870s is admirably captured in Robert Louis Stevenson, "The Old Pacific Capital," in *Travels and Essays of Robert Louis Stevenson* (1907). Those who wish to pursue the intriguing biographies of Fanny and Robert Stevenson will enjoy Margaret McKay, *The Violent Friend: The Story of Mrs. Robert Louis Stevenson* (1968), and Anne Fisher, *No More a Stranger* (1946). The latter work is entirely concerned with the Monterey period of Stevenson's life.

The history of Pacific Grove is recorded in Lucy Neely McLane, *A Piney Paradise* (1958). The book is based on interviews with old timers and liberally larded with newspaper quotations. For the Carmel Valley and the south coast, no published historical material exists. But a fine fictional account of the valley is afforded by Anne Fisher's novel, *Cathedral in the Sun* (1940), and there are several works of fiction that will deepen the reader's appreciation of events that occurred on the wild and rugged southern coastline.

Among these are Robinson Jeffers, *Selected Poetry* (1938) and Lillian Bos Ross, *The Stranger* (1942). The latter is a lusty novel laid in the early days of the Big Sur country and embellished with a wealth of authentic detail. Because the setting for Jeffers' narrative poems is along the sea from the Carmel River to Pfeiffer Point, his verse is alive with the charisma of the coast. For precise information on the location and plot of each of the poems, an exciting reference is Lawrence Clark Powell, *Robinson Jeffers: The Man and His Work* (1934).

A superb chronicle of Carmel's halcyon days as an artists' and writers' colony can be found in Franklin Walker, *The Seacoast of Bohemia* (1966). For cozy details told in a chatty style, an entertaining little book is Daisy Bostick, *Carmel—At Work and Play* (1925). Excellent descriptive passages on early Carmel, as well as a sensitive biography of Robinson Jeffers, are provided in Melba Berry Bennett, *The Stone Mason of Tor House* (1966).

Ranchos of Monterey County

The following information is taken from Robert Grannis Cowan, *Ranchos of California*, Academy Library Guild, Fresno, 1956.

Name of Rancho	Date of Grant	To Whom Granted	To Whom Patented	No. of Acres[*]
Aguajito	1835	Gregorio Tapia	Gregorio Tapia	3,323
Alisal	1823 & '34	Feliciano Soberanes	Basilio Bernal	5,941
Alisal or Patrocinio	1834	William E. Hartnell	María Teresa de la Guerra de Hartnell	2,971
Arroyo Seco	1840	Joaquín de la Torre	Joaquín de la Torre	16,523
Buena Vista	1822–3	Santiago and José Mariano Estrada	Mariano Malarín, atty. for S. Estrada	7,726
Buena Vista, Llano de	1822–3	Santiago and José Mariano Estrada	David Spence	8,446
Carneros (e. of Prunedale)	1842	María Antonia Linares	F. A. McDougal et al.	1,629
Carneros (n. of Prunedale)	1834	David Littlejohn	Heirs of David Littlejohn	4,482
Carpenteria, Cañada de	1845	Joaquín Soto	Heirs of Joaquín Soto	2,236
Chamisal, El	1835	Felipe Vasquez	Heirs of Felipe Vasquez	2,737
Chualar, Santa Rosa de	1839	Juan Malarín	Mariano Malarín, executor	8,890
Coches	1841	Joséfa Soberanes	Joséfa Soberanes	8,794
Cock's Tract	1840	Estéban Espinosa	Henry Cocks	1,106
Encinal y Buena Esperanza	1834 & '39	David Spence	David Spence	13,391
Escarpines, Bolsa de or San Miguel	before 1828 & again in 1837	Salvador Espinosa	Salvador Espinosa	6,416

(*) The original land grants were given in leagues and frequently were vaguely defined. For purposes of simplification the number of acres patented is used in the text as the number of acres granted, although the two figures sometimes differed.

Name of Rancho	Date of Grant	To Whom Granted	To Whom Patented	No. of Acres*
Familia Sagrada or Bolsa del Potrero Moro Cojo	1822	José Joaquín de la Torre (sold to John B. R. Cooper in 1829)	John B. R. Cooper	6,916
Gatos or Santa Rita	1820 & '37	Trinidad Espinosa	Domingo Perez	4,424
Gavilan or Gabilan	1843	José Yvez Limantour	J. D. Carr	48,781
Guadalupe y Llanitos de los Correos	1833	Juan Malarín	Mariano Malarín, executor	8,859
Huerta de la Nacion or Noche Buena	1835	Juan Antonio Muñoz	J. and J. Monomany	4,412
Laguna Seca or Cañadita	1833 & '34	Catalina Manzanelli de Munrás	Catalina Manzanelli de Munrás	2,179
Laureles or Cañada de los	1835 & '39	José Antonio Romero; José Boronda et al.	José Boronda et al.	6,625
Laureles, or Cañada de los	1844	José Agricia	L. Ransom	718
Meadows Tract	1840	Antonio Romero	James Meadows	4,592
Milpitas	1838	Ignacio Pastor	Ignacio Pastor	43,281
Monte, Rincon de la Punta del	1836	Teodoro Gonzales	Teodoro Gonzales	15,219
Moro Cojo, Bolsa del (Bolsa Nueva was added to this by Castro)	1825, '36-7 & '44	Simeon Castro	M. Antonia Pico de Castro et al.	30,901
Nacional	1839	Vicente Cantua	Vicente Cantua	6,633
Natividad	ca. 1830 & '37	Manuel Butrón & Nicolás Alviso	Ramón Butrón et al.	8,642
Nueva Bolsa (combined with Moro Cojo by Castro)	1829 & '36	Francisco Soto	--------	-----

Name of Rancho	Date of Grant	To Whom Granted	To Whom Patented	No. of Acres*
Ojitos	1842	Mariano de Jesús Soberanes	Mariano Soberanes	8,900
Pajaro, Bolsa del	1837	Sebastián Rodríguez	Sebastián Rodríguez	5,497
Pajaro, Vega del Rio de	1820	Antonio Maria Castro	F. A. McDougal et al.	4,310
Paraje de Sanchez	1839	Francisco Lugo	Juana Briones de Lugo et al.	6,584
Pescadero	1836	Fabian Barreto	David Jacks	4,426
Piños, Punta de	1833 & '34	José M. Armenta and José Ábrego	H. De Graw et al.	2,667
Piojo	1842	Joaquin Soto	Heirs of Joaquin Soto	13,329
Pleyto	1845	José Antonio Chavez	W. S. Johnson et al.	13,299
Poza de los Ositos	1839	Carlos Espinosa	Carlos Espinosa	16,939
Rincon del Zanjon	1840	José Eusebio Boronda	José Eusebio Boronda	2,230
Salinas	1836	Gabriel Espinosa	Heirs of Gabriel Espinosa	4,414
Salinas, Rincon de las	1833	Cristina Delgado	Rafael Estrada	2,220
San Benito	1842	Francisco Garcia	James Watson	6,671
San Bernabe	1841 & '42	Petronilo Rios	Henry Cocks	13,297
San Bernardo	1841	José Mariano Soberanes	Mariano Soberanes	13,346
San Carlos, Potrero de	1837	Fructuoso del Real	Joaquin Gutiérrez et al.	4,307
San Cayetano, Bolsa de	1824	Ignacio Vicente Ferrer Vallejo	José de Jesús Vallejo	8,866
San Francisquito	1835	Catalina Manzanelli de Munrás	José Ábrego et al.	8,814
San José y Sur Chiquita	1835 re-granted / 1839 re-granted	Teodoro Gonzales Marcelino Escobar	Joseph S. Emery and Nathan W. Spaulding, administrators	8,876

Name of Rancho	Date of Grant	To Whom Granted	To Whom Patented	No. of Acres*
San Lorenzo or Peachtree	1842	Francisco Rico	Heirs of Andrew Randall	22,264
San Lorenzo	1841	Feliciano Soberanes	Feliciano Soberanes	21,884
San Lorenzo or Topo	1846	Rafael Sanchez	Rafael Sanchez	48,286
San Lucas	1842	Rafael Estrada	James McKinley	8,875
San Miguelito de Trinidad	1841	Rafael Gonzales	Mariano Gonzales	22,136
San Vicente	1835	Francisco Estéban Munrás	Concepcion Munrás et al.	19,979
Saucito	1833	Graciano Manjares	John Wilson et al.	2,212
Sauzal	1823	Agustín Soberanes	Jacob P. Leese	10,242
	1834–5 re-granted	José Tiburcio Castro		
Segunda, Cañada de la	1839	Lazaro Soto	Lazaro Soto	4,367
Soledad Mission Lands	1846	Feliciano Soberanes	Feliciano Soberanes	8,900
Sur	1834	Juan Bautista Alvarado	John B. R. Cooper	8,949
Tierra, Corral de	1836	Guadalupe Figueroa	H. D. McCobb	4,435
Toro	1835	José Ramón Estrada	Charles Wolters	5,668
Tucho	1795	José Manuel Boronda	David Jacks	400
	1835 re-granted	Boronda and Blas Martinez		
	1841	Simeon Castro	Heirs of Simeon Castro	113
Tularcitos	1834	Rafael Gomez	Heirs of Rafael Gomez	26,581
Vergeles	1835	José Joaquín Gomez	James C. Stokes	8,760
Zanjones	1839	Gabriel de la Torre	Mariano Malarín, executor	6,714

Index

Italics refer to photographs.